WATER AND THE
CALIFORNIA DREAM

WATER AND THE CALIFORNIA DREAM

HISTORIC CHOICES FOR SHAPING THE FUTURE

DAVID CARLE

COUNTERPOINT

Originally published as *Drowning the Dream: California's Water Choices at the Millennium* by Praeger, 2000

Published in paperback as *Water and the California Dream: Choices for the New Millennium* by Sierra Club Books, 2003

Revised edition published by Counterpoint, 2016

Library of Congress Cataloging-in-Publication Data is available.
ISBN 978-1-61902-617-9

Cover design by Kelly Winton
Interior design by Domini Dragoone

COUNTERPOINT
2560 Ninth Street, Suite 318
Berkeley, CA 94710
www.counterpointpress.com

Printed in the United States of America
Distributed by Publishers Group West

10 9 8 7 6 5 4 3 2 1

For Nick and Ryan, the future.
And for Janet, always.

CONTENTS

ILLUSTRATIONS

INTRODUCTION
CHANGES AND CHOICES

In an arid environment, water is the ultimate sovereign.
(McWilliams, 1946, 293)

In the '90s, there was increasing concern about the limited water supply for cities of California. Planners began investigating ways to transport water from the Sierra Nevada snowpack. By '05 a plan was presented to the public and a campaign began to convince voters to make the right choice. Water shortages for existing users were emphasized: "Will your tap run dry?" However, proposals were actually intended to do something other than serve existing users. Imported water could foster enormous population growth.

That describes California as the nineteenth century came to a close and Los Angeles maneuvered for Eastern Sierra water. Even before those Owens Valley water supplies could be used up, before increased demand no longer matched supply, the pattern was repeated. Colorado River water was "needed" for the entire Southern California metropolitan area and then Northern California water, delivered by the California Aqueduct.

This turn-of-the-century narrative, strangely enough, still fit California's circumstances a century later, as the twenty-first century began. Population growth projections were still being used to justify new water projects, as they had throughout California's history. The Golden State reached the year 2000 with 34 million residents, and by 2015 held 39 million, with the state's forecasters suggesting that there would be 50 million Californians by 2051. Planners work with those forecasts as if they are inevitable, but before such projections can come true the limited water supply must be stretched even further.

Campaigns to convince voters to approve new California water projects historically relied on misinformation. Scared voters, concerned about their personal water supplies, repeatedly approved projects that instead fostered enormous growth. Those choices ultimately damaged Californians' quality of life, and had increasingly tragic environmental consequences. The most benefit accrued to a few large landholders and developers, a loose cartel of growth promoters that drove much of California's development. Yet questioning the prevalent dogma of unlimited growth, irrigated by water, became "un-Californian"—heretical behavior in a state whose history was shaped by water choices.

In the new millennium, some encouraging adjustments finally began to appear in California's relationship to water, as recognition grew that the historic approach had produced unwelcome changes in the California Dream. This book explores those historic choices and debates as the state was transformed by the movement of water out of its original watersheds into Southern California, to the Bay Area, and onto farmlands of the naturally dry San Joaquin and Imperial Valleys.

[Los Angeles, 1904:] Los Angeles is one of the prettiest cities I have seen . . . every house is surrounded with large grounds that are planted with various trees. . . . The city is a bustling business town, over 100,000 people, fine blocks, elegant hotels, and real estate agents thick enough to walk on. (Powell, 1996, 20)

[Anaheim, 1910:] In those days . . . this northern part of the county was one continuous citrus orchard. A lot of us that are going to be here with what few years we have left still miss those green orchards. (Martenet, 1968)

[Owens Valley, 1934:] The . . . last apple crop went to relieve distress in the homes of the unemployed in the Great City. It was the last

generous gesture of this despoiled land. Today the trees that bore
that crop are again white with blossoms, but the petals of these blossoms will fall on parched ground. The boughs will never more bend
under their load of fruit. The water is gone. It flows southward to
the Great City. Be it so. The sin is not ours. (Parcher and Parcher,
[1934] 1970, 41)

The quotations are from a citrus scientist's letters to his wife
back East, from the oral history of an Anaheim pioneer who, as a
city councilman, helped shape the changes he wistfully recalls, and
from a resident of the Owens Valley after Los Angeles, "the Great
City," reached three hundred miles north for water.

G. Harold Powell's letters extolled climate, vistas and the
beauty of Los Angeles (a startling comment today, more than a
century later). Tellingly, in his first letter, after his very first day
in the city, he also felt compelled to mention real estate agents in
superabundance!

Morris W. Martenet, Jr.'s oral history interview relishes memories of Southern California's brief idyllic era of citrus and sunshine, and of a little town called Anaheim, before freeways, urban
sprawl and Disneyland.

The Owens Valley episode is a well-documented story of
water imperialism. But the changes for people there, after the
south extended its "watershed" hundreds of miles north, also
led ultimately to drastic changes for Los Angeles and the rest of
Southern California.

Three key years in California's water history were 1913, 1940
and 1971. In 1913, the Los Angeles Aqueduct began delivering
Owens River water to Los Angeles; the Colorado River Aqueduct
was completed in 1940 and, in 1971, the State Water Project's
California Aqueduct began transferring Northern California water
to Southern California cities and San Joaquin Valley farms.

It was the bloom time of the year. . . . The landscapes of the Santa
Clara Valley were fairly drenched with sunshine, all the air was

quivering with the songs of the meadowlarks, and the hills were so
covered with flowers that they seemed to be painted. (Muir, 1912, 2)

These temple destroyers, devotees of raging commercialism, seem
to have a perfect contempt for Nature, and, instead of lifting
their eyes to the God of the mountains, lift them to the Almighty
Dollar. (Muir, 1912, 181)

To bring water to San Francisco and other parts of the Bay
Area, the city's Hetch Hetchy system was authorized by Congress
in 1913, despite a vigorous campaign led by John Muir against a
dam on the Tuolumne River inside Yosemite National Park. Water
deliveries began in 1931. The orchards and fields of the Santa Clara
Valley would, in the late twentieth century, give way to growth
made possible by imported water; today the area is better known as
"Silicon Valley." The Mokelumne Aqueduct began importing water
from the Sierra Nevada to East Bay cities in 1929.

Long time 'go, lots salmon in San Joaquin River. My people—
maybe 2–3 thousand . . . catch more salmon can haul in hundred
freight wagons. Dry 'em—carry 'em home. [Since 1909] no
salmon in river. White man make dam at old Indian Rancheria
. . .—stop fish—now Indian got no fish. (Pahmit, a Yokut Indian, in
Yoshiyama et al, 1996, 318)

The wedding of the Colorado River with the desert bearing its
name, the birth of the Imperial Valley and its miraculous growth,
were not commonplace. (Woehlke, 1912)

Critical moments of choice preceded each decision to construct
another aqueduct and to import water. California's history followed
no inevitable path. The state's environmental and quality of life
changes were driven by human choices. Yet the tendency is to consider the status quo, at any point in time, as the inevitable outcome
of history. There were times of decision that could have pushed

California in very different directions. Water choices have been the most potent forces shaping population growth. It is time to consider how, and why, such choices drowned so many California Dreams.

Water choices may seem a surprising approach to California's history. Most historians emphasize Gold Rush immigration, railroad and real estate company boosterism and their heavy promotion of "the California Dream," Southern California and Santa Clara Valley orchards expanding, then surrendering to freeways and suburbs, the Hollywood movie industry growing up and spreading images of the sunny southland, World War II bringing heavy growth of aircraft and military industries and the growth of the computer industry in Silicon Valley. But growth of the major urban centers after the early 1900s, beyond limits set by local sources, could happen only because of imported water.

> The emergence of Los Angeles as the leading metropolis of Southern California was in splendid defiance of all visible logic. (Watkins, 1983, 246)

> There was never a region so unlikely to become a vast metropolitan area as Southern California. It is . . . man-made, a gigantic improvisation. (McWilliams, [1946] 1973, 13)

What if development had followed a different path? In some alternate reality, some parallel universe, perhaps water engineer William Mulholland was successful when he begged Los Angeles' power elite to stop deifying growth. Perhaps they listened when he grumbled that the only way to solve the city's water problem was to kill the overzealous leader of the Chamber of Commerce.

It is intriguing to imagine the Eastern Sierra as it might be today, if Owens River water had remained in its natural watershed. For nineteen years I worked as a ranger at Mono Lake, participating in the effort to save that inland sea from the effects of Los Angeles' stream diversions. I heard opinions expressed, again and again, that today's sparsely populated Eastern Sierra was preserved by the water imperialism of Los Angeles; saved from the overdevelopment rampant elsewhere in the state.

The Owens Valley town of Bishop might, in the twenty-first century, be an urban center, not the equivalent of Los Angeles, but akin to Carson City, Nevada (which shares a similar climate and setting), with agriculture still dominating nearby valley lands. In this imaginary reality, Bishop's small town atmosphere might be lost. But consider the Los Angeles basin and Orange County within that same scenario. Picture urban enclaves far smaller than today's, and still encircled by rural farmland . . . still scented by the blossoms of nearby citrus orchards. The south coast would, as always, attract tourists, but to far less crowded beaches, moving along far less congested highways, breathing air far less polluted by the "people fumes" we call smog.

This book's focus begins with Southern California because the watery tentacles of that region reached the entire state. What would the rest of California be like in that reality? Where would its largest cities be? Would the state's overall population approach anything like the current 39 million, or might those people be spread among other states, or other nations? It is certain that they *could not* be in Los Angeles.

Why bother with such questions? After all, those decisions bringing water—bringing people—are behind us now. Their consequences have been faced. Do history and imaginary "what ifs" matter?

Honesty and self-interest make a review of California history imperative. The choices Californians make every day shape alternative futures. Population projections, in truth, are not inevitable. How many people, where they will live, and what their quality of life will be are matters of choice, just as they were throughout California's last 165 years. Californians may seek a hopeful legacy for their children and grandchildren, preserving the good that still remains in their quality of life.

In the face of today's remnant of the California Dream, does anyone other than shortsighted developers and land speculators seriously look forward to more than 50 million people in the state?

Undoubtedly, yes, some do. Unlimited growth is "the California Way"; a 165-year-old custom. Breaking that custom to achieve a stable population seems impossible. Some wish to avoid the demographic challenge of fewer young people supporting large cohorts of aging elders during a transition to long-term sustainability. Politicians shy away from population issues. The term "control," when coupled with "population," conjures draconian images of interference with reproductive freedom.

Though people are wary of the consequences of unlimited population growth, few have faced the problem directly. Yet water limits can be an impetus toward a stable population without any need for unpalatable reproductive or draconian immigration restrictions. William Mulholland was correct when, campaigning for more water for Los Angeles, he pointed out that his city would ultimately be limited by its water supply. He was just as correct when he said, "Whoever brings the water, brings the people" (Los Angeles Department of Water and Power, 2016b).

When four years of extreme drought hit California between 2012 and 2015, and climate change models forecast a dryer future for the region, grandiose plans that had long grown dusty were mentioned again, to bring Columbia River water from Oregon, or Canadian waters, or even to tow polar icebergs down the coast. Anything, it seemed, to keep the status quo in place. Yet, improved water recycling technology and conservation measures existed by 2015 that demonstrated that a pathway already exists for cities to back away from reliance on imported water.

Massive tunnels to serve the aqueducts that carry water south of the Sacramento–San Joaquin Delta became the twenty-first-century version of the "Peripheral Canal" that was defeated in a voter referendum back in 1982. The latest project's mixed objectives, through more than four decades of planning, were to isolate diverted freshwater from the Delta tidewater, reduce reversed flows within the Delta due to powerful pumps sucking fish their way, and improve reliability of water deliveries by restoring the damaged estuary ecosystem. The complex and controversial project, characterized by some as "fish versus people," could become the nation's most expensive water project ever.

In the early 1970s, when the state had 18 million fewer people and its population seemed to be stabilizing, historian Remi Nadeau wrote:

> Today Southern California has lost its booster spirit. It has vanished along with the clear skies, the uncrowded beaches, the unjammed streets, and the delightful countryside that made Los Angeles the mecca of tourist and settler. [Our] culture . . . turned its original objective—to settle the vacant land—into a blind dogma that persisted long after its reason had disappeared. Indeed, one might say that . . . they have brought in too much water. For if California now has enough water to more than double in population, then much of California is doomed to become insufferable. (1974, 5, 265)

If Nadeau had been right about the end of boosterism, then, forty years later, the process should have closed down. Yet when he wrote those words, newly available Sacramento River water had just come on line, and Nadeau had not seen the growth that would foster.

The blind dogma Nadeau described still has its proponents. It shaped the first 165 years as a state, often making environmental nightmares of California Dreams. Today we again hear startling warnings of water shortages—exacerbated by climate change—and are asked to approve additional water storage and export infrastructure. Will the measures assure water supplies for the present population in a sustainable way? Or will they allow unimpeded urban growth and expansion of thirsty orchards to continue until, once again, demand outreaches supply?

The changed environment and quality of life in California can be discovered in the first-person voices of its pioneers—the Spanish and Mexican *rancheros*, the gold-seeking '49ers, and the tourists and citrus farmers before the turn of the century. Each decade of the state's history brought its own pioneers, as successive water developments irrigated new waves of population growth. With the people came smog and traffic gridlock, suburban sprawl and urban crowding, extinctions and endangered species, toxic wetlands and paved-over farmland.

The shape of the future is not inevitable but a matter of choice—as it has been throughout the State of California's first 165 years. Californians do not have to continue drowning their California Dreams.

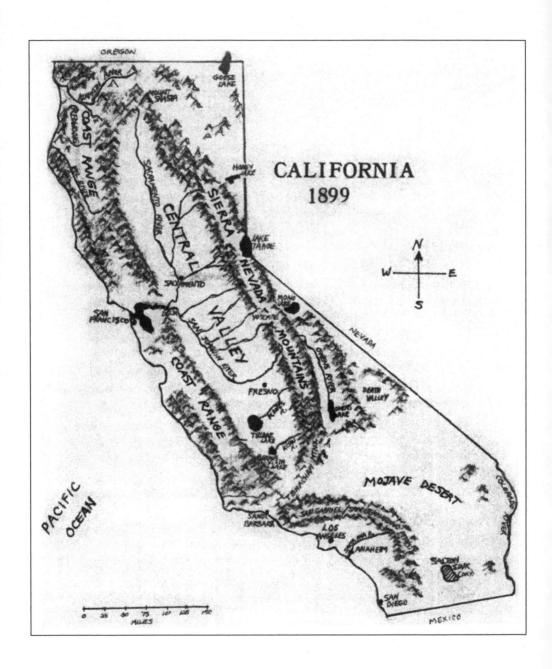

PART I

FRONTIERLAND TO FANTASYLAND

1769 Spanish settlement at San Diego; the native Indian population is about 300,000

1781 Pueblo of Los Angeles founded

1820 Alta California has 3,270 settlers and soldiers, with about 30 large *ranchos*

1822 Authority transfers from Spain to Mexico; hide and tallow trade starts

1830 Grizzly bear population near its peak, at about 10,000

1846 Bear Flag Revolt; the United States goes to war with Mexico

1848 James Marshall discovers gold at Sutter's Mill in January; the population of San Francisco in April is 850

1849 90,000 Forty-niners arrive in one year; the population of San Francisco reaches 25,000 by December

1850 Statehood; state population about 100,000; Indian population (not counted in census) is down to about 30,000

1851 Land commission appointed to transfer land grants to new hands

1857 Anaheim vineyard colony founded

1869 Transcontinental railroad completed

1870 State population at 560,000

1873 Two navel orange trees planted in Riverside

1875 Southern Pacific Railroad reaches Southern California

1880 First commercial grove of Valencia oranges planted in Orange County

1886 First trainload of oranges leaves Los Angeles for the East

1887 Atchison, Topeka and Santa Fe Railroad arrives in Los Angeles

1890–1900 L.A. population doubles to 102,000; Orange County population is 19,696

1903 Last record of a grizzly bear in Orange County

1922 Last confirmed kill of a grizzly bear in the state

ONE

IN GRIZZLY DAYS

> What a countryside it must have been. Oak woodland in the valley
> and foothills, extensive meadows of wildflowers, running streams
> in the canyons, and estuaries rich with shore life along the coast.
> (Leopold, 1985, 1)

To the left, as you face Sleeping Beauty's Castle in Disneyland, there is an oak tree. It is a young tree, only half a century old. Yet it is a special oddity in that fantasy landscape. Uprooted and transplanted to this location (a venerable California tradition), this tree is, nevertheless, one of the few California native trees growing in the park.

There was a time when massive coast live oaks, the ancestors of that tree, grew not far away on grasslands near the Santa Ana River, while others were scattered across the coastal plains of Southern California. The acorns they dropped each autumn became food for woodpeckers and jays, deer, grizzly bears and humans.

Today it is incredibly hard to picture that earlier scene. From a high viewpoint, one of the castle turrets, perhaps, you would see man-made objects in all directions. Two hundred years ago, when grizzlies were common here, the oaks and a few other native trees were some of the tallest things in sight upon the plain. Looking south and east from that fantasy viewpoint, a line of cottonwoods, alders, sycamores and willows marked the course of a river. It has been called the Santa Ana River since 1769, when the expedition led by Don Gaspar de Portola gave it that name.

Fourteen days out of San Diego the Spanish explorers camped by a broad, tree-lined stream. Father Juan Crespi, diarist for the expedition, named it "the River of the Sweet Name of Jesus of the Earthquakes," because, "we experienced here a horrifying earthquake, which was repeated four times during the day" (Bolton, 1927, 142). But the plain through which the river ran they named "The Valley of Saint Anne," or Santa Ana.

Crespi's alternative name has a prayerful honesty to it. But someday real estate developers would hold powerful sway in this part of the world, and it is difficult to imagine the City of Santa Ana becoming the eventual county seat if it had, instead, been named for "Earthquake River."

The shapes of the coastline and the inland hills, defining boundaries of this coastal plain, have not changed very much. On the hills you still find chaparral, the dense, flammable shrublands of steep dry slopes. On lower, more accessible slopes, there is only a remnant of the coastal scrub, the "soft chaparral." And the perennial grasslands and marshes that covered the plain itself, flowing from the hills to the sea, are almost entirely gone.

> At all seasons there was a variety and abundance of food, both animal and plant . . . whales, water birds, fish, elk, deer and antelope were common. . . . Clovers . . . grew to unbelievable height and density in both mountain and lowland valleys. Berry-producing vines and bushes screened numerous stream borders and hill regions that have long since been made bare by overgrazing, fire and water manipulation. Oaks . . . covered many valley flats and slopes . . . and afforded acorns for several months each year. (Storer and Tevis, 1955, 56–57)

That description of the environmental richness of early California—for grizzly bears—could just as well have been meant for the first humans living here. California Indians and grizzlies competed for similar resources, yet coexisted for thousands of years.

California's early human population numbers sound extremely small today. Yet within the state's boundaries, Indians lived in the greatest population density anywhere in North America. About 300,000 people, speaking one hundred different dialects—people of over one hundred differing cultures—lived among the state's rich resource diversity. Home for the *Gabrielino* Indians included the watersheds of the Los Angeles, San Gabriel and Santa Ana Rivers, and the Channel Islands offshore. Estimates of their population numbers range from 2,500 to 10,000. More accurate numbers will never be possible; the estimates come from village sites, totaling 50 to 100, each home to 50 to 100 people. Ten thousand people, at most, in the place where over thirteen million Southern Californians today reside in what are now Los Angeles and Orange County.

Almost all of the early peoples lived as hunter-gatherers. Agriculture—planting and irrigating crops—was only practiced in the relatively harsh environments of the Eastern Sierra and eastern Mojave Desert. We know relatively little about the *Gabrielino*. They were located in the path of change, devastated by forces that destroyed their culture and their environment. The foreign name given to them simply means they came under the influence of the San Gabriel Mission. We do know that they were homebodies, specialists in one place, their place. Anthropologist Theodora Kroeber saw the California Indians as "true provincials," whose most conspicuous defining trait was a preference for "a small world intimately and minutely known" (1976, 23–24).

They knew how to harvest the oak tree's acorns, leaching their bitter tannin to make them edible. The women were the specialists in basket-making, gathering and preparing plant materials and weaving cooking baskets for preparing acorn mush. They knew when and where to harvest chia and other edible flower seeds.

Southern California life has always centered on the beach. It did then, too, but in different, richer ways. Seals, sea otters, surf-fish, clams, mussels—the ocean was a "supermarket" in ways we can barely appreciate today. Fully half of the diet for early Southern Californians came from the ocean.

The marshes and estuaries adjoining the sea attracted uncountable numbers of migratory ducks, geese and shorebirds. Though the great salmon runs were only in Northern California's rivers, steelhead trout were trapped, speared or hooked as they returned from the sea to spawn in south coast streams, including the Santa Ana, San Gabriel and Los Angeles Rivers.

Inland, the people shared the landscape with wildlife. Central Valley grasslands, to the north beyond the mountains, were grazed by herds of Tule elk and pronghorn antelope. Elk ranged up north, but the lands surrounding Los Angeles and Disneyland were also home to pronghorn. Herds roamed wherever there was open terrain in California—everywhere except the Sierra Nevada forests and high country and the northern redwood forests.

Today only black bears are left in the state. They are mountain dwellers, so it comes as a surprise to most people that grizzly bears lived in the lowlands. Grizzlies roamed the chaparral and oak woodlands all along the coast and throughout the interior valleys. They were omnivores, interested in many of the same foods that attracted people. Grizzlies had a diet that varied with the seasons and with the variable fortunes of the hunter.

Early explorers wrote of bears in groups, feeding on dead whales on the beach. But can you picture them, again in a gathering, in south coast woodlands in the autumn, snuffling and snorting beneath one of the ancient, spreading oaks whose acorns have ripened and are dropping? The mature adults' feet leave prints over ten inches long and six inches wide, and also the marks of long, hooked claws.

The *Gabrielinos* would have stood back and let these massive bears feast. There would be other trees bestowing other harvests. The Indians' first preference was for black oak acorns, which they brought down from the higher mountains for storage, but they took advantage of readily accessible coast live oaks too. Grizzlies, however, were at the top of the food chain and, particularly in a group, would feel little intimidation from men with arrows or spears. That kind of fearlessness would hasten the bears' extinction, once men arrived with more efficient killing tools.

In Grizzly Days by Krista Ward

In 1830, the grizzly population may have reached a peak of about 10,000. By then, Spanish *ranchos* and missions had released thousands of free-roaming cattle: good grizzly food, but generally eaten as carrion, rather than taken alive. The grizzly bear population, like other wildlife hunted by humans, plummeted after the 1849 Gold Rush. The bears were first killed as a food source. Commercial hunters sold the miners jerky made from deer and elk, but grizzly bear jerky was most popular and brought the highest price. "One of the people that contributed most to the extermination of the grizzly bear was Grizzly Adams," according to wildlife biologist A. S. Leopold. "I was amused to watch the television series about him where he is set up as a sort of St. Francis in buckskins. In point of fact he was one of the deadliest of hunters in California history. He spent all of his time shooting grizzly bears for the tallow . . . and for the meat." (1985, 84).

Those times, those changes, lay ahead. The Bear Flag Revolt, the selection of the grizzly bear as the official state symbol and the last sighting of a live California grizzly in 1924 in Sequoia National Park, are historic moments unimagined by—and unimaginable to—the Indians keeping their wary distance from those feeding bears under that oak tree, one autumn day.

Autumn in Southern California does not mark as pronounced a seasonal transition as comes to the state farther north, but it does herald change. Winter's cold rains are yet to come, but first the hot winds of autumn blow. When skies are clear and fair in the Great Basin and high deserts, air moves away from that high pressure and drops into the south coast basin, warming and drying as it descends, funneling through canyons, picking up speed, and finally, howling across the flat coastal plain and out to sea. These currents are called "Santa Ana winds," and they bring the wildfire season.

The chaparral shrublands of California evolved with fire—an adaptation to the Mediterranean climate type, where rains are limited to the winter while summer and early fall bring six months of drought. Many local plants not only endured periodic burning, but also adapted to fire as an evolutionary force on the landscape. Today, some depend on fire to assure long-term species survival. "Fire-adapted" could also describe the Indians who used fire as a land management tool. Today, Californians *fight* fire, and they rage against the disasters of periodic, inevitable firestorms. They have not learned to be fire-adapted Californians—just one example of a quixotic struggle by humans to reshape the state on their own terms.

Chaparral plants shut down during hot dry summers and awake to a brief growing season during the winter rains. Leathery leaves with waxy coatings minimize water loss in the long arid seasons. But wax is flammable, ensuring that, eventually, intensely hot fires *will* sweep through the shrublands.

Fire benefits this plant community by recycling nutrients otherwise locked up in dead stems and leaf litter. Organic matter that would rapidly break down in wetter regions may simply mummify in the desert (modern-day post-picnic litterbugs seem oblivious to this fact). Throughout California's arid regions, fire is actually the primary force of plant decomposition.

Only particularly hot fires, the kind fostered by the plant wax, can break tough seed coats. So germination coincides with the clearing away of competing overgrowth during fires and proceeds when the soil is well-fertilized by ash. Thick root crowns, just below the surface of some shrubs, are designed to survive fires. Sprouts will emerge from those charred crowns and rapidly grow, taking advantage of the pre-existing root system.

Lightning storms and the climate, including the annual Santa Ana winds, mean wildfires are a natural force here. But for thousands of years California Indians regularly set fires too. They burned to keep the grasslands open, to drive rabbits and to favor plants used by deer or used in basketry.

Whether set by Indians or started by lightning, and whether in chaparral or grassland or oak woodland, the frequent fires were often smaller than those today. The ironic explanation, the reason for some of our uncontrollable, devastating wildfires, is the effective fire suppression practiced since the early 1900s. Less than one percent of today's wildfires escape early control. Smokey Bear's message of strict fire prevention turned out to be shortsighted.

Southern Californians live in a "semi-arid" climate. An average year brings fourteen or fifteen inches of rain to Los Angeles—almost, but not quite, placing the region in the "desert" classification. Elevational bands of plant communities—pine forests in the mountains, chaparral lower on the foothills, coastal scrub and valley grasslands—apportion themselves to a given elevation, to soil variations and to terrain. But ultimately it is the relationship to *water* that is of paramount importance.

The coast live oaks that provided acorns for bears and other animals sank their roots into well-watered valley soils. They towered over native grasses and wildflowers of the coastal plain. Those grasses, too, produced a scene far different from today's. Almost no native grasses survive today, so it took clever "detective work" to reveal the character of the original grasslands and understand how they were transformed. Adobe bricks, in structures built by the early Spanish, helped unravel this mystery. They also heralded the first era of environmental change for California.

TWO

SAVE THE COWS ...
HORSES OFF THE CLIFFS

Remarkably, the totality of environmental change in colonial
California was initiated and sustained by just a few thousand foreign human beings. (Preston, 1998, 289)

In the year 1825 California was overstocked with horses, and
horned cattle, and sheep, and the [*Californios*], considering
horses of less value ... killed off many thousands ... that room
might be left, and pasture for the other kinds. (Garner, [1846]
1970, 103)

The adobe recipe calls for straw as binder, so an Indian laborer
gathers dried grasses from the meadows and hills near the mission.
He chops and breaks it into manageable pieces. Before treading it
into the adobe mud with his bare feet, he rolls up the long pants the
padres want him to wear. He stops to pluck a half-dozen seeds clinging to the cuff. Twisting corkscrew stems emerge from the points of
the stickers.

This Indian remembers a time when different grasses than
these grew nearby. Almost all he gathered today are the new type,
those that sprout only from seeds when the winter rains come. When
he was a child, before the *padres* arrived, most grasses grew from
root masses that re-sprouted every year. They went dormant during the long dry summers, their tops turning brown, but the rains

always woke those roots again. With so many changes coming to the Indian's people—to his world—the grasses seem a small thing.

He tosses the seeds into the doughy mud with the rest of the adobe mix.

Two hundred years later, scientists identified the leaves and cork-screw seeds of filaree (*Erodium cicutarium*) within adobe bricks from some of the earliest Spanish structures in California. They also noted diminishing signs of the native perennial bunchgrasses, like the needle grasses and rice grass.

Earth, water and straw binder are the ingredients in adobe. Also sunshine and time; about thirty days are needed to dry the mud mixture after it is formed into bricks. Adobe structures built with this recipe became the signature architecture of the Spanish and Mexican eras in California.

Such buildings appeared first in San Diego, when Portola's 1769 expedition founded a *presidio* (military garrison), and the first Roman Catholic mission for Alta California. By 1775, when the American Revolutionary War was just beginning on the far side of the continent, five Spanish missions had been established under Father Junipero Serra's leadership, and another *presidio* at Monterey was the region's capital. Twenty-one missions would be completed by 1823, none very far from the coast, scattered between San Diego and Sonoma.

The grasslands alterations that accompanied mission-building were so rapid and thorough that it has taken "detective work" to reveal what was here, and when and how the vegetation changed. The clues were sealed in the bricks of Spanish and Mexican build-ings. Adobe brick analysis began in the 1930s, on buildings covering a range of dates, including San Antonio de Padua (built in Jolon, in 1771), San Fernando Rey de España (1797), Mission San Jose (1797), San Francisco de Solano (in Sonoma, 1824) and Rancho Vallejo (in Petaluma, 1834–45). Others were added to the list more recently, as techniques for identifying tiny pollen grains were developed to supplement the search for larger plant structures. Pollen, blown in from surrounding areas, can reveal the presence of plants growing nearby that were not purposefully mixed into the adobe.

Analyzing material encapsulated and preserved in adobe bricks of different ages reveals three major waves of invasion. Mustard (with its bright yellow flowers) and wild oats may be two of the most recognizable "weeds" on California's wildlands today. They became widespread before 1845. The second phase, from about 1855 to 1870, brought filaree, mouse barley, and nit grass. Barleys and bromes dominated after 1870. Each successive wave of invaders trended to be decreasingly palatability for grazing animals, as annual "weeds," well protected by burs and barbs, took over.

San Gabriel Mission, founded in 1771, became the most prosperous mission. Two years earlier Father Crespi had described the Portola expedition's discovery of "a spacious valley, well grown with cottonwoods and alders, among which ran a beautiful river from the north-northwest. . . . We halted not very far from the river, which we name *Porciúncula*. . . . The plain where the river runs is very extensive. It has good land for planting all kinds of grain and seeds, and is the most suitable site of all that we have seen for a mission" (Bolton, 1927, 146–47).

That description of the Los Angeles basin seems not at all familiar and entirely out of context today. The equally unfamiliar name, *Porciúncula*, was soon dropped in favor of the "Los Angeles River." Water was the key to successful colonizing of that arid region. Father Palou, traveling with colonists about to found the San Gabriel Mission, wrote in his diary:

> Besides the water of the [Santa Ana] river, which can easily be taken out to irrigate much and good soil that is there, the plain has various [*arroyos*] of running water. Likewise to the west there is a great forest of live-oak and much good soil and several creeks with water. A league and a half from the Mission toward the said west is the *Rio de Señora de Los Angeles de Porciúncula*, which the whole year round has a sufficient volume of water with which much land can be irrigated. (Cooper, 1968, 19)

Near the new Mission a farming pueblo was founded a decade later, in 1781, with the ungainly name *El Pueblo de Nuestra Señora la Reina de Los Angeles de Porciúncula.* That would be shortened, in common usage, to Los Angeles, or, in time, simply to "L.A."

The pueblo began with forty-six settlers. Accounts suggest that it was hard to find people willing to move north from Mexico. Alta California was distant from the "civilized" portions of Mexico. Rather than a pioneer life of frontier freedom, the first settlers were under complete government authority regarding the places each settled and the market for their agricultural output. Spanish colonialism gave way to Mexican governance in 1822, which led to secularized missions and grants of land to some individuals. The romantic image that persists of that time centers around the life of *Californios* on those vast *ranchos.*

"We were the pioneers of the Pacific coast, building towns and Missions while General Washington was carrying on the war of the Revolution, and we often talk together of the days when a few hundred large Spanish ranches and Mission tracts occupied the whole country from the Pacific to the San Joaquin" (Vallejo, 1890, 183). Mariano Guadalupe Vallejo's memoirs were published in 1890, the year he died. He was born in Monterey in 1808. By 1820, when Vallejo was twelve, the mission system was well established, though only 3,270 settlers and soldiers lived in Alta California. And yet, by the end of that decade, a transformation of grasslands in California's coastal valleys had been unwittingly contrived. The *Californios* were discovering the harsh reality of California's changeable climate, with wet years followed by dry. Severe drought between 1828 and 1830 helped the landscape transition, as overgrazing paved the way for European annual grasses.

"In 1773 . . . all the Missions, taken together, owned two hundred and four head of cattle and a few sheep, goats, and mules. By 1800 all this was changed: the flocks and herds of cattle of California contained 187,000 animals . . . and large areas of land had been brought under cultivation, so that the Missions supplied the presidios and foreign ships" (Vallejo, 1890, 183).

The livestock numbers continued to multiply. When a severe drought began in 1828 (with no rain for twenty-two months in coastal Southern California), there were about 400,000 cattle, 300,000 sheep and an uncountable number of horses (uncountable because so many were roaming wild). Livestock grazed freely over the unfenced valleys and coastal hills, and some roamed wild into the interior grasslands of the Central Valley. Overgrazing and the seeds of European annual grasses began to transform the state.

Just a few decades later, by 1862, there would be an incredible 3 million cattle and 9 million sheep! The state's original "pastures" had been grazed by elk, pronghorn antelope and deer. Animal numbers and their impacts on the native grasses were kept in balance through long-evolved relationships between the vegetation, climate and local predators.

If horses and cows could do so well, why had native elk and pronghorn herds never reached similar numbers? Predators helped control populations, but the predator whose influence most declined during the mission years was the human. California Indians must have played a role in the predator–prey balance that limited the big grazing mammals. The Spanish harvested some of their own cattle and sheep, of course (though not horses, at first). But realize the relative numbers: only a few thousand newcomers were spread along the coast of California on land where Indian hunters once numbered in the tens of thousands. Those native hunters were being swept away by the European invasion.

Many of the changes within California during the Spanish and Mexican eras were unintentional. Certain plants arrived adventitiously, traveling in livestock fodder, carried in sheep wool, "planted" by animal droppings or transported by hooves. They spread rapidly once overgrazing had cropped away native competitors. Likewise, viruses and bacteria leaped from European to more susceptible Indian hosts, whose immune systems put up little or no resistance. Deadly diseases radiated through the Indian communities. Smallpox, tuberculosis, typhoid, dysentery, influenza and pneumonia were part of the deadly mix, common within the newcomers' society, but measles, chicken pox and others also swept through the native populations with devastating consequences. Between 1806 and 1810, a measles epidemic killed one-third of the Indians in the missions around the San Francisco Bay Area. Georg von Langsdorff, a naturalist with a Russian expedition that sailed into San Francisco Bay in 1806, wrote in his diary that "The measles had been very general here for some months, with fatal results to the Indians, and some thousands of them in *Nueva California* died of the disease" (Langsdorff, 1927, 126).

Cowhides became the moneymaking industry for the missions and *ranchos* once Yankee sailing ships began to visit the coast to trade. As cattle were more valuable, the great, free-roaming horse herds became a competitive liability. The hands-off approach to animal husbandry took a grim turn.

"In 1806 there were so many horses in the valleys about San José that seven or eight thousand were killed. Nearly as many were driven into the sea at Santa Barbara in 1801, and the same thing was done at Monterey in 1810" (Vallejo, 1890, 188).

The same harsh practice became a picturesque part of the family memoirs written by actor Leo Carrillo:

> Near the beautiful old adobe ranch house [on the old Rancho Santa Margarita], which now is the headquarters of the Marine General commanding Camp Pendleton, was the bluff where horses were driven to their death so that there would be more grazing land for the cattle. The vaqueros would spread out into a long line and start the wild horses running ahead of them. Gradually the vaqueros would close in closer and closer on the horses, keeping them headed in one direction. Suddenly the wild horses would realize that they were trapped between the hated men and a great cliff which lay ahead. Hundreds of them . . . plunged over the cliff to their death. (Carrillo, 1961, 253)

Environmental changes during this era were most profound along the coastal corridor from San Diego to San Francisco Bay, where the missions and *ranchos* concentrated. Richard Henry Dana did not travel more than a few hours inland from his ship during the 1834–35 visit he detailed in *Two Years Before the Mast*. But his descriptions show that native wildlife still remained impressive. Near San Diego, he wrote, "Hares and rabbits . . . were abundant, and, during the winter months, the waters are covered with wild ducks and geese. Bears and wolves are numerous in the upper parts, and in the interior, (and, indeed, a man was killed by a bear within a few miles of San Pedro, while we were there,) but there were none in our immediate neighborhood" (1949, 154).

As the horse-killing episodes show, the pastoral life of the *rancheros* was not a gentle one. Encounters between bears and vaqueros became one way to spice up the tranquility of early California life. Grizzly bear numbers probably increased due to the hide and tallow trade because so much beef carrion was discarded after the valuable hides were stripped. Vallejo described how grizzlies "used to come by night to the ravines near the slaughter-corral where the refuse was thrown by the butchers. The young Spanish gentlemen often rode out on moonlight nights to lasso these bears, and then they would drag them through the village street . . . and when they were tired of this sport they could kill him. But sometimes the bears would walk through the village on their way to or from the corral of the butchers, and so scatter the people" (1890, 189).

Bloody bear-and-bull fights became popular. They are an intriguing metaphor for the struggle that was underway between native species and the newcomers. Vallejo noted that the fights were held at Easter and on fiesta days to celebrate the patron saint of a mission. A hind foot of the bear was often tied to the bull's forefoot, "for a large grizzly was more than a match for the fiercest bull in California, or indeed of any other country" (Vallejo, 1890, 190).

Handicapping the grizzly upset Englishman W.R. Garner, who complained in an 1846 letter, "Should the first bull not kill the bear . . . a second one is brought in, and sometimes a third, but the bear never has fair play; as he is made fast by the hind leg . . .

Detail from *Lassoing a Bear* by A.F. Harmer, 1865. Courtesy of University of Southern California, on behalf of the USC Library Department of Special Collections.

[and] the bear is destined to be killed whether he conquers or not" (Garner, 1970, 154).

The Spanish and Mexican eras spanned almost eighty years in California. Though the *padres* and *rancheros* confined most of their activity to the coast, changes were inexorably spreading into the interior. Wild livestock roamed into the Central Valley. Diseases spread along Indian trade routes. Parties of mountain men—trappers seeking beaver and otter skins—slipped into loosely held Mexican territory by backdoors: over the mountain passes of the Sierra Nevada and the northern Cascades. In 1832, John Work's Hudson's Bay Company trapping party (over one hundred men, women, and children) came down through Oregon to the Central Valley. Near Marysville Buttes, north of present-day Sacramento, Work wrote in his diary: "We have been a month here and we could not have fallen on a better place to pass a part of the dead winter season. . . . There was excellent feeding for the horses and abundance of animals for the people to subsist on; 395 elk, 148 deer, 17 bears, and 8 antelopes have been killed in one month" (Work, 1945, 31).

Yankees had begun to join the Mexican *Californios*, occupying roles as merchants and traders in the pueblos, some marrying into ranchero families. "We find ourselves suddenly threatened by hordes of Yankee emigrants, who have already begun to flock into our country, and whose progress we cannot arrest," Pío Pico, a prominent Californian, lamented in 1845. "They are cultivating farms, establishing vineyards, erecting mills, sawing up lumber, building workshops, and doing a thousand other things which seem natural to them, but which Californians neglect or despise" (Fogelson, 1967, 12).

Much of California, though changing, was still wide-open frontier. During the 1840s, American soldier John C. Frémont led several scientific explorations that eventually touched on every region of California. His diaries describe the wildlife, trees and flowers, including orange fields of native poppies, blue-flowering lupines growing head high, and almost everywhere he went, lush fields of filaree—the exotic grass with corkscrew seeds.

> Between the head of the Tulare lakes and the mouth of the San Joaquin, from the 19 January to the 12th February [1846] . . . the evergreen oaks were in flower, *geranium cicutarium* [filaree] was generally in bloom . . . making on all the uplands a close sward. The higher prairies between the rivers presented unbroken fields of yellow and orange colored flowers, varieties of Layia and Eschscholzia Californica [poppy], and large bouquets of the blue flowering nemophilia nearer the streams. (Spence, 1984, 517)

In early April, along the upper Sacramento River, "The salmon crowd in immense numbers up the Umpqua, Tlamath [Klamath], and Trinity rivers, and into every little river and creek on the coast north of the Bay [of] San Francisco" (Spence, 522). In late May, they camped near the same Buttes where Hudson Bay trappers had wintered more than a decade before: "Game was very fat and abundant; upwards of eighty deer, elk, and bear were killed in one morning" (527).

In mid-September 1846, the Salinas Valley's "good range, grass and acorns, made game abundant, and deer and grisly [sic] bear were numerous. Twelve of the latter were killed by the party in one thicket. . . . We saw among the upper boughs [of Valley Oaks] a number of young grisly [sic] bears, busily occupied in breaking off the smaller branches which carried the acorns, and throwing them to the ground" (Storer and Tevis, 1955, 63).

Frémont was near the pueblo of Los Angeles in February 1847: "[B]y the end of the month, the face of the country was beautiful . . . covered with a luxuriant growth of geranium . . . and along the foot of the mountains, bordering the San Gabriel plain, fields of orange colored flowers were visible at the distance of fifteen miles from Los Angeles" (Spence, 1984, 545).

Colonel Frémont played a supporting role in the Bear Flag Revolt in the summer of 1846, when a short-lived California Republic declared its independence from Mexico. He was an active participant when the United States successfully went to war with Mexico that same year. In February 1848, the Treaty of Guadalupe Hidalgo made California a U.S. territory (along with territory that would become the states of Nevada, Utah, New Mexico and portions of Arizona and Colorado). The new border with Mexico extended far enough south to include the valuable harbor of San Diego.

Meanwhile, up in the Sacramento Valley, Captain John Sutter had been building a personal agricultural empire since 1839. After his employee, James Marshall, discovered gold along the American River, the pace of environmental change suddenly accelerated.

THREE

GOLD FEVER: AFFLICTED FOREFATHERS

The idea of a mighty river being taken up in a wooden trough, turned from the old channel, along which it has foamed for centuries, perhaps, its bed excavated many feet in depth, and itself restored to its old home in the fall, these things strike me as almost a blasphemy against Nature. (Clappe, 1970, 162)

The sawmill being constructed by James Marshall's crew for John Sutter in 1848 would harness some of the American River's flowing water to power a large blade. Trees from the Sierra foothills could then be cut into planks for building barns and houses on Sutter's lands or to be sold to settlers arriving in the Sacramento Valley. Adjustments were needed to the millrace, through which water flowed to turn the mill wheel, so on the morning of January 24, James Marshall walked along the race, shutting off the water.

"It was a clear cold morning; I shall never forget that morning . . . my eye was caught with the glimpse of something shining in the bottom of the ditch. There was about a foot of water running then. I reached my hand down and picked it up; it made my heart thump, for I was certain that it was gold" (Kirsch and Murphy, 1967, 291). Marshall's heart "thumped" at the very possibility of gold. A few months later, hearts by the thousands were thumping with gold fever. Within a year a mass migration followed that catapulted the new U.S. territory into sudden statehood. The Gold

Rush has been considered the phenomenon that gave California a "running start" toward greatness. It certainly produced the first of many population booms.

The population of the formerly Mexican *ranchos* and pueblos was numerically overwhelmed. Only 13,000 *Californios* and anglos combined were in California when Marshall made his find. A staggering 90,000 gold seekers arrived in 1849. By 1852, the population of the young State had climbed to 250,000. Only twelve years after Marshall's gold discovery, the rush was over as a force fueling immigration, but the population was near 380,000. From 1848 to 1853, because of the rush to California, the geographical center of the U.S. population shifted eighty-one miles west. (Statistics like these ignore the California Indians. Their numbers, roughly 300,000 before the Spanish arrived, fell to 30,000 as early as 1850.)

The Forty-niners were not intentional "state-builders" and not the pioneers one might prefer for California, if given a choice. They were men (even by 1852 only 15 percent of the population was female), mostly young men, caught up in a mania of gold fever. Sheer numbers and a harvest of wealth accelerated the territory's transition to statehood, but the Gold Rush years left a physical legacy of environmental loss and a "mine the wealth" mindset that shaped the following decades. Writer Bayard Taylor saw the California environment under the miners' assault as being like "a princess, fallen into the hands of robbers, who cut off her fingers for the sake of the jewels she wears" (Taylor, 1862, 155).

Some of the Forty-niners recognized the effects of gold fever in themselves. Miner William Swain, in an April 1850 letter to his family in New York, wrote: "The emigration to this country has been marked with a different stamp and character from any other emigration. It has generally been the emigration of individuals, not families. Their hearts have been left at home. . . . They have considered that as this is but a temporary stopping place for them, they have not been called upon to do anything for California but all for themselves" (Holliday, 1981, 369–80). J.S. Holliday's book,

The World Rushed In, is built around the diaries and correspondence of Swain and other miners. Holliday notes that "These people came as exploiters, transients, ready to take, not to build . . . they found themselves surrounded by crowds of hurrying men concerned only with how to make the greatest amount of money in the shortest time. With that common motive, they also shared an indifference toward California and its future" (1981, 197).

The fever did not heat up overnight. News of Marshall's find, at first kept secret by Sutter and his workmen, leaked out and was reported in San Francisco newspapers, but was received with general skepticism. In the spring, Sutter sent the military governor some gold samples. First Lieutenant William Tecumseh Sherman, then stationed in Monterey, later wrote: "I took the largest piece and beat it out flat, and beyond doubt it was metal, and a pure metal. Still, we attached little importance to the fact, for gold was known to exist at San Fernando, at the south, and yet was not considered of much value" (1945, 30).

Belief, building to excited conviction, came only after a cunning entrepreneur began "beating the drum" in San Francisco, and after government officials, including the president of the United States, certified to the nation the rich character of the gold deposits.

Sam Brannan was one of California's earliest "boosters." A Mormon elder, he was part owner of a store not far from Sutter's Fort, with ties to the Mormon crew building the sawmill. He also owned a San Francisco newspaper, the *California Star*, and would eventually expand his business interests from that port city to include flour mills, warehouses and extensive real estate holdings. In May 1848, poised to sell hardware and camp supplies to prospectors, he stepped off a boat at San Francisco holding a bottle of gold gathered from the workmen at Sutter's Mill. Waving the bottle overhead and waving his hat in the other hand, he hollered, "Gold! Gold! Gold from the American River!" (Dillon, 1981, 284).

It was effective. Brannan's *California Star*, on Saturday, June 10, 1848, reported:

Every seaport as far south as San Diego, and every interior town, and nearly every rancho from the base of the mountains in which the gold has been found, to the Mission of San Luis, south, has become suddenly drained of human beings. Americans, Californians, Indians and Sandwich Islanders, men, women and children, indiscriminately. There are at this time over one thousand souls busied in washing gold, and the yield per diem may be safely estimated at from fifteen to twenty dollars, each individual. (June 10, 1848)

Sherman's commander, Colonel R.B. Mason, the military governor of California, made a personal inspection of the gold fields later that summer, and sent a report to the Secretary of War on August 17. Apparently a believer in completed staff work and the adage, "Seeing is believing," Mason sent 230 ounces of gold to Washington, D.C., along with his report:

We reached San Francisco on the 20th [of June], and found that all, or nearly all, its male inhabitants had gone to the mines. The town, which a few months before was so busy and thriving, was then almost deserted. At the time of my visit [to the American River], but little more than three months after the first discovery, it was estimated that upwards of four thousand people were employed. . . . Two ounces were considered an ordinary yield for a day's work. . . . The discovery of these vast deposits of gold has entirely changed the character of Upper California. Its people, before engaged in cultivating their small patches of ground, and guarding their herds of cattle and horses, have all gone to the mines, or on their way thither. No capital is required to obtain this gold, as the labouring man wants nothing but his pick, shovel, and a tin pan, with which to dig and wash the gravel, and many frequently pick gold out of the crevices of rocks, with their butcher knives on pieces from one to six ounces. (Mason, 1848, 1–6)

The final skeptics were convinced, at last, when President James K. Polk told Congress, on December 5, 1848, "The accounts of the abundance of gold in that territory are of such an extraordinary character as would scarcely command belief were they not corroborated by the authentic reports of officers in the public service" (Jackson, 1980, 64).

Overland travelers had to wait for spring, but boats began leaving the east that winter, taking miners to California "around the Horn" or to land crossings at Panama or Nicaragua. They made up new verses to sing to the popular song "Oh! Susanna":

> I soon shall be in Francisco, and then I'll look all round,
> And when I see the gold lumps there I'll pick them off the ground.
> I'll scrape the mountains clean, my boys, I'll drain the rivers dry,
> A pocket full of rocks bring home, so brothers, don't you cry!
> Oh! California, that's the land for me,
> I'm going to Sacramento with my washbowl on my knee.
>
> (Jackson, 1980, 69)

A picture of the Forty-niners mindset is revealed in those simple song lyrics: they would scrape the mountains, drain the rivers, get rich, then head back home.

> [February 17, 1850, South Fork of Feather River:] Here all know and feel that our acquaintance is of short duration, and almost all expect some day to return to the States. . . . Probably nine out of ten of the miners are calculating someday to return to the States. (William Swain, in Holliday, 1981, 329)

Many made it back home. Many who stayed did so because they had not found enough gold to pay their way back. Yet more kept arriving, attracted by hope and hype, by the real wealth of gold being shipped out of the state, and by this early manifestation of the California Dream. Nineteenth-century technology had begun to shrink the world. Ship sails were being replaced with steam engines.

News spread more quickly and long-distance travel was suddenly more feasible. Gold-seekers came from Mexico, Chile, Peru, China and Europe.

This growing population had to be fed. Fortunes were made selling supplies to the miners, but farming was not on the agenda for Californians during the early years of the Gold Rush. Sutter's laborers abandoned him for the gold fields. His agricultural holdings were seemingly ideally located to serve the demand, but rather than growing rich off the miners, he was overwhelmed. "Whoever wanted meat killed one of his sheep, hogs or steers. Dismayed, he observed the near ruin of his fort: 'Stealing began. Land, cattle, horses, everything began to disappear.' His fences were torn down piecemeal for firewood to allow hungry horses into his grain fields to graze" (Dillon, 1981, 297). Sutter's version of the California Dream drowned beneath waves of miners with other aspirations.

The miners came armed, and they hunted to feed themselves. The pre–Gold Rush abundance of wildlife disappeared. Swain, in an April 21, 1850, letter described the scarcity of game. Too many hungry miners crowded the riverbanks, so that deer "cannot go to the river to drink, or graze among the neighboring hills without hearing the crack of some hunting rifle" (in Holliday, 1981, 366).

Commercial hunters, responding to the demand, made enormous inroads into the wildlife populations. Grizzly Adams was the most famous of them. He specialized in killing grizzly bears in the Sierra foothills, which he sold for meat and tallow. Market hunter F.A. Isbell harvested the massive flocks of waterfowl in the San Jose valley, in the winter of 1852:

> We hunted ducks and geese; there were thousands of them; we could load the cart in two days. . . . I did not shoot at a single goose often. I have killed twelve at a shot, with both barrels; many a time have killed from four to six. One day I killed forty-four; at another time I killed twenty-five ducks at a shot with both barrels. They were all the same kind called widgeons. . . . From there we went to the Foot Hills to hunt deer and quail. We could get four

dollars a dozen for quail and twelve cents a pound for deer meat. I could kill from two to four dozen [quail] a day. (Isbell, [ca. 1871], in Thelander, 1994, 29)

Indians were hurt by this competition for resources, but inadvertent causes like wildlife declines and disease introduction were no longer the primary forces dooming native populations. Deliberate genocide arrived along with the Gold Rush. California historian Hubert Bancroft, from a perspective only four decades old, wrote that "the savages were in the way; the miners and settlers were arrogant and impatient; there were no missionaries or others present with even a poor pretense of soul-saving or civilizing. It was one of the last human hunts of civilization, and the basest and most brutal of all" (Bancroft, [1890] 1967, 474).

Water was the key to early gold mining. Gold Rush–era "mines" were actually the rivers themselves. Just as Marshall's discovery happened after water washed through the millrace, the miners used pans, and then increasingly sophisticated sluice-box systems, to wash river deposits. Besides the direct disturbance to riverbanks and riverbeds, and to the plant, insect and animal life of those riparian systems, the miners' "washings" became an erosive force that turned rivers dark with silt and mud.

In 1848 and early in 1849, gold was found by simply using picks, pans and shovels. Once hundreds of thousands of miners were digging at the banks of the Sierra rivers, those easy pickings were gone, so the earth needed to be dug and washed in greater volume. Riverbed mining developed as miners began to cooperatively build diversion dams to expose the beds of even the largest rivers. Work could not begin until the spring runoff ended. Once flows dropped, temporary dams and flumes would be constructed with timber logged from the nearby hills. Then came a frenzy of digging and sluicing in the dry bed, with an eye to the weather. The first heavy rains of autumn usually swept away all that year's construction.

William V. Mells, in "How We Get Gold in California," called riverbed mining, "'jamming' or turning a river." He wrote: "Every

River "turning" for placer mining, Middle Fork, American River, 1859. Photograph by Charles L. Weed, Courtesy of US Bureau of Reclamation.

bend or shallow place in the numerous mountain streams of the gold region has been thus attacked, the waters diverted from their course, and made to pass through artificial channels, leaving the old course dry for mining operations" (Mells, [1860] 1978, 10–11).

By 1852, the riverbed technique was widespread. "There is nothing which impresses me more strangely than the fluming operations. The idea of a mighty river being taken up in a wooden trough, turned from the old channel, along which it has foamed for centuries, perhaps, its bed excavated many feet in depth, and itself restored to its old home in the fall, these things strike me as almost a blasphemy against Nature" (Clappe, 1970, 162). Such objectivity was unusual in that time and place, but author Dame Shirley (Louise A.K.S. Clappe) was an observer, not a participant in the activity. She and her husband tried their hand at some casual panning, but he was a physician and she accompanied him to mining camps on the Feather River in 1851 and 1852.

Dame Shirley, from her perspective, saw the manipulation of mighty rivers as blasphemy. But the consequences to "Nature" went beyond the diversion of water. Modern riparian environments have taken on a special status because they have been so diminished, and are extremely rich biological resources. In drying and then digging up riverbeds, the miners killed plant and animal life that had formed the basis of river ecosystems. Fish, birds and mammals feed on insects, like stoneflies, caddisflies, or mayflies, whose larvae find niches in the riverbed itself. The food chain of a river begins with plants—algae growing on riverbed substrates and material dropping in from bordering plant communities. Though "turning" a river was temporary, the life in the rivers would not quickly return to the status quo when the water was back in its channel.

"The country is rapidly changing here in appearance," Hubert Burgess wrote in the early 1850s. "In going down the M[okelumne] River, [we] were several times stopped by the grandeur of the scenery. The only drawback to the view is the color of the water. So much work being done up the river, its color is brown instead of, as I have seen it, clear as crystal. The salmon still pass up, but to certain death" (Mumma, 1998, 23).

Mercury was commonly used to help capture all of the gold passing through sluice boxes. The mercury-gold amalgamation could later be separated by heating, with most of the mercury recaptured as vapor and cooled to be used again. Today we know that mercury is an extremely toxic metal. Yet it was in widespread use by the miners, who called it "quicksilver": Eugene Ring was disconcertingly casual about "the lively metal trickling" away into the river on his first day of prospecting, in April, 1850.

> Having accumulated quite a pile of earth, we pumped and rocked, and shovelled away untill [sic] near sundown. The drawers containing the quicksilver were then emptied into a pan from which the dirt was washed . . . in running water. . . . I took the Quicksilver which we fondly immagined [sic] rich with "oro" to the river and proceeded to strain it through a Chammois [sic] skin, a process to

> get rid of all the quicksilver but such as adhering to the particals [sic] of gold, for the amalgam.
>
> I squeezed and strained; the lively metal trickling through the pores of the Chammois [sic], the bulk growing smaller—smaller . . . certain misgivings entered my mind that it was all going through; and after giving the skin a last wrench I gently opening it, & discovered—amalgam—a little roll about the size of a duck shot and worth perhaps half a dollar. (Ring, Ring and Ring, 2008, 92)

By one estimate, 7,600 tons of mercury were lost into Mother Lode rivers. We cannot know how many miners' afflictions were actually related to such regular, close exposure to mercury. Symptoms of mercury toxicity are subtle and may affect many organ systems. Scurvy, due to diets without fruits and vegetables, and cholera, from poor sanitation, were more common complaints.

Today, mercury is just one of the heavy metal mine drainage issues of concern to the State Water Resources Control Board. Mercury standards for aquatic life and human health are occasionally exceeded in the Sacramento River, which receives water from all of the northern Mother Lode rivers. U.S. Geological Survey estimates show average deposits of seven ounces of mercury being carried daily toward San Francisco Bay. During the severe floods of 1997, on one day alone, "70 pounds of mercury, some 160 times greater than the dry season average, had been washed . . . down into the San Francisco Bay area" (Chatterjee, 1998, 19).

The eventual transition to hardrock mining in California would add another category of toxic discharges to watersheds: acid mine drainage, ". . . as corrosive as battery acid," seeping from mineshafts and tailing wastes into ground and surface water. Late in the twentieth century, the Sierra gold country experienced a real estate boom, with foothill communities becoming commuter suburbs for Central Valley cities. Homes were built on top of mine tailings, still toxic from miners' arsenic "in concentrations up to 50 times higher than the level deemed safe by government. Californians are discovering the poisonous persistence of their roots" (Greenwald, 1995, 36).

Would Eugene Ring or the other gold miners care about the environmental consequences passed down from their quest for wealth? That seems unlikely. Gold was their objective and very few saw their personal futures linked with California's fate. The ultimate manifestation of this tunnel vision was the development of hydraulic mining. Water, again, became the tool. It was gathered in reservoirs high in the mountains, dropped through flumes and pipes to develop a great head of pressure, then shot from iron cannons, called monitors, to carry away entire hillsides. The goal, as in a miner's pan, was then to use sluices to separate the light, "waste" material and reveal the heavy ore.

Focus on the land as you read miner William Mell's description, which appeared in 1860, in *Harper's* magazine, in the article, "How We Get Gold in California." Do not forget those hills, or their soil, grasses, shrubs, trees, insects, rodents, the birds that nested there and the larger mammals that passed through. And remember the rivers that carried the muddy "wastes" downstream, after the material passed through long sluice boxes.

[The water] is thrown with such force as to eat into the hill-side as if it were made of sugar or salt. Several of these streams directed upon a hill-side bring down more earth than a hundred men with shovels and picks could throw. But the art of the miner does not rest here. It is his constant aim to undermine as well as to break down; he consequently works, in a single day, huge caverns into the hill-side with his 'water-batteries,' until . . . a 'cave in' is about to take place . . . and hundreds of tons of earth are leveled down for washing.

The entire face of the country is being changed by the removing of hills and filling up of flats and canons, while some of the large mountain affluents [sic] of the Sacramento and San Joaquin rivers are becoming filled with the deposits. . . . The muddy current extends the entire length of the Yuba into the Feather River, and thence into the Sacramento far below Marysville. (Mells, [1860] 1978, 19–20)

Hydraulic mining, Malakoff Diggins. Courtesy of State Museum Resource Center, California State Parks.

An intriguing point about Mell's description is that it was published at least fifteen years before hydraulic mining saw it widest use. Charles Shinn, writing in 1885, was able to summarize effects of the actual peak years, when over 400 hydraulic mines were operating: "[after] 1876 a hundred million cubic yards of gravel, sand, and clay . . . washed into the Yuba and its tributaries; . . . in 1880 some 15,220 acres had been seriously injured" ([1885] 1948, 255).

The "injured" acres reference has nothing to do with the hillsides eaten away. It refers, instead, to farmland acreage downstream, near Marysville and Sacramento. By the 1880s, farmers and townsmen had settled in the Sacramento Valley, with interests diverging from those of the miners. The injury inflicted on the former was enormous. Total debris delivered to the valley, from all the rivers carrying hydraulic mine runoff, was close to 1.5 billion cubic yards—a staggering eight times the volume of earth moved in constructing the Panama Canal (Gilbert, 1917).

One month before the 150th anniversary of Marshall's discovery, in a story headlined GOLD'S TARNISHED LEGACY, a Bay Area newspaper described how hydraulic mining deposits sit beneath the eastern supports of the San Francisco–Oakland Bay Bridge, having washed from mines in the Sierra Nevada foothills, 150 miles away (*Alameda Times-Star,* December 29, 1997).

Our Gold Rush forefathers were afflicted with gold fever. The state of California, with early laws made by miners and for miners, will always carry the "pock-marks" of the pathology that shaped its early history. But hydraulic mining finally became too controversial. The mining industry was shocked when Sacramento Valley farmers won their lawsuit against a hydraulic mining company upstream. "Of that great struggle, which has been to all intents and purposes a suit between valley counties and mining counties, it is yet too soon to speak, for a generation must pass away before its results are manifest, but it will always rank as one of the most important judicial decisions ever made in an American state" (Shinn, [1885] 1948, 255).

FOUR

STATEHOOD, STATE WATER AND STATE LAWS

> Once admit that the highest use of the soil was to yield gold, and the rest follows as a matter of course. (Shinn, [1885] 1948, 254)

> This Spanish grant land-title system is one of the great drawbacks of this country. One man will make an immense fortune from that ranch, but the public suffers. (1861 journal entry, in Brewer, 1966, 170)

On September 9, 1850, President Millard Fillmore signed the act that made California the nation's thirty-first state. Another drought was occurring in 1851, and one of the first acts passed by the new state legislature required that a state surveyor be appointed to plan for improvements to navigation, irrigation, and drainage on the state's major rivers. They also adopted the English common law doctrine of riparian water rights, a decision that would eventually come in conflict with water appropriations by some miners and ranchers.

The first legislature's primary constituency was, at that time, overwhelmingly concentrated in the gold country and the city of San Francisco. If, up to then, the Gold Rush had been the compulsive mania of a hundred thousand men, now, through government deliberations, the miners' aims and their environmental impacts became institutionalized choices. California was born a gold-seeking state with a gold-seekers' legislature. More than thirty years had to pass before a judicial decision would finally say "no" to miners.

That message was finally delivered when Judge Lorenzo Sawyer, in January 1884, ruled in favor of valley farmers in their suit against a hydraulic mining company. Writers of that period were astonished. It was like an icy bucket of water being tossed into the face of a feverish miner, at long last lifting his attention beyond the personal fixation on gold-gathering. A pamphlet written in the year *before* the Sawyer decision, while the court deliberations went on, summarized the hydraulic miners' viewpoint: "It is not reasonable to presume that hydraulic mining will cease" (Evans, [1883] 1981, 16). How, the pamphleteer asked, could a business activity be ended that generated so much wealth, was fostered by the laws of the state and nation, and lawfully carried on? He conceded that there were real issues, including the "right" of a person to damage another's property, the maintenance of navigable rivers, the support of a growing population in the valleys, even the "influence on climate through the denudation of the forest land of the Sierra" (16). Yet, even in the face of those problems, it remained unimaginable that the practice should ever end.

Hydraulic mining was not banned outright by Sawyer's decision, but could no longer be practiced in ways that damaged downstream interests. Runoff material had to be confined on the mining site—an effectively fatal requirement. The judge's decision was anti-pollution rather than pro-environment. Mining site environments and river water quality were not specifically protected. However, deposition onto farmland, flooding of towns and obstruction of navigable waterways would no longer be allowed.

In 1884, the Sawyer decision was shocking because California law had, until then, placed mining rights above all others.

> At an early date the state courts of California decided that "agricultural lands, though in possession of others, may be worked for gold. . . . All persons," it is held, "who settle for agricultural purposes upon any mining-lands in California, so settle at their own risk."

[In 1850, in Grass Valley] two men fenced in a natural meadow. Here they could annually cut two heavy crops of hay, which was worth eighty dollars per ton. . . . However, . . . a prospector climbed the brush fence . . . struck "pay gravel," and in less than twenty-four hours the whole hay-ranch was staked out in claims of fifty feet square. . . . The tract was not property, in the miners' definition. (Shinn, [1885] 1948, 248, 251–52)

It was acceptable—and legal—for miners to undercut houses. Entire towns were moved. "Once admit that the highest use of the soil was to yield gold, and the rest follows as a matter of course." Substitute "environment" for "soil" and "fortunes" for "gold," and Shinn's summary of the prevailing thinking explains most of the environmental destruction throughout California's history.

Once surface mining was played out, the hunt for gold went underground. Hardrock miners did not claim parcels of land, but rather the right to follow a vein of ore wherever it might lead. A house or town might be undisturbed by tunneling far below—unless the vein led to the surface. Then, once again, mineral rights came first in the law.

In 1882, a mining company patented a claim on federal land north of Mono Lake, in the Eastern Sierra. Mining there was never profitable and shut down in a few years. Today, my house sits in a subdivision within that patent. The title documents to my home and my neighbors' contain this clause detailing "the right of the proprietor of any lode claim . . . which . . . may be found to penetrate, intersect, pass through, or dip into said land through the side lines of said lode claims, to enter said land along the dip of said vein or lode for the purpose of extracting and removing the ore therefrom."

Our real estate agent laughed when asked about the provision. "Don't worry. It's a holdover; language that is common on gold country deeds. But no one is mining in this location now." The legalese, we are told, is just an interesting anachronism. California society has changed in the last 150 years. Sluicing away homes or undercutting a subdivision is no longer acceptable in California.

Yet old mining laws continue to shape our lives, no matter how irrational they seem today. The federal government codified mining practices that originated in the California gold fields. The 1872 Mining Law still applies on federal public lands, allowing miners to stake claims and pay no royalties on the minerals extracted. Once a claim is patented the miner or (more commonly today) the international mining corporation, can own the property outright. The 1872 Mining Law makes no provision for environmental protection, says nothing about pollution or restoration of public land. It was written, after all, in a different era, when the government aimed to build the western states through mining.

California water law was also shaped by mining. Water had to be moved to process ore, first for washing gravel through sluice boxes, later to "turn" rivers from their channels to mine the beds, and eventually through dam construction and "appropriating" water by moving it through miles of flumes to supply hydraulic mines.

> The storage capacity of artificial reservoirs constructed by those engaged in hydraulic mining in California is estimated at 7,600,000,000 cubic feet. In older countries, where law and custom establish what is known as riparian rights, such a diversion would be impossible. What was at first the custom, was subsequently recognized by the law, special acts of the legislature being passed granting the hydraulic mining companies water-privileges unknown in other countries. (Evans, [1883] 1981, 11–12)

The riparian doctrine governing water rights conflicted with this new "appropriation doctrine." Miners and, eventually, irrigation farmers acquired rights by diverting water for use elsewhere. Under riparian law, however, water ownership came with the property through which a river passed. Eventually, court decisions created the hybrid California Doctrine, applying either concept based on which came first, land title or water diversion. Lawyers, as always, benefited greatly from the resulting confusion.

The California Doctrine emerged from an 1886 court case between land speculators in the Central Valley: irrigation water appropriator James Ben Ali Haggin versus Henry Miller and Charles Lux, ranch owners holding riverbank properties with riparian rights. These three men all came to California because of the gold discovery, but built fortunes outside the Mother Lode country. They, and a few others, followed an acquisitive path to land monopoly that still shapes California's development and water policies.

Haggin ultimately acquired more than 400,000 acres in the Central Valley, using "dummy entrymen" to circumvent acreage limits on federal and state lands. Miller and Lux used the same technique to build their land empire. Along with fifteen Spanish/ Mexican *ranchos* in Northern California, Miller/Lux holdings eventually totaled 750,000 acres. Familiar with the riparian doctrine governing water law in the rest of the nation, they purchased land along both sides of the San Joaquin River for one hundred miles, and a fifty-mile stretch along one bank of the Kern River. Their business, in the early years, was raising cattle for meat, as Miller was a butcher in San Francisco while Lux was the city's major meat packer. Lux handled financing for their partnership and Miller was out on the ground, buying land, managing ranches and constructing irrigation canals.

Federal mining laws, the Homestead Act, the Swamp Land Act and the Timber and Stone Act were all fraudulently violated, so that a few men, or their corporations, were able to acquire holdings greater than lawmakers had intended. Acreage limits existed so that public property would theoretically transfer to many small landholders, but hired "locators" were paid a few hundred dollars apiece to file on 160-acre parcels, and then transfer title to a single company. By 1871, nine million acres within California were held by just 516 men. It was a society dominated by a few powerful individuals.

California's Spanish and Mexican eras had established the pattern of vast land holdings, but those *ranchos* were now ripe for takeover. That opportunity, coupled with the exploitative mindset of the Gold Rush, may explain the prevalence of so much land acquisition larceny. With the addition of water, dry land eventually would be increasingly valuable real estate. The consequences of this concentrated land control are still felt in twenty-first-century California, though corporate, rather than individual identities, help to obscure that reality today.

The treaty ending the war with Mexico had declared that "property of every kind, now belonging to Mexicans . . . shall be inviolably respected." *Californios* would be "admitted . . . to the enjoyment of all the rights of the United States according to the principles of the Constitution; and . . . shall be maintained and protected in the free enjoyment of their liberty and property" (Robinson, 1948, 251). That language was not honored. Instead, the legal system itself became the tool for prying ownership away from the *rancheros*.

On March 3, 1851, Senator William Gwin's "Act to Ascertain the Land Claims in California" passed in Congress. *All* titles had to be proven with surveys and documentation. Land commission hearings were held from January 1852 to March 1856, but the commission findings were nearly meaningless, because all decisions had to be reviewed by an appellate court *and then again* by the Supreme Court. Claim settlements before the board *averaged* seventeen years. The original owners usually went bankrupt during those long years. Their attorneys sometimes became owners of the very land they had been hired to protect, when the grantholder had no other way to pay hefty legal fees.

Some of the land was taken over by squatters during the long delays. The northern California *ranchos*, in particular, were too close to the Gold Rush population boom. The City of Oakland, in the East Bay, began as a squatter's town. Its first mayor, Horace Carpentier, subdivided the town of Oakland on Rancho San Antonio. The Peraltas took legal action to recover their land, but it was 1910 before the case was settled.

Jackson A. Graves, attorney and banker, moved to Los Angeles in 1875 and was still working to settle land claims decades after the land commission hearings ended. "One can readily understand what a prolific source of litigation was the settlement of the title and the partitioning of these various grants among their numerous owners," he wrote (1927, 166). Graves's legal practice persisted so long in Southern California because there, outside the frenzy of the northern California Gold Rush, *rancho* lands stayed intact longer.

At first the "cow counties" reaped windfall profits from sales of beef to the mining districts. Within a few decades, Southern California *ranchos* held under such family names as Abila, Sepulveda, Pico and Yorba would transfer to a few Yankees—including Temple, Stearns, Forster—who would then give way to Flint, Bixby, Irvine and others.

Taxes, mortgage interest, chicanery and drought drove the changes.

> Parker H. French . . . using forged power of attorney . . . sold and mortgaged nearly "every ranch in the county worth the trouble." . . . Pío Pico in 1862 had paid moneylender Abel Stearns the principal on the $19,500 mortgage on Los Coyotes Rancho, but still owed him nearly as much interest. Meanwhile, Don Pío Pico and his brother Andres had entangled so many backers . . . [that] many rancheros of Los Angeles county with sound finances also were ruined." (Pitt, 1971, 107–9)

Besides legal fees and interest payments, the tax structure added to the *rancheros'* financial woes. "*Familia mia,*" Don Andres [Machado] said . . . "We must awaken to reality. Our holdings have been encroached upon by a new thing called taxes. . . . I have been compelled to meet my tax bills with coupons of land. Our thousands of acres have been reduced to a small area hardly large enough for the *casa*" (Carrillo, 1961, 48).

Spanish and Mexican *ranchos* had essentially been subsistence operations, generating income only through sales of tallow and hides, and later, for a few years, by selling beef to miners. But tax assessments *necessitated* profit-making operations. Even at twenty-five cents an acre, 10,000-acre pastures became a heavy burden.

Assessments based on cattle numbers were a greater problem when herds were shifted between counties.

Benjamin Hayes, who came to California in 1849, was an attorney and judge in Los Angeles, holding circuit courts in San Diego and San Bernardino. In 1856, during another drought, the judge visited John Forster, who owned much of what would later become southern Orange County, including the lands around Mission San Juan Capistrano.

> Since March 1st [Don Juan Forster] has removed . . . fifteen hundred head of cattle to a rancho in San Diego County, designing to remove another thousand now perishing here for grass. All of his cattle were assessed by the Assessor of Los Angeles. The Assessor of San Diego assessed to him 2500 head in that county; and he received notice that a sufficient number of them would be sold on August 10th to pay the tax. He hurried sixty miles to Los Angeles City for his certificate of assessment; thence to San Diego, 140 miles, to present it before the Board of Equalization. . . . [It] was concluded to await the session of the district Court. He says he has already traveled 260 miles on this business, been long delayed, with detriment every day to his stock; now has to travel another 120 miles; perhaps, employ a lawyer; lose more valuable time. His neighbors are in the same situation; indeed, the question has become of general interest, the inadequacy of pasturage having compelled many to remove their stock to San Diego, San Bernardino, Santa Barbara, or even Tulare. (Hayes, 1929, 114)

Drive the freeways across Orange County toward Disneyland and you are traveling over lands once held by one man. Bernardo Yorba's holdings included Rancho Santiago de Santa Ana (62,516 acres), Rancho Cañón de Santa Ana (4,449 acres) and Rancho Lomas de Santiago (47,226 acres). "Bernardo Yorba . . . in the day of his glory . . . might have traveled fifty to sixty miles in a straight line, touching none but his own possessions. His ranches . . . were delightfully located where now stand such places as Anaheim,

Orange, Santa Ana, Westminster, Garden Grove and other towns in Orange County—then a part of Los Angeles County" (Newmark, 1916, 177). Between the Lomas de Santiago and the ocean was Jose Sepulveda's Rancho San Joaquin (48,808 acres). Almost all of this ranchland, and more acreage farther north, was eventually acquired by venture capitalists (and sheep ranchers) Jotham and Llewellyn Bixby, Thomas and Benjamin Flint and James Irvine.

An exception occurred to that pattern when, in 1857, Yorba sold a relatively small piece of land near the Santa Ana River to a group of Germans, who named their agricultural colony "Anaheim." The farmers established a mutual water company to build small dams and a canal system to bring water to shareholders from the river, and they fenced their settlement with a dense willow hedge. During droughts, Anaheim remained green due to irrigation. "It is told that it became necessary for the citizens of Anaheim . . . to post men to fight off the inrush of the famished cattle" (Bixby-Smith, 1925, 82).

A transition to sheep rearing was forced by drought. Heavy rains in 1861 were followed by two years of drought severe enough to nearly finish the cattle industry (and bring the final demise of native grasslands). Perhaps 3 million cows died of starvation by 1864 in Los Angeles County. A rash of mortgage foreclosures followed.

Up in Sonoma, in Northern California, winter rainfall in 1875 would be just half the long-term average. Mariano Guadalupe Vallejo, doing his best to adapt to the demands of this new society, helped manage a water company in Sonoma. A letter in the Sonoma State Historic Park archives was sent on September 15, 1875, signed by Vallejo and James Forsyth, and is startlingly similar to exhortations made to customers by California water agencies during each modern drought:

> Dear sir: You are hereby respectfully requested to make an economical and judicious use of the water of the Sonoma Water Works for your domestic purposes, so that all subscribers may be equally benefitted thereby. Any extravagance and wastefulness

or gross carelessness in leaving the faucets open all night [will] be charged for accordingly. *M.G. Vallejo [and] James Forsyth*

Land acquisitions across the state, whether of *ranchos* or government lands, resulted in enormous monopolies. Most new owners, attracted to California by the Gold Rush, did not hold the land for social standing, as the *Californios* had, but evaluated acreage on profit-and-loss balance sheets. The laws of the young state and the nation fostered the transfer from owners who valued the land for itself, to speculators and land developers. Before the land investments would really pay their way and satisfactorily accommodate those changed values, one more land monopolist would emerge. The Southern Pacific Railroad would introduce mass marketing to the equation. An image of California needed to be widely propagated, to attract buyers for all that valuable real estate.

FIVE

RAILROADS AND REAL ESTATE, CITRUS AND SUNSHINE

CALIFORNIA, Cornucopia of the World—Room for Millions of Immigrants; 43,795,000 Acres of Government Lands Untaken; Railroad & Private Land for a Million Farmers; A Climate for Health & Wealth, without Cyclones or Blizzards. (California Immigration Commission poster, 1883)

This morning I was out at 6:30 and went to Hollywood again to look over lemon groves. (1904 letter, in Powell, 1996, 21)

The founders of the Central Pacific Railroad, known as "the Big Four," oversaw construction of the western portion of the transcontinental railroad to connect California to the East. Soon Huntington, Hopkins, Crocker and Stanford's corporation owned 11 million acres of unpopulated land within this state, granted to them by the federal government. One of them, Leland Stanford, was elected California's governor. The railroad company was poised to move real estate marketing into high gear.

Train tracks tied Sacramento to the rest of the nation after the golden spike was driven at Promontory Point, Utah, in 1869. Seven years later as the Southern Pacific Railroad (SP) they extended lines into Southern California. The Pacific Railway Act, July 1, 1862, " . . . granted to the said company . . . every alternate section of public land, designated by odd numbers, to the amount of five alternate

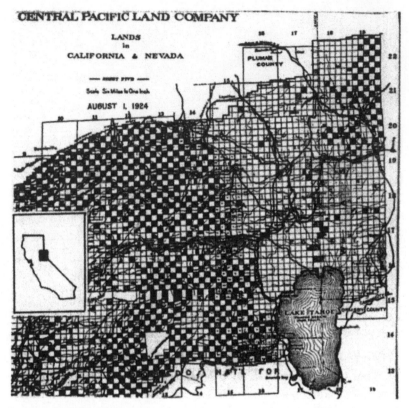

Detail of a 1924 map of railroad grant lands (alternate sections) near Lake Tahoe. Courtesy of U.S. Bureau of Land Management.

sections per mile on each side of said railroad . . . within the limits of ten miles on each side of said road." Later, the ten-mile zone on either side of the track was expanded to twenty miles. For every mile of rails it laid, the railroad company acquired up to 12,800 acres of federal land.

Not all the land through which tracks might be routed was public domain. So it was no surprise that SP, at first, avoided the coast, which had been in private hands since *rancho* days. Their first extension to Southern California came south over public property in the Central Valley. Land grants to railroads eventually totaled 11,585,534 acres—more than 11 percent of California's total acreage.

Here was land monopoly on a grand scale. It fostered wealth and potent political power for the railroads, particularly SP, the *sole* rail provider to the state from 1869 to 1887. The great scale of railroad real estate interests helped clarify the consequences of California's broad pattern of absentee land ownership. Big land-holdings, however acquired, did not point to one inevitable future for California. Dividing the property among many people through real estate sales would have been consistent with a populist ideal. For a while, then, California flirted with an idyllic vision of rural farms surrounding small urban communities. Los Angeles County became the nation's agricultural leader. Nevertheless, those farms and remnant wildlands would, in the next century, be drowned beneath relentless suburban sprawl and concentrated farmland ownership, made possible via long-distance water aqueducts.

The urban changes were driven by a growth dogma, known as "boosterism," in the final decades of the 1800s. The philosophy was proselytized so successfully that it became a seemingly unstoppable force. Marketing took the place of mining as the favored way to exploit California land values. Until the twentieth century, however, water would limit the market value of dry southern real estate. The attractive quality of life that went with small urban enclaves surrounded by farmlands only succumbed to the growth dogma of the land barons after ways were found to push past watershed limits.

Los Angeles' population stood at 11,183 in 1880. The great real estate "boom" of the 1880s pushed it to 50,000. In the final decade of the century the city's population doubled, reaching 102,000 by 1900. "During those boom years Los Angeles was having its first experience of rapid growth, and we were almost as proud and boastful then as we are now,—at least in quality if not in quantity. It seemed just as exciting to suddenly grow from ten to fifty thousand, as it does to aim at a million or two" (Bixby-Smith, 1925, 149).

The boom really took hold when SP's competitor, the Atchison, Topeka and Santa Fe Railway, laid track into the area in 1887. Fares dropped, and kept dropping, until the rate war between the Santa Fe and SP allowed travel from the Missouri River to California for only one dollar. Return fares were not so cheap. The "war" served the shared purposes of both competitors' long-term goals: marketing real estate while hauling freight for the growing region.

Advertisements saturated the Eastern states and even Europe, presenting a range of themes: tourism, health, agriculture, land for immigrants. The transcontinental railroad meant that the Western wilderness could now be crossed in relative comfort in about a week. Winter tourists, seeking escape from Eastern snowstorms, were courted. The health benefits of the climate, particularly for respiratory illness sufferers, were so successfully marketed that, for a time in the 1880s, Los Angeles hotels could not meet the demand for rooms for invalids. Land syndicates platted a hundred communities with 500,000 lots—many without a water supply. Construction never occurred on many of them.

Climate tied all of the subthemes together. Books, pamphlets and posters extolled "semitropical" Southern California and "America's Italy." The Southern Pacific Railroad staffed not only land offices, but also a literary bureau. Major Benjamin C. Truman authored *Semi-Tropical California: Its Climate, Healthfulness, Productiveness, and Scenery*, in 1874. Truman owned the *Los Angeles Star* newspaper, and became the chief of the SP's literary bureau in 1879.

Perhaps the most widely read publication (fostered by SP) was journalist Charles Nordhoff's *California: For Health, Pleasure, and Residence*:

> California is our own. . . . There, and there only, on this planet, the traveler and resident may enjoy the delights of the tropics, without their penalties; a mild climate, not enervating, but healthful and health-restoring; a wonderfully and variously productive soil, without tropical malaria; the grandest scenery, with perfect security and comfort in traveling arrangements; strange customs, but neither lawlessness nor semi-barbarism. (1873, 11)

Nordhoff touched all the themes, including the comforts of the railcars on the cross-continent trip, the must-see sights for tourists once in California, information for invalids, details about growing crops in the "semitropical" climate, and advice for settlers wishing to form cooperative agricultural colonies. He used the successful vineyard colony of Anaheim, established sixteen years earlier, as a model. Nordhoff strongly recommended that prospective settlers come to the railroad's land office

> . . . in the great San Joaquin Valley, which is just being opened by the building of the Southern Pacific Railroad, there are three millions of acres open to settlement. . . . There Government land can be had in eighty-acre tracts, under the Homestead Act, for nothing, and one hundred and sixty acres at . . . two dollars and a half per acre; while the railroad sections can be bought at low prices, and on five years' credit, in whole sections of six hundred and forty acres. If any . . . person in the East . . . should ask me what I would advise . . . I should . . . direct him first to . . . the land-office of the Central Pacific Railroad Company.
>
> If any Eastern mechanic, feeling the oppression of his circumstances, desires independence for himself and his children, he has, I verily believe, in this Southern California, and especially in the San Joaquin Valley, the best opportunity in the world to acquire it. . . . [S]oil and climate yield many of the costliest products of commerce; the climate is so mild that his children may play out-of-doors almost every day of the year, and his animals need no shelter in the winter, while his house need not be as stout as in the East. (1873, 177–78, 180–81)

As part of the California promotion, a giant sequoia was felled in 1891 at the request of Collis P. Huntington, one of SP's Big Four founders. Huntington had given his considerable support to the creation of the new Sequoia and General Grant National Parks in the Sierra Nevada mountains. The Mark Twain Tree was far too massive to actually be sent by rail across the country. Only two basal cross-sections of the 1,340-year-old tree were used; one was shipped to New York City for display at the American Museum of Natural

History and the other to the British Museum in London. The rest of the wood, from a tree that had been growing since AD 551, became fence posts and grape stakes.

SP was not alone in the marketing campaign. The Santa Fe Railroad created a "California Excursion Association." In 1885, oilman Thomas Bard and H.H. Boyce of the *Los Angeles Times* headed the Southern California Immigration Association, promoting the region throughout the nation. The association was replaced by the Los Angeles Chamber of Commerce in 1888. A five-man committee (four real estate men plus *Los Angeles Times* publisher Harrison Gray Otis) crafted the resolution that set forth the group's commitment to "permanent expansion." A year later the Merchants and Manufacturers Association was formed, another contrivance of Otis's promotional zeal. *Sunset Magazine* began publication that same year, 1896, founded by SP to promote westward travel. The name *Sunset* came from the *Sunset Limited* train, which ran between New Orleans and Los Angeles.

The extravagant marketing claims and frenzied real estate boom produced some local detractors. "Right here we must observe that thousands and tens of thousands are coming, not chiefly because we have a glorious climate, but simply because we have a boom," Mary C. Vail wrote in *Both Sides Told, or Southern California As It Is . . .*, a pamphlet appearing in 1888. She wanted to caution readers about unrealistic claims being made by promoters. The ultimate impression Vail gave of Southern California remained positive, but as a resident, she revealed discomfort at the effects of boosterism. "The great crowds who have hurried thither, seem to have come to build towns and cities, and a wonderful extent of these fertile valleys are staked off in town lots. It certainly would have been much better if these expectant townsites were yet under the direction of the intelligent plowman. All around the growing town-centers, land is too valuable to be devoted to farming" (1888, 8, 16).

Yet the scale of "urban sprawl" in the 1880s was minuscule compared to what would later come. In fact, agricultural growth had not yet peaked. Citrus orchards had been present since the Mission days, but in 1873 two navel orange trees were planted in Riverside. They were a new variety for the region. A few years later the Valencia orange was introduced to Orange County. The two varieties were ideally suited to differing microclimates of the coastal plains and foothills, so long as irrigation water was applied, and since they ripened in different seasons, were not direct competitors. Southern California's varied soils and conditions supported a full range of crops, but citrus became "king." Its success was aided by partnership with the railroads, building on their expertise at marketing.

> This they say—the happy dwellers,
> In that land of flowers and gold—
> That the orange is the symbol
> Of their health and wealth untold.
>
> If long life you would be having,
> Knowing naught of human ills,
> Daily eat at least one orange,
> Brought from California's groves.
> (Jacobs, in Caughey and Caughey, 1977, 216)

A poem competition was part of the 1907 Iowa advertising campaign of the California Fruit Growers' Exchange. With a matching grant from SP, the growers' slogan, "Oranges for Health—California for Wealth," spread across Iowa in a five-month test campaign. The marketing trademark, "Sunkist," emerged from this successful first effort at cooperative marketing. Colorful banners marked the sides of citrus railcars and crate labels became a new art medium. Though each citrus brand had unique labels, most depicted common elements: bounteous harvests, sun-drenched vistas with abundant water, all done in warm, lush colors. Across the nation, the labels marketed an Eden-like image of California, as well as the fruit inside the crates.

Citrus label, Arlington Heights Fruit Company, Riverside. *Artesia*, ca. 1893. Reproduced by permission of The Huntington Library, San Marino, California.

Southern California responds like magic to this chance to send her fruits to the East, and the area planted month by month is something enormous. It is estimated that the crop of oranges alone in 1891 will be over 4500 [train]car-loads.

Take Riverside as an example. In 1872 it was a poor sheep ranch. In 1880–81 it shipped 15 car-loads, or 4290 boxes, of oranges; the amount yearly increased, until. . . . In 1890 it rose to 1253 car-loads, or 358,341 boxes; and an important fact is that the largest shipment was in April . . . at the time when the supply from other orange regions for the markets East had nearly ceased.

The city of Riverside occupies an area of some five miles by three, and claims to have 6000 inhabitants; the centre is a

substantial town with fine school and other public buildings, but
the region is one succession of orange groves and vineyards,
of comfortable houses and broad avenues. Pomona [west of
Riverside] is a pleasant city in the midst of fine orange groves,
watered abundantly by artesian-wells and irrigating ditches from a
mountain reservoir. From the top of San Jose Hill we had a view of
a plain twenty-five miles by fifty in extent, dotted with cultivation,
surrounded by mountains—a wonderful prospect. (Warner, 1891,
119–20, 123–24)

The newspaper *Bradstreet's Weekly* published a survey in 1895 that
pronounced Riverside the richest place, per capita, in the nation
(Farmer, 2013, 223).

Despite the town-building frenzy of real estate agents and sub-
dividers, farmers created a society of small family plots and cooperative communities across the Southland. "Rarely . . . has such beauty
and civility, such luxuriance and orderly repose been achieved on
an American landscape as that brought about by citrus on the landscape of Southern California . . ." (Starr, 1985, 143). This emerging
citrus industry brought government pomologist G. Harold Powell
to Southern California in 1904 and 1909, to help growers reduce
spoilage during shipping. Powell's letters to his wife "back East,"
detailed a quality of life in Los Angeles and its rural surroundings
that appears enormously attractive today:

Los Angeles is one of the prettiest cities I have seen, and its beauty
is due to the large grounds and yards around the houses. In the
residence sections every house is surrounded with large grounds
that are planted with various trees, mostly orange, pepper, eucalip-
tis [sic] and Eng. walnut. The city is a hustling business town, over
100,000 people, fine blocks, elegant hotels, and real estate agents
thick enough to walk on.

This morning I was out at 6:30 and went to Hollywood again to
look over lemon groves . . .

The orange trees are a wonderful sight laden with their golden

fruit, set off against the rich green back ground [sic]. I wish you
could see them as you can have no real conception of their beauty
in any other way. (1996, 20–21, 31)

Starting with two navel oranges in 1873, their number grew to
more than five million trees by the turn of the century. Few imag-
ined, in 1900, that anything could seriously threaten the way of life
that came with citrus farming. For over seventy years, citrus groves
would provide beauty and wealth to Southern Californians, until
"inevitable progress" drowned their fertile soils beneath a flood of
housing tracts and asphalt.

As the nineteenth century closed, however, limits to local water
supplies threatened to limit the alternative future hoped for by
developers. The railroads felt the problem directly. They had millions of arid acres to market. With their potent political influence,
they helped push for solutions.

In the area of water policy, enlightened corporate self-interest
led the Southern Pacific to identify with "the public welfare" and
to work vigorously to solve water problems. Southern Pacific
[owners] approved the spending of funds and energy in water
promotion, placed their prestige and political influence behind
community efforts to build large water systems, and invested
private capital in irrigation and land subdivision projects. While
pursuing these goals, the Southern Pacific became a major influence on regional and national irrigation movements after 1880.
(Orsi, 1991, 49–51, 60)

In the opening years of the new century, Southern California's
native grasslands were a fading memory, but orange poppy fields
still blossomed on the arid upland valleys following winter rains.
Wildlife numbers were greatly diminished, but much of the native
diversity of species still existed in increasingly isolated populations. "In 1875, ranging in the Baldwin Hills and on the Sausal
Redondo, were seven wild antelopes, the remnant of a great herd

that once inhabited this portion of Los Angeles County. In the next few years they were all killed off" (Graves, 1927, 154). Rivers still ran in unconfined, willow-lined channels, jumping their banks during particularly wet seasons, and romping across floodplains. A few wetlands had been drained and planted to water-tolerant crops, but the shape of the coast had not been greatly altered. "Sportsman" Charles Holder could still write, in 1906, about water birds in great numbers:

> [A]ll the country to the south of the Palos Verde, near San Pedro, and extending to Long Beach, is a shallow back bay . . . often running back into the country to form some little pond or lake. At Alamitos, where the San Gabriel River reaches the sea, and at Balsa [sic] Chica . . . we shall find these lagunas, or sea swamps, the home of the duck, goose and swan. The season begins in November. . . . The air is clear, and the distant mountains stand out with marvelous distinctness . . . ducks, geese, and cranes are going south and . . . the winter shooting season has arrived. No more beautiful sight than this can be seen in Southern California when these vast flocks pass up and down, silhouetted against the chaparral of the mountain slopes. (1906, 51–52)

Those ancient, patriarch oak trees that had been spared the axe, valued for their shade and stately beauty, continued to drop acorns each fall. Raucous woodpeckers and nervous deer ate some of the harvest, but the grizzlies that once feasted below the trees had been driven into isolated pockets of wilderness. No California grizzly remained alive in Orange County after 1903. The species, though, kept a precarious hold on existence in mountains farther north.

Also at the turn of the century, certain people in Southern California began to wonder how to circumvent local limits to growth. A "water choice" would soon be offered to the people of Los Angeles.

Los Angeles Aqueduct System. Courtesy of Los Angeles Department of Water and Power.

PART II

HISTORIC CHOICES— EASTERN SIERRA WATER

1905 Los Angeles voters authorize Owens Valley project

1910 Los Angeles city population is 319,000

1913 Los Angeles Aqueduct starts delivering Owens Valley water

1920 Los Angeles population is 576,000, surpassing San Francisco for the first time

1920–1923 The city buys additional land and water rights in Owens Valley

1924 Valley men blow up aqueduct; Owens Lake is dry due to Los Angeles water diversions

1930 In prior decade, Southern California adds 1,368,000 people; $40 million bond issue passes in Los Angeles to build Mono Basin aqueduct and buy rest of Owens Valley water rights

1941 Water diversions from Mono Lake streams begin to Los Angeles

1970 A second barrel of the aqueduct is completed and groundwater pumping and Mono Basin diversions increase to keep it full

1972 Inyo County sues Los Angeles under CEQA over groundwater and irrigation issues

1976-1979 Court rejects two EIRs prepared for Los Angeles' operation of second aqueduct

1984 Inyo County/Los Angeles interim groundwater pumping agreement

1994 Los Angeles' water licenses are modified by the State to protect Mono Lake

1998 Los Angeles and Air Pollution Control Board agree to resolve Owens Lake dust storms by 2006

We are gathered here today to celebrate the coming of a king— for water in Southern California is king in fact if not in name. (First speaker at the opening ceremony for Los Angeles Aqueduct, 1913)

There it is. Take it. (William Mulholland's speech at same ceremony; *Los Angeles Times*, November 6, 1913)

SIX

MELODRAMA ON THE RIGHT SIDE OF CALIFORNIA

When I was a child I can remember the Bishop area as being a place where everything was green and lush. I can remember— but what's the use? The Valley had a grandeur then, equal to its mountains. Thank God, Los Angeles can't monopolize nor diminish Mt. Tom just yet. (Evaline Perry Penpraze, in *Saga of Inyo County*, 1977, 111)

The Sierra Nevada has two faces. The western slope rises gradually. Grassy foothills with oak tree clusters give way to expansive pine forests. Higher, still west of the crest, is backpackers' country. Gnarled trees survive there, clinging to patches of soil in granite basins. Streams pool in those basins to form blue lakes. High country scenery is stark—the beauty of clean edges and lines. But the sharpest line defines the crest itself and divides the two faces.

At the Sierra crest, snow and ice loom over a sudden, sheer drop into high desert basins—the "right side" of California. Only twenty miles to the east, the White and Inyo Mountains parallel the Sierra Nevada, rising nearly as high. The Owens Valley is a 90-mile-long trough nestled between the looming mountain ranges. A falcon launching itself from Mount Whitney (the highest peak in the Sierra Nevada range at 14,494 feet above sea level), could plummet 10,700 feet before reaching the valley floor.

Melted snow-water was once carried by the Owens River the length of the valley to finally spread into Owens Lake. Farther north, five smaller streams fed Mono Lake within its own separate basin. Both lakes, through the eons, became inland seas, salty with minerals washed in from surrounding lands. Both developed unusual natural ecosystems—salt-tolerant algaes eaten by brine shrimp or alkali flies that, in turn, became traveling fuel for millions of migratory birds.

On September 4, 1904, William Mulholland and Fred Eaton left Los Angeles in a buckboard, traveling north across the Mojave Desert toward the Owens Valley. The idea for the trip was Eaton's. Formerly superintendent of the water company that served Los Angeles, and later mayor of the city, Fred Eaton is credited with the original dream of bringing Owens River water 230 miles to Los Angeles. The audacious concept was worth investigating because of its powerful appeal to the local power-elite, the handful of land barons who owned most of Southern California.

For ten days, Eaton and Mulholland explored the valley and charted the river. Owens Lake, on those days in early fall, must have been teeming with waterfowl. Eight thousand people were living in the towns or scattered farms of the Owens Valley, while Los Angeles, after several decades of real estate booms, still had only 200,000 residents.

A true-life melodrama was about to begin in which Los Angeles, playing the villain's role, would appropriate the water of the distant agricultural valley. The city would expand its limits; San Fernando Valley real estate developers would grow richer; eventually 3 million citizens of Los Angeles would have a quality of life vastly changed from the population at the turn of the century.

Owens Valley homesteaders, farmers and townsfolk unsuccessfully fought eviction. Irrigated farmlands reverted to sagebrush while Owens Lake dried and died. In time, the City reached farther north and tapped creeks feeding Mono Lake.

This water melodrama, with aqueduct bombings, a "David and Goliath" theme, accusations of conspiracy and deception, and poignant personal losses, has kept versions of the story alive in print and film. The human theater remains compelling. But the environmental consequences at *either* end of the aqueduct also pose intriguing questions. What was it like in the Eastern Sierra 100 years ago, before its water was taken away? Was the Owens Valley, where the land was purchased by a distant city, actually "saved" from the rampant urbanization that diminished the quality of life in other parts of California? If so, what does that say about Los Angeles? What was accomplished there with imported water?

The Los Angeles Aqueduct was completed in 1913. Its costs were paid by bonds that city voters approved in two elections in 1905 and 1907. The city acquired water rights by purchasing Owens Valley land, and the federal government cooperated by withdrawing public lands in the valley from new settlement and approving the right-of-way where the 233-mile aqueduct crossed federal property.

South of the spot where the Owens River was diverted into pipes, the river channel went dry. By 1924, the once vast, living Owens Lake was a dead dustbowl. For a few decades, farmers and residents upstream of the diversions hoped they might be unaffected by Los Angeles' take of "surplus" water. But in the 1920s the City's purchasing program moved relentlessly north. Violent, but ultimately futile resistance developed.

In 1930, Los Angeles voters approved another bond act to finish buying land and water rights. Ultimately, Los Angeles acquired 300,000 acres in the Owens Valley, about 98 percent of all privately held lands. The new bond also funded an extension of the aqueduct north to the Mono Basin. Additional plumbing began diverting stream water away from Mono Lake in 1941. The effects on Mono Lake would foster a great environmental battle in the 1980s, and a victory for the lake supporters in 1994 that shocked the West's water establishment.

Owens Valley pioneer T.E. Jones was apparently blind to internal contradictions in his 1885 description of Owens Lake: "No living thing abides the surface of this water, perfectly clear as ever it is, neither fish nor fowl nor reptile nor anything, save millions of small white worms from which spring other myriads of a peculiar kind of fly. . . . Legions upon legions of a so-called duck . . . lived on the lake." These "Dead Sea" waters—which were actually teeming with life—exerted a sinister attraction for Jones's "so-called ducks" (probably eared grebes). "They are web-footed but have a bill like a common chicken. . . . These birds migrate from other regions, alighting on the Lake perfect birds, only soon to become bereft of feathers and even the physical power to prevent themselves from drowning whenever the surface of the water becomes ruffled by a continuous breeze" (Jones, 1885, in *Saga of Inyo County*, 1977, 10).

A toxic lake that could attract "legions" of birds to their deaths would certainly become a drain on native waterfowl populations. Jones failed to see that Owens Lake was an enormously productive food source, feeding vast numbers of migratory birds. Owens Lake, when it was alive (like Mono Lake today), served up enough food energy that grebes could undergo a complete molt and replace feathers in a very short time. Incidents of dead birds along the shore, even in the thousands, would not be uncommon, though usually statistically insignificant when a lake hosts millions of birds at once.

The odd chemistry of Owens Lake produced an ecosystem that seemed very strange to Jones. Mark Twain visited Mono Lake in the 1860s, and succumbed to the same "dead sea" terminology— followed by amazed descriptions of the numbers of brine shrimp and brine flies being fed upon by "countless" birds. Twain's book, *Roughing It*, so exaggerated the caustic quality of the alkaline water that today some visitors to Mono Lake are afraid to dip their fingers in, let alone swim in the lake.

Lakes that are too salty to drink, with no fish to eat, were deemed worthless by some human observers. That value system may partly explain what happened in the Eastern Sierra in the years to follow. Yet not all observers were so blind.

In the valley just under the Alabama Gates, the river divided and came together a mile or more downstream. This . . . was a sanctuary and feeding ground for migratory geese. Long V-shaped lines of the beautiful birds could be seen circling and settling for the night, or they continued on ten miles, to Owens Lake. The lake was alive with wild fowl, from the swift flying Teel [sic] to the honker goose. Ducks were by the square mile, millions of them. When they rose in flight, the roar of their wings was awesome. In the still, cold winter it could be heard on the mountain top at Cerro Gordo, ten miles away. It's hard to visualize all this as reality, unless one lived back there. (Beveridge R. Spear in *Saga of Inyo County*, 1977, 9)

Spear had lived there and knew it as a reality. Born in Lone Pine in 1894, she was not a humor writer, like Twain. Her family settled in the area in 1874. During the drought years of the 1860s, cattlemen had begun driving herds into the Owens Valley. By the 1870s, 200,000 head of cattle were using the area for winter range, but farmers and townsmen were also settling the Eastern Sierra.

The Paiute Indians of the Owens Valley had developed an extensive system of ditches and channels for watering crops. Within California's state boundaries, only the Owens Valley Paiute and Mojave Indians living along the Colorado River practiced irrigation-agriculture. In both places, plentiful river water ran through dry desert landscapes.

The new farmers and ranchers, in the final decades of the nineteenth century, expanded Owens Valley irrigation so that "by 1890 more than a dozen canals and ditches, with a cumulative total length of 250 mi (400 km) had been completed . . . over 46,000 acres were being irrigated (14,000 acres of cultivated cropland and 32,000 acres of pasture land)" (Babb, in Hall, Doyle-Jones and Widawski, 1992, 265).

It was fall [1901] when we arrived and the orchards were loaded with luscious peaches, pears, plums, and apples, and the arbors hung heavy with ripening grapes. The creeks were running full, even so late in the year, and nearly every yard had an icy stream diverted from the main ditch. (Charice Tate Uhlmeyer, in *Saga of Inyo County*, 1977, 212–13)

Farming and grazing began to spread over the flat valley floor, but the mountains were always close, a physical presence making wilderness a constant neighbor.

The fruit trees and the green fields with the high mountain peaks in the background were spectacular. Some of the mountains that surrounded us were over 14,000 feet high. I have often wondered what effect the mountains have on a person. I cannot imagine that anyone who lives under these noble peaks with such beautiful scenery could help but be happy. This valley would probably have been even more beautiful if they had not taken the water away. (Alcorn, 1991, 63)

The first water was taken in 1913. Changes that came to the Owens Valley were not widely felt, at first. Early land purchases by Los Angeles focused on the south end of the valley, near the Owens River diversion point. In fall 1911, when the Alcorn family arrived, the primary agricultural region around Bishop and Big Pine had not been touched. The Alcorns eventually lived on Tinemaha Ranch near Big Pine. "When we first moved to the ranch, there was a dairy herd of about 130 Holsteins cows. The dairy cows were on the ranch from the time we moved there until 1920. In later years, we had over 100 white faced Hereford cows and 10,000 sheep" (Alcorn, 1991, 35).

Climate and landscape gave a unique feel to life in the Eastern Sierra, differing from the west side of the mountains, the prairie farmlands of the Central Valley or California's coast. Descriptions of daily life in those first decades of the twentieth century regularly intermixed with details of the human settlements and the natural wilderness surrounding those towns and farms: the mountain vistas, streams, lakes and wildlife.

Owens Valley agriculture; Red Mountain Ranch near Big Pine (ca 1920). Courtesy of the County of Inyo, Eastern California Museum.

It seems only yesterday, really it was August, 1918, that my sister and I rode the little "Slim Princess," narrow-gauge railroad into the station of Laws, five miles from Bishop, and took a hard-rubber-tire bus over to Bishop. I was only eleven years old and water problems had no meaning for me. However, I had been impressed by the blue and sparkling water of Owens Lake as we had come by it on our trip up through the valley. I'm always glad that I have this memory as I drive by the dry and dusty lake bed today. Owens Valley was still a beautiful agricultural area at that time. As a high school boy at Bishop, I remember working during the summer vacations on the fine dairy ranches with their large fields of alfalfa. In my free time, I amused myself by spearing enormous carp in the large irrigation ditches that took the sparkling Sierra Nevada snow water from the Owens River and transported it to the arid lands of the Valley. (Wood, 1973, 1)

Richard Wood grew up in town (Bishop); Frank Madina was a farm laborer of Mescalero Indian background. He also recalled the mix of pastoral abundance and wild nature.

I came to Owens Valley many years ago. I was very young. The Owens Valley was very beautiful great big apple orchards pears and peaches and many other fruits, there was plenty water for irrigation, pure drinking water that came from springs and snow from the mountains . . . most of the farmers raised cattle sheep and hogs, . . . they raised chickins [sic] duck turkeys and rabbits . . . the farmers had beautiful Jersey cows for fresh milk and butter and cream. Bishop had a big creamery, all surplice [sic] milk that the farmers did not use was sold to the creamery and made into butter and cheese, and it was sold in L.A. or Frisco. . . . Fishing license was one dollar, fifty fish was the limit. . . . Deer, you could see them feeding along the river banks, deer season we use to go at the foot of the mountains and get a big four pointer buck, quail and grouse all over the valley, if you went high in the mountain you could get mountain quail, beautiful bird very big, and you could run into mountain sheep, you don't see them anymore, most of that animals were shot by greedy men. (Madina, 1990, 22–24)

On Owens Valley farms in 1910, there were 43,000 sheep; 5,000 horses; 20,000 cattle; 5,800 colonies of bees; 20,000 apple trees and 40,000 grapevines. Moreover, 58,000 bushels of corn were raised that year; 51,000 bushels of wheat and 53,000 bushels of potatoes (Smith, in Putnam and Smith, 1995, 254). At the end of that decade, the Bishop Chamber of Commerce described the valley's largest community as "a good town to live in" with "three banks, three hotels, two lumber yards, a flour mill, a creamery, an ice plant, five garages, a theatre and moving picture house, three weekly newspapers, and mercantile establishments representing practically every line of business" (Bishop Chamber of Commerce, 1920, 19).

All this activity made the water supply to the Los Angeles Aqueduct vulnerable. Too many water users were upstream of the Owens River intake. The early system had no storage reservoir above the diversion point to supply water through the inevitable drought cycles. And the thirsty, sprawling city was still growing. In the '20s, the melodrama reached a crisis.

By 1920, local irrigation for agriculture within the Owens Valley reached its peak, with 50,000 acres of pastureland and 25,000 acres of cropland. But flow into the Los Angeles Aqueduct also reached full capacity that decade. The city moved its land acquisitions program north, buying a patchwork of key parcels, then pressuring nearby neighbors to sell. A series of aqueduct bombings occurred in the 1920s, focusing the attention of media and legislature on the valley's plight. Outside interests condemned the methods and morality of the city's land and water grab. "The city concerned reverted to ruthlessness, savage disregard for moral and economic equations, to chicanery and faith-breaking. . . . The municipality became a destroyer, deliberately, unconscionably, boastfully" (*Sacramento Union*, April 3, 1927).

However, despite the ugly adjectives, the takeover was legal, at that time.

The unique farm valley reverted to desert scrubland, punctuated by a string of traveler-service communities. The economies of Lone Pine, Independence, Big Pine and Bishop converted to tourism, offering rest and refreshment for Southern Californians passing up the valley to mountain resorts. Yet the melodrama metaphor falls apart when it comes to a happy ending. No hero vanquished this "villain," "saved the ranch," married a rancher's daughter and lived happily ever after. In fact, this melodrama has not yet seen the curtain drop.

Los Angeles' control of Owens Valley river and groundwater is still contended today because of the environmental consequences of the dewatering. The difference in the modern desert valley is that dry uplands are no longer punctuated by wet streams and corridors of riparian vegetation. Pumping has lowered groundwater levels, killed trees and dried the few zones of marshland. Owens Lake quickly plummeted past the "Dead Sea" effect of increased salinity to become that oxymoron—a dry lake. Its alkali flats began plaguing the southern end of the valley as the source of unhealthy dust storms. To comply with air quality standards, Los Angeles began spreading water with delivery pipes and "bubblers" in 2002. In 2014, the city and the local air pollution control district agreed to a waterless dust control system of plowed furrows.

At the close of the twentieth century, lawsuits and negotiation finally returned some water to the lower Owens River channel, restoring a corridor of life (until the water is diverted, again, back into the aqueduct, and sent south to Los Angeles). Groundwater pumping is being managed under an agreement between Inyo County and Los Angeles, to minimize impacts on vegetation.

In human terms, the quality of life within the Owens Valley was forever altered when the Eastern Sierra became subservient to a distant, thirsty metropolis. Along the way, some of the melodrama's victims left poignant memorials:

"A Message From Owens Valley, The Valley of Broken Hearts"
To the legislature and People of California:
    We, the farming community of Owens Valley, being about to die, salute you!
                    Owens Valley Property Owners Protective Association
                            (opening words of paid notice in *Sacramento Union*
                                    and *Sacramento Bee*, March 19, 1927)

I don't want to go away. I love the hills and the sky, the sunshine and the desert, the flare of autumn and the promise of spring. I love the mountain lakes and the rushing streams; the song of the birds, the croak of the frogs, the call of the wild things. I love my home and the neglected garden, and I don't want to go. The . . . last apple

crop went to relieve distress in the homes of the unemployed in the
Great City. It was the last generous gesture of this despoiled land.
Today the trees that bore that crop are again white with blossoms,
but the petals of these blossoms will fall on parched ground. The
boughs will never more bend under their load of fruit. The water is
gone. It flows southward to the Great City. Be it so. The sin is not
ours. (Parcher and Parcher, [1934] 1970, 24, 41)

And oh, it was a wonderful farming country. Oh, it don't look like
anything now. The water's gone. . . . [A]ll that sweep from Manzanar
down there and all this over here by the White Mountains was all
farms, cattle, farms. And the people were really pretty well-to-do,
you know, that had those farms. But you know the water went,
well, the farms went. And you know down here at Manzanar they
had an apple orchard that they had started there . . . but you know
the water was taken away and the trees began to wither and die,
and finally they were all pulled out.

So you see, now when I came out of the mountains the other
day, came down off of the hills . . . we were looking at the valley
and you know, it's all withered and gone. You can see a house here
and there and all, but you don't see those farms—alfalfa farms,
corn fields, grain, why it's all gone and there's no water any more.
They can't do anything about it, you know. (Bulpitt, 1954, 29–31)

Was the Owens Valley actually "saved" from the relentless
urbanization that inflicted so much damage to the California
Dream elsewhere in the state? The mirror image of that question is just as intriguing: Without Owens Valley water, might Los
Angeles still offer the attractive quality of life of the small urban
center it was at the turn of the nineteenth century, surrounded by
agricultural land?

Today's sparsely populated Owens Valley *did* avoid the ugliness
of overdevelopment. Its open space, today, stands as an appealing
contrast to urban and suburban sprawl. But to accept that the natural character of the Owens Valley was "saved" means ignoring dead

streambeds, ignoring the killing of Owens Lake and the toxic dust storms generated off its salty bed, overlooking the effects of ground-water pumping on vegetation and wildlife, and accepting the threat that almost made a "dead sea" of Mono Lake. And that acceptance would disregard the aspirations of Owens Valley's early settlers.

Eastern Sierra water flows, now, to Los Angeles. The changes that resulted were enormous at *either* end of the aqueduct. They were changes forced on Owens Valley residents, but chosen by the power-elite and the voters they influenced in Los Angeles. Understanding the scare tactics used to convince voters to support the real estate hierarchy's vision of long-term growth is one key lesson from this historic melodrama.

SEVEN

LIFE IN THE BIG CITY—HOW DID THEY GET AWAY WITH IT?

One point emerges clearly . . . Los Angeles did not need the aqueduct to rescue it from immediate drought, but rather to allow it to grow. (Hundley, [1992] 2001, 152)

If Los Angeles does not get Owens water now, she never will need it. (William Mulholland, in *Los Angeles Times*, August 18, 1905)

In 1900, Los Angeles was a small urban center serving a rural county. The former "Queen of the Cow Counties" now held more farmers than cowboys or vaqueros. Fruit and vegetable harvests made Los Angeles County the number one agricultural producer in the nation, a positive result that emerged from several decades of "California Eden" promotions. But another outcome was a business community enamored by never-ending real estate booms. Local water limits threatened those dreams of the few men who owned almost all of the undeveloped land in Southern California.

On July 29, 1905, the *Los Angeles Times* headline read TITANIC PROJECT TO GIVE CITY A RIVER. Mulholland and Eaton's plan was revealed. Just five weeks later, on September 5, voters were asked to approve $2.5 million in bonds for purchasing Owens Valley water rights. A second election to authorize $23 million in construction bonds followed in 1907. Voters overwhelmingly passed both bonds. The first vote was 10,693 YES to 754 NO—14 to 1 in favor. The larger bond issue was approved by a 10 to 1 margin—21,923 to 2,128. Perhaps the "lopsided votes reflected the public's commitment to growth and the widespread belief that the entire community would benefit from the project" (Hundley, [1992] 2001, 149).

Or perhaps, rather than an enthusiastic endorsement, the votes are better interpreted as the successful result of an intensive propaganda campaign. The style of the campaign aimed at voters suggests that the outcome was not such an apparent certainty to those pushing the water project. Their message became inflammatory to the point of dishonesty. If the public was so committed to the purposes of the water project, why was it sold so aggressively? If the benefits were real and for everyone, why were people misled?

To ensure the right vote on the Los Angeles Aqueduct bonds, a public panic campaign was instituted. Similar campaigns by water agencies and growth promoters would repeat such tactics in California throughout the next century. The propaganda campaign told current users that *their* water supply was in imminent danger, yet the scale of the project was designed to enable future growth on undeveloped lands. The Los Angeles Department of Water and Power (DWP), ostensibly created to serve its water customers, became the essential tool of real estate developers. William Mulholland, superintendent of the water agency, served as the prime mouthpiece for the propaganda campaign.

"If we could only make the people see the precarious condition in which Los Angeles stands!" Mulholland told one gathering. "If we could only pound it in to them! If Los Angeles runs out of water for one week, the city within a year will not have a population of 100,000 people. A city quickly finds its level and that level is its water supply!" (in McCarthy, 1937, 31).

There were double that number of people living in Los Angeles at that time. The implication was that the present 200,000 people were already twice as many as local water supplies could actually sustain. Yet, despite Mulholland's dire predictions, and before any outside water ever did reach Los Angeles, the population would grow to 500,000, without shortages occurring.

"If you don't get the water now, you'll never need it. The dead never get thirsty," Mulholland ominously warned in a *Times* article on August 18, 1905. The *Los Angeles Times* joined Mulholland in "revealing" a dire shortfall facing the city's water users. "Facts relating to water development which would have been kept secrets lest they create a panic are now freely discussed" (July 31, 1905).

But panic was just what was intended. The *Times* publisher, Harrison Gray Otis, was one of Southern California's major real estate developers, and a member of two San Fernando Valley real estate groups that would profit enormously from the new water. Otis was not shy about using his paper to further his personal financial interests. When reading the newspaper or listening to Mulholland's speeches, citizens of Los Angeles heard that they were in the midst of a water shortage that had become critical. The drought was a surprising revelation, however, because during recent years, rainfall averages had been normal.

Some historians dismiss the fakery of the campaign's "drought," pointing out that dry years had been interspersed between wet ones and water conservation measures *were* needed— and instituted—during that period, to stretch local supplies to meet increasing demand. Yet, the revelations to voters, before the election, differed from weather and hydrology statistics in the permanent, official records. They were statements designed to influence the election.

> By the summer of 1905, when Mulholland discovered his drought, the city was in the midst of an especially wet year, with precipitation running more than 25 percent above normal . . . his sudden announcement of a lingering drought must have come as something of a shock to any residents of the city who had been following the water department's affairs. Mulholland warned that "Los Angeles could run dry in only a few weeks." (Kahrl, 1982, 85)

If the well-respected head of the water agency was making pronouncements that Los Angeles could "run dry," locals might understandably grow concerned, whatever their personal experience of local weather suggested to the contrary.

Here are the National Weather Service's rainfall totals for the Los Angeles Civic Center from the turn of the century (in inches, for twelve-month seasons ending June 30):

1900–01: 16.29
1901–02: 10.60
1902–03: 19.32
1903–04: 8.72
1904–05: 19.52 (the winter preceding the first bond election)
1905–06: 18.65
1906–07: 19.30 (the winter preceding the second bond election)

The average rainfall measured at the Civic Center over 135 years between 1877 and 2012 has been 14.98 inches. Note, in particular, the rainfall totals for the last two seasons; the second, larger bond election followed three wet years.

The city's business, real estate and political leaders formed the Owens River Campaign Committee to handle the election campaigns and get out the vote. Those institutions that had been so successful at promoting Los Angeles and Southern California to the world were in the right place to refocus expertise and attention toward influencing, now, a hometown crowd. The Chamber of Commerce, the Merchants and Manufacturers Association and the Municipal League became the core of the Owens River Campaign Committee.

On the day of the 1905 election, cars and carriages by the hundreds shuttled voters to the polls. The vehicles were paid for by the San Fernando Valley real estate group (known as "the Syndicate") and the other civic groups pushing the campaign. Why such extraordinary efforts for a water plan that would be enthusiastically endorsed by the citizens?

There were doubters; enough to be given a disparaging tag by the pro-aqueduct press. They were called "knockers." The *Times* newspaper competitor, the *Los Angeles Examiner*, initially took an editorial stance hostile to the proposal. A member of William Randolph Hearst's national chain, the *Examiner* was a newcomer in the city (since December 1903), and willing to question the unquestionable—the boosterism "gospel" proselytizing unlimited growth in Southern California. The paper termed the real estate speculation story the "Scandal of the Century," pointing out that the Syndicate—with inside information (probably supplied by Board of Water Commissioner Moses H. Sherman)—had completed its purchase of 16,000 acres of San Fernando Valley ranchlands *on the same day* that the commission heard via telegraph from Fred Eaton that he had secured the key land options in the Owens Valley. Other, even larger investments would follow, but on this first scheme alone, the *Examiner* foresaw Syndicate members making a profit of $5.5 million, after dry Porter Ranch lands received imported water.

If serving the city's population had been the primary criterion, alternatives to Owens Valley water existed that would have kept imports within the watersheds of Southern California. On August 2, 1905, the *Examiner* suggested "that Piru and Alamos Creeks, in Ventura County, could provide 4,000 inches of water over a distance of fifty-seven miles for only $3.3 million." That was a more environmentally sound option that might have served the needs of the existing population, plus allowed for reasonable growth. But it was an option that meant acquiescing to a limited vision of Southern California's future, one that would have left much of the former ranch landscape too dry for its current, speculative owners. Besides, that local water could be committed to the south coast's regional development, provided eight times as much was imported for the city from the Owens Valley. Boosters were not at all interested in the more constrained vision. Growth *within limits* and long-term stabilization were never tenets of their dogma.

Increased groundwater pumping from neighboring basins, like the San Fernando Valley, was another option. Agriculture within the south coast region could give way to the "needs" of the city, rather than Owens Valley agriculture. But Otis's *Times* explained to its readers the folly in that kind of thinking: "To take more water for the city from the underground reservoir would stop the growth of the surrounding country . . . [and] set a limit to the growth of Los Angeles" (Gottlieb and Wolt, 1977, 133). Of course, local agriculture ultimately would give way to the insatiable demands of urban sprawl within the Los Angeles Basin, anyway.

On election eve, September 6, 1905, the *Times* made its position crystal-clear: "It is not too much to say that every person who votes in the negative on Friday night will be placing himself in the attitude of an enemy of the city and will be opposing its progress and prosperity."

Even the *Examiner,* which had diligently questioned so many aspects of the aqueduct proposal, finally came out in favor, following a personal visit from its publisher. William Randolph Hearst, at that time, had strong presidential ambitions. After a meeting with city business leaders on September 2, he wrote an editorial for the *Examiner* endorsing the water project, and directed his staff to support it from then on.

Despite all of the clamor and controversy, despite the fleet of vehicles to shuttle voters, and despite the importance of this water choice for Los Angeles, only 11,447 ballots were cast in a city of 200,000 people. The decision to build the Los Angeles Aqueduct was made by a pathetically small number of voters.

The campaign to then approve construction bonds culminated in another election in June 1907. "On the morning of June 12 . . . the aqueduct forces began harvesting their votes. Some eighty-four autos and twenty carriages, donated for the cause, shuttled through the precincts all day long to bring supporters to the poll" (Nadeau, 1974, 34).

The water that the people of Los Angeles agreed to pay for reached the city six years later, on November 5, 1913. The new aqueduct itself reached only to the San Fernando Valley. From that high point, it was said, much of the water could be used to replenish groundwater supplies of the entire coastal basin. The ceremonial arrival of the first water in San Fernando, where the aqueduct terminated, attracted a crowd of 43,000 people to hear dignitaries' speeches. Mulholland's comments, before the water gates were opened, were short. Afterwards, as the torrent spilled down a foaming cascade-chute, the engineer's words had a fitting brevity that would ensure historical immortality: "There it is. Take it!" (*Los Angeles Times,* November 6, 1913, 1).

In 1905, in the year that the water choice was made, Los Angeles' population was 220,000. By 1910, with the aqueduct only half-completed, it reached 319,000. In 1920, the city surpassed San Francisco for the first time, with 576,000 residents. The population doubled yet again, in the next decade. The first half million was accomplished entirely with local water, but growth beyond that point, to over 3.8 million residents in 2015, came primarily with water taken from the Eastern Sierra. Beyond sheer numbers, in terms of environment and quality of life, what was accomplished with the water?

A real estate brochure was produced to publicize a new San Fernando Valley community called "Owensmouth" (a name that must have rubbed nerves raw in the Owens Valley, and was later changed to Canoga Park). The brochure's cover image artistically captured the promise of those early days: water poured from the mouth of an aqueduct pipe; the lines of falling water became the lines of an early twentieth-century business district, with blocks of homes nearby, then fields of row crops marching in the background toward mountain peaks. It was an idyllic mix, the California Dream come true. Developing and annexing San Fernando Valley communities, so that they could legally use city-owned water, were the next major steps toward that dream. In the 1920s, the artist's image seemed achievable. "From grain field to thriving community," read a 1922 account of Culver City, in the valley. "To appreciate Culver City . . . it is necessary to go back to the time when the townsite was nothing more than a field of grain on which a real estate man held an option" (Henstell, 1984, 15).

Mary DeDecker's family came to the San Fernando Valley in 1919. They had thirteen acres in fruit orchards in Zelzah (now called Northridge):

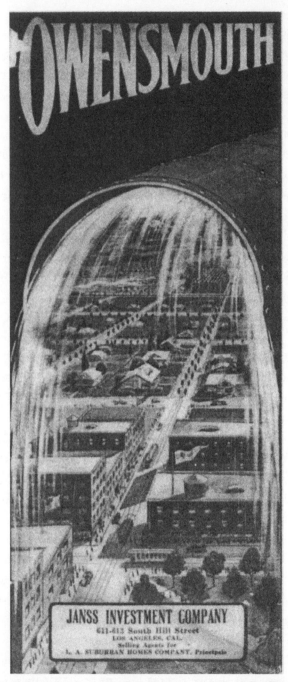

Owensmouth subdivision brochure cover. From Catherine Mulholland, *The Owensmouth Baby: The Making of a San Fernando Valley Town*, 1987. Courtesy of Catherine Mulholland.

It was farming and there were only two paved streets in the Valley at that time. . . . There were a lot of fruit orchards. They were growing citrus fruit, mostly oranges and some other things like melons, cantaloupes and watermelons. Around the borders of the Valley were lots of Oak trees in the hills and of course in the canyons they had a lot of native things. It was clean and just a pleasant place. The little town of Zelzah was not very big. We had a drug store, general store, a little grocery store and a service station and that was about it. (DeDecker, 1992, 2–3, 5)

The city's new water could only be legally used within the city itself. After all, it had been paid for by Los Angeles' citizens. So annexation campaigns to bring valley lands within the city limits were the next battles. Those campaigns degenerated to "big scare" tactics, also, including the delivery of bottles of smelly water to voters' doorsteps with notes attached, claiming that the foul fluid showed the quality of local water sources.

Existing valley towns—San Fernando, Burbank, Glendale and Lankershim—fought annexation. They were being asked to submerge their identities. Newspapers serving the towns newly created by the real estate companies were, not surprisingly, pro-annexation. Each decision to join the city added to the process that, ultimately, would create a sprawling megalopolis. The discovery of oil in Southern California and the Hollywood film industry accelerated the real estate boom of the 1920s, but water availability was the ultimate factor in facilitating continued growth. "The old carpet of gorgeous wild flowers is gone; cities creep over the plain and a network of roads covers the earth. . . . One beauty goes and perhaps another comes for those who have eyes to see—especially if they have a fair sized blind spot, which I find sometimes is a most satisfying possession" (Bixby-Smith, 1925, 172).

The 1920s, of course, also brought violent resistance in the Owens Valley. The next major move, meant to settle forever the city's problem in the Eastern Sierra, brought yet another bond issue before Los Angeles voters. These funds would buy the rest of the land and water rights in the Owens Valley, and extend the aqueduct north to tap streams feeding Mono Lake. Another fear campaign, the strategy that had worked before, was rolled out. Though Owens River water was enough to foster growth for many more decades, suddenly, again, the *Times* headlines screamed about a water shortage, only two or three years off!

CITY MUST VOTE BONDS OR THROTTLE EXPANSION

With Unchecked Population Gains Mono Basin Water Essential to Avert Shortage by 1932, $38,800,000 water bond to be voted on May 20; Bureau of Water Works and Supply issued a report so voters may know facts. . . .

In order to safeguard the city's present water supply in Owens Valley, and to develop additional underground water up there, the city must acquire additional lands and water rights, including the purchase of the towns. . . . Development and unchallenged control of these underground water resources requires the ownership by the city of all lands and water rights of every nature within the confines of the valley. (*Los Angeles Times*, March 16, 1930, 1)

Efforts of the business leaders and real estate interests were joined, this time by the Water Department, which had evolved into a major power in itself. The $40 million bond issue passed 8 to 1, in 1930. Purchases of Owens Valley land proceeded rapidly enough, but construction of the Mono Basin extension was not completed for ten years. No water shortage proclaimed itself during those ten years, despite the dire headlines of 1930.

The population of Los Angeles swelled to just under 2 million by 1950. Though Colorado River water was also beginning to be imported into other cities in Southern California after 1940, the growth of the city of Los Angeles in the thirty-seven years after 1913 was accomplished with Eastern Sierra water.

In 1959, Los Angeles Department of Water and Power (DWP) was told by the state that it could lose rights to Mono Basin streamwater if they were not used. Taking the additional water required building a second "barrel" for the aqueduct. Though the water itself was not then needed in Los Angeles, losing the rights for future use was inconceivable. Yet another bond was needed. It was issued in October 1963. No voter approval was required this time—water interests had succeeded in getting a charter revision in 1947 that let the board push ahead without an election.

In 1970, the second, parallel aqueduct was completed, doubling import capacity. It was to be filled by increasing diversions from the Mono Lake Basin, decreased irrigation of Los Angeles–owned pastures in the Owens Valley and increased groundwater pumping. Mono Lake's decline accelerated after the second aqueduct was completed. In the following decades, the salty inland sea lost half its volume and its salinity doubled. A citizens' campaign to "Save Mono Lake" began, and in 1978, the Mono Lake Committee and National Audubon Society sued Los Angeles. When courts ruled that the long-established water rights of Los Angeles must take into account environmental consequences, water agency executives throughout Southern California and the West expressed appalled amazement. The state was required to protect Mono Lake's natural values held "in trust" for the public. In 1994, DWP's state water licenses were ultimately amended, so that Mono Lake's unique ecosystem and the living streams that fed the lake would be protected. Once the lake recovered to a specified "management level," Los Angeles would be able to go on taking about 38 percent of the streamwater it had been diverting.

If only the idyllic Owensmouth image had held true. But the water falling from the pipe onto that landscape was unconstrained and unlimited; the image also conjures a flood, sweeping over the good life of Southern California. Were people blind to the consequences of this water choice? Or did the city they built match their dreams?

EIGHT

DID THEY SEE WHERE THEY WERE GOING?

Los Angeles is a real estate conspiracy rather than a municipality.
(Hearing comment, Commission on Industrial Relations, 1914, in
Mulholland, 1987, 78)

In 1905, the year when Los Angeles citizens were given the choice
to import Eastern Sierra water, Owens Valley author Mary Austin
went to Los Angeles. Her interview with William Mulholland led
to an article for the *San Francisco Chronicle*, published on September
3, 1905, in which she wrote: "Every considerable city in the State is
or is about to be confronted by a water problem. But what is to be
gained by the commonwealth if it robs Peter to pay Paul? Is all this
worthwhile in order that Los Angeles should be just so big?"

Mulholland's reaction to the visit from Austin was, "By God,
that woman is the only one who has brains enough to see where
this is going!" (Kahrl, 1982, 107). Clearly, Mulholland saw where
things were headed for the Owens Valley. But did he, and the prime
movers behind the water project, also have an accurate vision of
the consequences for their own city? Who were these driven men—
bankers, railroad tycoons, utility magnates, real estate developers,
newspaper publishers, politicians—and their effective engineer,
Mulholland? What motivated them?

They were the twentieth-century beneficiaries, directly or
indirectly, of the land legacy inherited from the Spanish and

Mexican eras. Land grants led to ownership patterns different from anything possible in the Owens Valley, which was never claimed by *rancheros*. In the Eastern Sierra, federal acreage limits applied to homesteaders. President Theodore Roosevelt explained the Progressive philosophy in his Annual Message to Congress, on December 3, 1907:

> Especial attention was called to the prevention of settlement by the passage of great areas of public land into the hands of a few men. . . . [W]here the small home-maker cannot at present utilize the land . . . the government shall keep control of it so that it may not be monopolized by a few men. The government should part with its title only to the actual home-maker, not to the profit-maker who does not care to make a home. Our prime object is to secure the rights and guard the interests of the small ranchman, the man who ploughs and pitches hay for himself. (Roosevelt, 1907, 2)

This philosophy makes the Federal government's participation in the Owens Valley water grab astonishing—fathomable only if the phrase was actually inverted in the minds of the power-cartel. "The greatest number equals the greatest good" better states the perception of land developers (and better describes the dogma that has shaped most of California's growth). Lofty motives for acreage limitations never stood a chance in California, where private land monopolies had been carried over at statehood and then expanded during the latter half of the nineteenth century.

Morrow Mayo, in his 1933 history of Los Angeles, incorporated a personal letter from Gifford Pinchot explaining why National Forest status had been extended onto non-forested federal lands within the Owens Valley.

> It is perfectly true that I did what in me lay to prevent the people of Los Angeles from being held up by a handful of people—and a very small handful of people—living along the line of the proposed

canal. The essential fact is that I used the power that lay in me for the greatest good of the greatest number, and that the results have abundantly justified my action. (1933, 236)

Mayo's conclusion, in contrast, was that the greatest good for the greatest number would have been a water project protecting Owens Valley agriculture while sending *surplus* water to the city. He harshly concluded: "The Federal Government of the United States held Owens Valley while Los Angeles raped it" (1933, 246).

Investors in the San Fernando Mission Land Company, usually referred to as the Syndicate, included Henry Huntington of the Pacific Electric Railway, E.H. Harriman of Union Pacific, Moses Sherman of the Los Angeles Pacific Railroad, W.G. Kerckhoff of the Pacific Light & Power Company, Joseph Sartori of the Security Savings Bank and Trust Company, L.C. Brand of the Title Guarantee and Trust Company, E.T. Earl of the *Los Angeles Express* newspaper and Harrison Gray Otis, publisher and editor of the *Los Angeles Times*. The Syndicate closed the deal on their 16,000-acre purchase immediately after Fred Eaton informed the water commission that key parcels had been acquired in the Owens Valley. The project had been, until then, a closely guarded secret, but Sherman, besides being a member of the Syndicate, was a Los Angeles Water Commissioner. The timing of the San Fernando Valley land purchase was, undoubtedly, more than coincidence. But there were no applicable laws against civic authorities profiting from such insider trading, at that time.

Competitors set aside business differences for common profits in the Syndicate. Sherman's trolley cars were competing with Huntington's "Red Cars," and both were rivals of Harriman and the still powerful Union Pacific Railroad company. Sartori and Brand were rivals in banking and title insurance (a business that was invented during the region's real estate booms of the late nineteenth century). Earl's *Express* regularly faced the fierce competitive journalism style of Otis, at the *Times*.

An even bigger land deal quickly followed, when the Los Angeles Suburban Homes Company bought 47,500 acres in San

Fernando Valley. As with the Syndicate, this company was most commonly referred to with a byname: "the Board of Control." The purchase was from the Los Angeles Farm and Milking Company, controlled by Lankershim and Van Nuys interests. James Lankershim originally purchased the ranch in 1860 from former California Governor Pío Pico. His dryland wheat farming was the bridge between the Mexican land grants and the new era of real estate speculation. The Board of Control included Otis, his son-in-law, Harry Chandler, and Sherman, plus Otto Brant, of the Title Insurance and Trust Company and Hobart Johnstone Whitley (a.k.a., the Great Developer).

> For all their individual differences, they shared an uncommon acquisitiveness for land, and had already done a great deal of business together. They had all invested in Whitley's first subdivision of Hollywood in 1901. Some were involved in Whitley's development of Corcoran, while others were partners in the C&M Company, a spread of almost a million acres along the California–Mexican border. They all held interests in the 270,000-acre Rancho El Tejon in Kern County. (Mulholland, 1987, 11)

Were they the region's benefactors, serving the community as they personally prospered? Should they be perceived as builders and providers who facilitated the California Dream for the masses? There is no question that a small group (fewer than ninety land barons) dominated Southern California's development in the early decades of the century. Chandler, in particular, amassed enormous real estate holdings. Following Otis's death in 1917, he deliberately (some say "shamelessly") used the omnipotent voice of the *Los Angeles Times* newspaper to push his personal agenda for the region: unlimited expansionism to be accomplished through aggressive boosterism.

In April 1896, the *Los Angeles Times* editorialized: "It is evident to the most superficial observer that no human agency could keep back the city from a career of astonishingly rapid progress toward the position which nature has evidently assigned her, as one of the largest cities of the United States, and probably the most important city on the Pacific Coast" (Gottlieb and Wolt, 1977, 64). Otis and Chandler's vision—the *Times* vision—perceived no limits for the real estate industry: "A boom which is destined to stay and grow and spread until the whole of Southern California, from the sierra to the sea, is one vast garden, dotted over with lovely homes." Note that this vision, though vast, was still of a garden "dotted" with "lovely homes" (Gottlieb and Wolt, 1977, 16). It called for all of Southern California to be developed, but forecast nothing of urban sprawl and congestion that might result from too much growth. "There is no room for knockers here," a promoter exclaimed in 1908. "We are too busy going ahead to listen to the man with a tale of woe. The fault-finders are not going to help matters by telling us things are going from bad to worse" (Fogelson, 1967, 190).

The great developers could have been benefactors, in fact, except for a failure of imagination. They did not recognize the actual consequences of too many people within the region. This blind spot in their vision may have been caused by the bright light of gold shining in acquisitive eyes.

John Anson Ford, one of Chandler's perennial foes in Los Angeles County issues, said, "If Harry Chandler had the same moral shrewdness and character as his commercial intelligence . . . Los Angeles would now be the finest city in America" (Gottlieb and Wolt, 1977, 121). The Chandler land empire totaled over 2 million acres by the 1930s, much of it suburban land, but even more consisting of agricultural and ranch lands with the potential of enormous profitability from subdivision and development. It included the 300,000-acre Tejon Ranch, sprawling north of Los Angeles into the southern Central Valley. That ranch would become a major agricultural beneficiary of future water projects within the state.

Chandler's empire even reached into Yosemite National Park. He was a stockholder and director of the park's concessionaire, the Yosemite Park and Curry Company. In the *Times* special

Panama-Pacific Exposition issue, January 1, 1915, marking the completion of the Panama Canal, a two-page photo spread described new concessions for Yosemite:

> *Ideal Hotel Conditions in Yosemite National Park, Club House, Music Room, Cottages, Swimming Pool, Dancing Pavilion, Bowling Alleys, to be opened to the public about May 1st, 1915.* For the first time in its history the world-famed Yosemite National Park will be conducted on a plan that will attract to it people who, while they love the wonders of nature to be found there, also demand hotel and living accommodations that will, in a measure, equal those offered at similar resorts throughout the European continent. The department [of the Interior] has granted a concession for a hotel and clubhouse in Yosemite National Park which will make it possible for tourists to follow the slogan, See America First, without having to suffer the hardships of pioneering.

Not surprisingly, the boosterism philosophy was practiced within the Curry Company, even when serving visitors to one of the nation's premier wildland preserves. The Curry Company's approach to national park promotion focused on developing hotels and shopping centers for tourists. "'A lot of people complain that there is not much to do except look at the scenery and camp,' one company official explained. 'We are going to give the people what they want'" (Gottlieb and Wolt, 1977, 159).

"Giving the people what they want," under the boosters' philosophy, was best accomplished through promotions to ensure that people wanted exactly what was for sale. Following World War I, yet another marketing organization was formed through Chandler's efforts, the "All Year Club," to push year-round tourism in Southern California and, of course, to attract more real estate customers.

Even when the vast land ownership monopolies were converted into many small landholdings, the objectives of Theodore Roosevelt's Progressive philosophy were not met. Much of the former *rancho* land was, at first, leased (rather than sold) for agriculture.

But that rural phase was temporary. There was far more money in subdivisions developed for many buyers than in a lesser number of farms and ranches. The speculators who acquired the former land grants pushed the subdivision process until it went too far.

There are indications that even Mulholland, the "high priest" of the water import effort, was unhappy with the actual changes he saw in the San Fernando Valley. "Instead of being developed as agricultural lands, the property has been subdivided into town lots and small 'rich men's country estates' at prohibitive values. . . . The capitalists who have brought up this property have looked forward to the time when the aqueduct would be completed and the plans for distribution of the water through this territory would enhance land values" (Mulholland, 1987, 74). In that complaint there is a hint of the agony of a man "just doing his job" and unhappy with the consequences, like an atomic scientist appalled by the bomb.

Mulholland is an enigmatic figure. As chief engineer of the water agency, he was the leading "mouthpiece" in the water campaigns. A self-made man, widely respected in his community, he appears, at times, to have been unwittingly used by the power cartel for its purposes. His personal motivations were those of a workman-like engineer, driven to solve problems and successfully complete projects. He projected an image of a gruff, self-educated man, the essence of practicality and common sense. Local newspapers played up Mulholland's image and quoted him prominently in editorials promoting the aqueduct. "By prominently featuring Mulholland . . . Otis and the Syndicate members believed that the charges of graft and corruption against them might be dissipated" (Davis, 1993, 29).

Mulholland came to Los Angeles in 1877. He grew up in Dublin, Ireland, later lived in New York City and Pittsburgh and passed through San Francisco on his way to Southern California, so he had a basis for comparison in his reaction to the city he would help change: "Los Angeles was a place after my own heart. It was the most attractive town I had ever seen. The Los Angeles River was the greatest attraction. . . . It was a beautiful, limpid little stream with willows on its banks. . . . It was so attractive to me that it at once became something about which my whole scheme of life was woven. I loved it so much" (Spriggs, 1931, 67). He began working as a ditch-tender for the private Los Angeles City Water Company in 1878. In the 1880s, living beside the Buena Vista Reservoir where he worked as a *zanjero* and dam-keeper, he spent his own money to buy and set out thousands of tree seedlings in the surrounding Elysian Hills.

When seasonal wildfires raged, he repeatedly turned down requests to send water department staff to help fight fires. He took a position against the nearly universal assumption, at the time, that brushfires must be totally suppressed.

> I know that my stand in this matter is not supported by any of the forest rangers, but I have come to this decision in regard to the damage done by brush fires, from observation. We have these fires every year, among the underbrush along the coast range. I have made close observation of the burned areas, the next year, and on the years following during the past twenty years.

His extensive quote ran in the *Los Angeles Times*, September 12, 1908, as wildfires were racing across the hills. "If a portion of the water shed burns off each year, then there is always a large majority of the shed covered with a new green growth that will defy any fire. . . . Experience has taught me that we cannot prevent [wildfires]." He repeated that his conclusions had been reached, "in the face of contrary opinions on the part of all the forestry men in Southern California," but he held to the wisdom of his own experience: "These brush fires burn until they get through and then they quit."

He was decades ahead of his time in his accurate appreciation of fire ecology relationships, but was preaching to a deaf congregation on most of those points. The chief engineer pushed for forest conservation, recognizing that a healthy forest on the city's watershed lands was essential to the groundwater supply of the entire Southern California basin.

Once he took on water import projects, however, he became a driven man. His career became focused on overwhelming whatever challenges lay in the way of bringing water to Los Angeles. The importance of his particular work and his gratifying effectiveness were recognized and rewarded. In time he became the highest paid public official in the entire state of California. But Mulholland is also remembered as arrogant, dictatorial, as one who savored combat and was ruthless about overriding perceived enemies to achieve his objectives.

> I remember how real hatred developed for the leaders of the Department of Water and Power in Los Angeles, especially William Mulholland. To the residents of Los Angeles he was the great hero engineer who had built the impossible 280-mile aqueduct bringing the waters of Owens Valley to San Fernando Valley. To the farmers of Owens Valley he represented greed, arrogance and overwhelming financial power that finally brought resistance in the valley to a halt. (Wood, 1973, 2–3)

Horace Albright, former director of the National Park Service, described a dinner conversation with Mulholland to *Cadillac Desert* author Marc Reisner. Mulholland told Albright that, in his opinion, Yosemite Valley should be photographed thoroughly, the images sent around the world, and then the valley's river should be dammed to "stop the goddamned waste!" (Reisner, 1986, 95). The appalling willingness to sacrifice the majesty of Yosemite Valley to human thirst stands in stark contrast to Mulholland's quoted statements about early Los Angeles and his reputation as a "nature lover." It seems probable that Mulholland took some pleasure in playing to his own notorious reputation at the dinner that night.

When his granddaughter was asked (for the public television version of *Cadillac Desert*) what William Mulholland might think of the extent of development that came to Los Angeles, if he could see it today and compare it to his personal hopes for the city, she said, "I think my grandfather, in his vision, pictured a city like Dublin—like his childhood—people knew each other. Growth sabotaged everything he did" (KTEH-TV Foundation, 1997). I asked her to expand on that answer; later, in a letter on May 30, 1999, she answered:

> I'm not too keen on speculating on another person's feelings, i.e., my grandfather's "possible reactions to Southern California today." In one sense, I don't have to speculate. I simply know he wouldn't like it. He wasn't too happy about the population surge in the 1920s, so you can imagine how the post-WWII world would strike him. Yet, like it or not, as an engineer committed to supplying water for his city, he would have been out there dreaming up designs for optimum use of existing supplies.

That kind of driven purpose, harnessed by the growth cartel, helped turn the California Dream into a marketer's ploy, with little concern for actual changes to the quality of life within the region. The growth machine, once up and running, was relentless. We are left to wonder what might have been. What if imported water had never come to Southern California?

NINE

WHAT IF THE LOS ANGELES AQUEDUCT HAD NEVER BEEN BUILT?

Just how important the citrus belt has been in changing the physical appearance of the land can only be sensed by trying to imagine what Southern California would be like were these green belts removed. They have contributed as much, perhaps, as any single factor to the physical charm of the region. (McWilliams, [1946] 1973, 208)

I used to like this town. A long time ago. There were trees along Wilshire Boulevard. Beverly Hills was a country town. Westwood was bare hills and lots offering at eleven hundred dollars and no takers. Hollywood was a bunch of frame houses on the inter-urban line. Los Angeles was just a big dry sunny place with ugly homes and no style, but good-hearted and peaceful. (Raymond Chandler's Los Angeles detective Phillip Marlowe, in *The Little Sister*, [1949] 1976, 183)

"The pilot has turned on the seat belt sign, as we make our final approach to the Los Angeles airport. Please return trays and seats to the upright position, and prepare for landing. Local air temperature is 67 degrees on this last day of 2015. Happy New Year to you all, and fly our airline again, soon."

Out the window, as the plane banks, the snow-capped peaks of the San Gabriel Mountains make a backdrop to geometric lines of orchards and rows

Poppy fields at Altadena, 1886; the trolley went to the bottom of Echo Mountain. Courtesy of University of Southern California Library, on behalf of the USC Library Department of Special Collections.

of field crops. Town centers poke their multi-story buildings above the rural landscape, like sand castles punctuating an expanse of otherwise flat beach. I close the internet connection on my laptop computer and crane to see the ocean as the plane completes its turn. There, offshore, through the famous clean air of Southern California, Catalina Island pops up on the southwest horizon. The tourist families near me are talking about their beach vacation.

"Oh, we've tried Florida, but the crowds are so bad. Southern California may offer less to do, without all the amusement parks that Florida has, but we like clean beaches. Not so awfully crowded. We always take some California oranges home with us, of course, when we go home. What's that? Northern California? Oh, the Bay Area's OK, but overbuilt. We drove from San Francisco across the Central Valley once, to Yosemite, and that whole corridor is just too much congestion and smog, you know?"

Strip away in your imagination all that came with the water imported from the Eastern Sierra. Set aside, for a moment, knowledge that additional water imports would follow after 1940. Visualize an alternate reality, some parallel universe, where Los Angeles moved through the twentieth century and into the twenty-first on a different path. There would still have been oil discoveries in the 1920s, but once the oil fields were depleted, they might have reverted to sheep ranches, rather than water-dependent subdivisions. A man-made harbor probably would have been developed serving Los Angeles, though it would not be as busy as today's harbor. World War II would have brought some West Coast military installations, but wartime and postwar military industry would go to regions with a larger workforce population, perhaps in Northern California. Freeways? They certainly would have come, but fewer in number and carrying far fewer cars. The entire region would be under less concrete and subject to very little smog. In the year 2016, details of life would differ, of course, from life in the first decades of the twentieth century. But with 500,000 people (instead of 3.8 million) in the city of Los Angeles, those differences brought by modern technology and conveniences would be experienced in a setting that had much more in common with life in Los Angeles a century earlier.

The rest of Southern California, in this scenario, would have felt less pressure to convert agricultural land to subdivisions. Overdrafting groundwater wells that served much of that agriculture would have become a critical issue. As the coastal plain's underground freshwater was over-pumped, saltwater intrusion would have been a problem. But those same problems developed and are being addressed in other California coastal basins today. Though irrigated acreage might have declined, better water conservation practices and groundwater recharging technologies may have become the norm in Southern California's citrus belt. Meanwhile, the natural environment might have survived intact in more locations around the fringes of this relatively minor metropolitan region.

Southern California's population increases after the early 1900s, beyond limits set by local sources, were possible *only* because of imported water. People who only know the Los Angeles of the twenty-first century may struggle with that concept. Surely the development of the mega-city, the reality of that vibrant sprawling global force known as L.A., was inevitable, wasn't it? The city certainly *must* have been fated to grow, sooner or later, some way or another. And what about those population figures? Where does the city population number of 500,000 come from? William Mulholland, after all, declared that without imported water the city could only sustain a population of 100,000. That, as history showed, was electioneering exaggeration, however. The city's water agency, DWP, acknowledged that local water sources—the Los Angeles and San Gabriel Rivers plus groundwater—could support about a half-million people (Los Angeles Department of Water and Power, 2016a). (Since the 1990s, actually, such effective water conservation measures were being introduced in Los Angeles that a common estimate for the number of urban users served by an acre-foot of water could be adjusted from five, up to seven or eight. If water conservation became the general practice, perhaps as many as 800,000 people could live in Los Angeles using local supplies.)

If an alternative historic path had been chosen for Los Angeles, life in the city would be far different today. What would the rest of California be like in that reality? Could the state's overall population approach anything like the current 39 million, if only 3 million were in the Southern California region? It seems more probable that those people, today, would be spread among other states or other nations. It is certain that they *could not be* in Los Angeles. The state's largest cities would be in northern California. Urbanization around San Francisco Bay would probably not be any more extensive it is saturated today, but development there might have been accelerated without the economic competition of the southern state. Urban sprawl into the agricultural regions of the Central Valley might be more widespread than today.

It is intriguing to imagine the Eastern Sierra as it might be if Owens River water had remained in its natural watershed. The Owens Valley town of Bishop might today be an urban center, though not the equivalent of Los Angeles. There is little reason to conclude that the 500,000 acre-feet (AF) of water used for 3 million people in Los Angeles would have inevitably transformed the Owens Valley into an urban city of that same scale. Location and climate are important differences.

One hundred fifty miles north of Bishop, in the Eastern Sierra, is Carson City, Nevada. The two towns share a similar climate and setting, with agriculture still dominating valley lands near Carson City. Nevada's state capital is at 4,660 feet above sea level; Bishop, at 4,147 feet. Annual precipitation averages only 5.76 inches in Bishop, but is 10.75 inches in Carson City. The Owens River flows past Bishop, while a similar river, the Carson, brings melting snow-water to the agricultural fields of the Carson Valley and the urban and suburban zones of Carson City. The population of Carson City is 54,000. Agriculture, including dairy and cattle ranching, has persisted into the twenty-first century near Carson City, though under pressure from sprawling subdivisions (ironically, most of the newcomers are emigrating Californians escaping their overcrowded state).

If the Reclamation Bureau had gone ahead with *local* irrigation development in the Eastern Sierra, enough assurance might have been added regarding water availability in dry years to spread more permanent cultivation, instead of intermittently irrigated pastures. More non-forage crops like wheat, corn, fruit trees and vegetables might have been grown in the Eastern Sierra, assuming the place of alfalfa and irrigated pasture. Modern reclamation technology and a bigger local population would have meant a strong local market for farmers. "Owens Valley with its rich soils and abundant water resources offered a far more likely prospect for agricultural development in 1900 than did the peat bogs of the Sacramento–San Joaquin Delta, the barren lands of the west side of the San Joaquin Valley, or the forbidding wastes of the Colorado Desert, all of which rank today among the richest centers of agricultural production in California" (Kahrl, 1982, 38–39).

Yet not all of the Owens Valley soil is fertile. Much of it is alkaline or rocky, and with the region's harsh climate, farmers on lands of lesser quality might have been inclined to sell out to developers. Industry might have invaded the area. The valley could today be fighting industrial air pollution issues as severe as those in modern Los Angeles. Owens Valley would still have the scenery, but might have congestion and pollution too.

As for its evolution into a service economy for recreational travelers, if there were no enormous population of Southern Californians just five hours to the south, the attractive mountain resorts would draw fewer people into the region.

The fate of Owens Lake is worth speculating about, because it touches on human nature and the way environmental controversies are resolved. In 1874, the deepest point of that salty inland sea was measured, from a steamboat, as fifty-one feet. But the lake naturally experienced wide fluctuations during wet and dry cycles. In that desert climate, an incredible six vertical feet of water evaporated away every year. Since the lake was quite shallow, a ten-foot drop could cut the lake's surface area in half. So, as farmers upstream diverted Owens River water to agriculture, Owens Lake quickly showed the effects, particularly in dry years. In 1899, the wharf that had served the steamboat was two miles away from a dropping shore. On August 4, 1904, the *Inyo Register* ran a story titled "Is Owens Lake Near Its End?" The lake was thirty-two feet lower than in 1874. The writer predicted that, at the rate of decline seen then, Owens might be dry in fifteen years. However, even with farm diversions continuing, the lake made a partial recovery during the following wet years, rising twelve feet between 1905 and 1913 (the years that the aqueduct was being constructed). Los Angeles' complete diversion of the Owens River, before it reached the lake, was the ultimate reason why the lake dried entirely by the 1920s.

Were Owens Valley irrigators going to kill Owens Lake anyway? Perhaps. Other farm communities destroyed major bodies of water through irrigation diversions. But the problems that followed, the loss of waterfowl and dust storms, would have been felt locally, and local diverters would have been directly affected, or directly under the pressure of the neighboring communities. A solution would have been forthcoming much more easily and rapidly than was possible for Eastern Sierra communities negotiating with a distant landlord—the city of Los Angeles.

In our imaginary, alternative reality, Bishop's small-town atmosphere might be lost. But one should never forget the Los Angeles basin within that same scenario. Southern California might still be a wonderful place; the images that sold the California Dream might still be essentially true. Honesty and self-interest make considering such historic alternatives a worthwhile exercise. Californians shape alternative futures every day. The future is no more inevitable now, no less a matter of choice, than it was throughout the last 165 years of California's statehood. If there is still good to be found in the California lifestyle, it, too, can be squandered if the lessons of history are ignored.

But, of course, the Eastern Sierra water choice was only the first of others to come. As Los Angeles' growth cartel and Mulholland assumed salesmanship and leadership roles again, Colorado River water spread new growth across the entire Southern California region.

There are the chances of developing from the Colorado River masses of power, alongside which the Owens production would be but a flash in the pan. The growth of Los Angeles that has astonished William Mulholland—he has expressed dread of that growth here in Fresno—has driven him on to new flights of the imagination, which probably makes him think with impatience of the Owens Valley as a minor feature of Los Angeles assets. But minor though it may be, it is still essential, for it is real and tangible while the Colorado River is speculative. (*Fresno Republican*, Nov. 29, 1924)

Colorado River Aqueduct. Courtesy of Metropolitan Water District of Southern California.

PART III

HISTORIC CHOICES— COLORADO RIVER WATER

1900 The Alamo Canal begins delivering water to Imperial Valley farms

1902 President Theodore Roosevelt signs the Reclamation Act, beginning a long series of investigations and reports on control and use of the Colorado River

1905–07 The Colorado River breaks through Imperial Valley Canal headgates; the Southern Pacific Railroad is finally, after two years, able to close the "leak" that forms the Salton Sea

1916 300,000 acres irrigated in the Imperial Valley

1925 Los Angeles passes $2 million bond act enabling surveys for Colorado River aqueduct route

1928 Metropolitan Water District of Southern California (MWD) formed; "vigorous campaign" launched to pass bond act for new aqueduct

1931 Voters approve $220 million bond to build Colorado River aqueduct

1933 Federal construction of Hoover Dam begins

1940 State population is at 6,907,387

1941 242-mile Colorado River Aqueduct completed by MWD, begins deliveries

1942 Imperial Valley receives first deliveries via the All-American Canal

1940–1947 State gains 3 million new residents

1950 State population 10,586,223; Los Angeles at just under 2 million; Orange County at 216,224

1955 Disneyland opens in Anaheim

1970 California least terns declared an endangered species, only 600 pairs are left

1985 MWD faces the loss of 800,000 acre-feet per year (AF/yr) of Colorado River water because Central Arizona Project is on-line

1988 MWD and Imperial Irrigation District (IID) agreement for 100,000 AF/yr transfer of water conserved by Imperial Valley farms

1999 MWD construct Diamond Valley Reservoir in an off stream valley near Hemet to hold Colorado River and State Water Project imported water

2002 When California fails to meet a deadline to end its reliance on surplus Colorado River water, the U.S. Department of Interior orders immediate cuts to MWD and IID; the state's population is about 35 million

2003 A Quantification Settlement Agreement is reached between California's Colorado River water users to comply with need to stop taking surplus water from the river; State agrees to take responsibility for impacts to the Salton Sea as agricultural drainage is reduced; San Diego County to receive 200,000 AF/yr after 2017

Water from the Colorado River: We Need It! Let's Go and Get It! A project that means the very life of our Southern California. (Citizens Colorado River Water Committee, 1931)

TEN

"AND LEST OUR CITY SHRIVEL AND DIE . . ."

Two men stagger across a desert landscape, wondering out loud if they can make it to water. They reach a waterhole, but it is dry. After a last shake of an empty canteen, one of the men dies in his partner's arms.

Those opening scenes in the movie *Thirst* were part of the 1931 campaign to bring Colorado River water to Southern California. As the parched man died on-screen, words suddenly appeared: "Presenting William P. Whitsett." The board chairman of the Metropolitan Water District of Southern California (MWD) used no subtlety in drawing the parallel facing Southern Californians: "This same tragedy has occurred many times in the history of man. The moral to be gained by it must be learned. For we here in Southern California are face to face with a water problem. While lacking the dramatic element, it is far more serious because it affects the lives and property of every man, woman and child in this region." All of Southern California, in his opinion, "was at one time a desert waste. We have reclaimed this desert and now we have in its place this growing empire." Images of citrus groves and downtown Los Angeles appeared to demonstrate his point of pride. "But the desert is ever around us, waiting and eager to take back what was once its own. And it *will* take it back, unless we bring in more water." Fountaining artesian wells were followed by a cartoon graphic of the declining water table, as Whitsett described the region's ground-water overdraft problem. "Unless we take immediate steps to bring in water from an outside source, the people of Southern California will be up against a serious water shortage. But we're fortunate at having within our reach a water source capable of supplying our needs. This source is the Colorado River" (MWD, 1931a).

In the early years, much of Southern California's farmland was irrigated from shallow wells that tapped water under so much pressure that it fountained freely to the surface. Pumps were not required. "There was an artesian well across the street." That was Henry Warne's first recollection, when asked how life in Orange County had changed since his birth there in 1914. He grew up on his father's sugar beet farm in Bolsa, and saw the transformations that came to the region, until his death in 1998. When he was forty-one years old, Disneyland opened five miles to the northeast. Millions of new residents who arrived during the second half of Henry's life would never realize that artesian wells and thousands of acres of wetland marshes were once part of the Orange County landscape. Freeways and suburbs thoroughly covered the county in 1997, when Henry considered my question. "One of the biggest changes," was his next thought, "You used to be able to see stars at night; the Big Dipper, Milky Way. Not anymore" (Warne and Warne, 1997).

Changes spreading across Southern California in the second half of the twentieth century, whether the obvious urban sprawl or the subtler characteristics of daily life, were primarily the result of Colorado River water. In 1931, south coast residents of "Thirteen Golden Cities" were targeted by a vigorous campaign effort. The decision reached by the voters of those cities had profound conse-quences for Southern Californians in every neighboring town and throughout the rural counties.

State Engineering reports reveal that Southern California is now actually consuming 170 million gallons of water each day MORE than either Man or Nature is replacing. A few years ago there was an artesian well belt in Southern California underlying 315 square

Colorado River Aqueduct campaign literature, 1931. Reproduced by permission of The Huntington Library, San Marino, California.

miles. Today artesian wells practically have disappeared. Instead, our cities and ranches are pumping water from depths varying from 120 to 350 feet. There is no substitute for water. (MWD, 1931b)

Particularly, there was no substitute for Colorado River water—this was the additional message in a widely distributed brochure. The cover invoked the patriotic image of Uncle Sam pointing at the reader, as on a military recruitment poster: "Uncle Sam Says to us: IT'S YOUR MOVE . . . I am building BOULDER DAM to save the WATER you need—YOU must build your own METROPOLITAN AQUEDUCT." An additional diagram headed, "Yesterday—Artesian Wells," depicted ripples of water beginning just below the ground surface. Beside that diagram was another: "Today—120 to

250 Feet to Water," with a well pipe penetrating through ground, past the words, "dry . . . dry . . . dry . . . dry," until finally tapping the lowered water table (MWD, 1931b).

Groundwater depletion was a real concern of Henry Warne's farming community and of townsfolk like Charles Pearson, the mayor of Anaheim:

When we first came here [in 1906] there were artesian wells in places from a mile and a half west of the city limits of Anaheim in different areas clear to the ocean. During the winter espe-cially between Anaheim and the beach areas, there was a lot of surface water which supported thousands of ducks and geese. As pumping increased, the water . . . dropped, and by 1920 people began to worry a little, because as the water went down they had to lower their wells, and had to put on bigger pumps. (Pearson, 1968, 34)

Pearson's observation that "people began to worry a little" is an interesting counterpoint to the MWD campaign hysteria. There is no question that the artesian belt was being overdrafted. Thirty-one wells in Westminster had average flows of 2,500 gal-lons per hour, according to the July 5, 1873, issue of *The Southern Californian*. Eventually 250 artesian wells were at work near that community, lowering the water table of the coastal peat lands where Henry Warne's family farmed.

Less than fifty years ago [in the 1870s], the now famous peat lands of the Westminster and bolsa country, known as *cienegas*, were regarded as worthless. In the fall and winter these marshy lands were the resorts of millions of wild geese; they were also the haunts of wild ducks and other water fowl, and were the favorite hunting grounds of sportsmen of that day. The early settlers counted the *cienegas* as so much waste land, or rather as worse than waste, for the drier portions of these swamps were

the lurking places of wild cats, coyotes, coons and other prowlers, which preyed upon the settlers' pigs and poultry. (George W.
Moore, in Armor, 1921, 165)

The Federal Drainage Act of 1881 produced funds and authority for ditches to carry water off Bolsa wetlands. Reclaimed land
began to grow celery and sugar beets. One hundred years later,
government agencies and environmental groups would scramble to
salvage a few remnant coastal marshes. "No net loss of wetlands"
would become official policy of state government, recognizing the
rich biological diversity (including "prowlers") of marshlands. By
1910, some well pumps were being used even in the wet peatlands
of Westminster, yet Henry, born in 1914, remembered that artesian
well flowing across the street.

Groundwater overdraft images became the "poster-boy" for
the campaign to bring water from the Colorado River. This time,
not only Los Angeles citizens, but also voters in twelve other cities
scattered across the southland were asked by their new water agency,
the Metropolitan Water District of Southern California (MWD),
to approve bonds to pay for a 240-mile aqueduct. MWD's original thirteen member cities were Anaheim, Beverly Hills, Burbank,
Compton, Fullerton, Glendale, Santa Monica, Long Beach, Los
Angeles, Pasadena, San Marino, Santa Ana and Torrance.

Ideas for using Colorado River water had been percolat-
ing ever since President Theodore Roosevelt signed the 1902
Reclamation Act. That started federal engineers on a long series
of Colorado River studies and reports, primarily meant to tame
periodic floods and provide irrigation water to farms in the valleys near the river. A long-distance aqueduct to the Southern
California coast was a dream inserted late in the process. William
Mulholland led the initial effort—his final campaign in the service of Los Angeles' growth. Mulholland retired in 1928 and died
seven years later. His lasting legacy became the water hierarchies
he molded, DWP and MWD, which shaped Southern California
through the rest of the century.

Snow falling high in the Rocky Mountains gives birth to the Colorado River, which ultimately travels 1,400 miles, tapping a watershed over one-twelfth the area of the lower 48 states. Before any dams were built, the river flowed through parts of Wyoming, Colorado, Utah, New Mexico and Arizona. It formed the border between California and Nevada, crossed into Mexico, and finally deposited a heavy load of nutrients into a delta at the Gulf of California. Spanish explorers named the river for its red color, which was caused by sediments picked up as it carved through the desert landscape (creating the Grand Canyon, along the way).

On average, 14 million AF of water pass down the Colorado each year. By comparison, Eastern Sierra streams tapped for the Los Angeles Aqueduct carry an average of only 600,000 AF, annually. The Colorado River became the key to dreamers with *big* plans for California.

Native fish in the river's warm water included humpback chub, bonytail chub, razorback sucker and a minnow called the Colorado squawfish. That particular minnow was the largest in that fish family within North America, up to six feet long and one hundred pounds! Squawfish were sometimes called "Colorado salmon," because they migrated upriver each season to spawn. For a time, they were so abundant along the length of the Colorado and its tributaries that they were pitchforked directly out of irrigation ditches linked to the river, and used to fertilize fields.

The southeast corner of California holds the Imperial Valley, where more than 100,000 acres were being cultivated in 1905 with Colorado River water delivered by the Alamo Canal. That ditch, completed four years earlier, extended sixty miles, for most of that length passing through Mexican lands south of the border. The desert climate allowed as many as three consecutive crops to be harvested every year. However, the silt-laden Colorado kept plugging the diversion point of the canal. During an effort to clear the intake, more than 90 percent of the river's flow jumped into the northward opening. The water settled into the Salton Sink, a basin 227 feet below sea level. Finally, in 1907, the Southern Pacific Railroad, new

owners of the headgates, were able to plug the "leak," but the flooding was a clear message to Reclamation engineers that the wild
river needed to be tamed.

Though caused by human error, the 1905 event recreated a
natural phenomenon that had occurred at least four times between
the years 700 and 1580, when the Colorado River had temporarily
changed course and flooded the sink. Each time, freshwater from
the river gradually became salty after the river turned back toward
the ocean and each lake evaporated. The twenty-first-century version, named the Salton Sea, has remained full because of agricultural drainage off surrounding farmlands.

The silt-prone Alamo Canal had a geographical and political
problem: its route passed through Mexico and American farmers were forced to share half the diverted water with that nation.
With 360,000 irrigated acres and more than 15,000 people living
in the Imperial Valley by 1919, the Imperial Irrigation District
(IID) began lobbying Congress to authorize construction of a new
canal. This one would stay north of the border—it would be the
"All-American Canal."

It took decades of negotiation before both the IID and the
MWD realized their separate hopes for the Colorado River. Seven
states and Mexico had competing interests and rights to the river's
water. California, with almost no contributing watershed, might
have had one of the weakest claims among the states, yet it had the
most voters and political clout at that time. The other states had
neither California's population nor the momentum of its booming
growth. While cautious and acrimonious negotiations for federal
dams on the river moved through Congress, in 1925 Los Angeles
held yet another water bond election, this time for $25 million to
fund surveys for an aqueduct route across the desert.

William Mulholland had traveled to the remote little town of
Las Vegas in 1923 to view the river. Although, by then, his city
was consolidating holdings in the Owens Valley that would ensure
enough water for a half-century of city growth, he posed for pho-
tographers beside the Colorado River and declared, "Here's where

we get our water" (Nadeau, 1974, 192). For the 1925 campaign, he proclaimed: "And lest our city shrivel and die, we must have more water, we must build a great new aqueduct to the Colorado" (Ostrom, 1953, 3). Here was the familiar dire message, the campaign rhetoric of overstated threats. Either build this aqueduct, or shrivel and die!

The region's normal pattern of variable rainfall provided a convenient drought cycle to fuel the new campaign's fire. After an exceedingly dry winter in Southern California in 1924, Mulholland proclaimed: "This drought is one of the most appalling things that could happen. We have never even half conceived of such a thing" (Nadeau, 1974, 192). California's growth proponents were never eager to embrace the idea that droughts *will* occur, preferring to characterize them as astonishing surprises. They were also never shy about using droughts as proof of the need for additional water imports. In 1926, Los Angeles returned to a better-than-average 17.66 inches of rain.

Six of the seven Colorado Basin states approved a Colorado River Compact in 1929 (Arizona refused to participate at that time). The Boulder Canyon Project Act authorized construction of a high dam with electrical-generating capability and an All-American Canal into the Imperial Valley. Southern California was the only customer for electricity then, so MWD obligated itself to purchase all of the power, helping to justify the costly project. The negotiated compact allocated 4.4 million AF to California—3.3 million for Imperial Valley farms and another 1.1 million to urban MWD uses.

Unfortunately, time revealed that the annual river flow averaged 2 million AF less than the 16 million allocated, in total, among the states. Exacerbating the over-allocation mistake, in 1944, a treaty with Mexico obligated 1.5 million AF to flow across the southern border.

Those problems were not immediately felt, however. After President Hoover signed the Boulder Canyon Project Act in June 1929, the immediate focus in California became the campaign to fund the new aqueduct. MWD was conceived to spread the costs of aqueduct construction and water distribution among the cities of the south coast. A bond election was set for September 29, 1931. The dry heat of September, once again, made it the ideal month for a water election in California.

Prominent leaders formed the Citizens Colorado River Committee. Speakers spread out to community groups. A special newspaper, *Water News,* carried the committee's message. This campaign incorporated modern innovations, including automobile stickers and, three nights a week, radio broadcasts. The "It's Your Move" brochure contained the program schedule: "Listen! Metropolitan Water District Radio News. KGER—Every Monday Evening—8:15; KMTR—Every Tuesday Evening—7:00; KNX—Every Friday Evening—7:30." It also advertised a public exhibit in the Title Guarantee and Trust Building in downtown Los Angeles (real estate interests, as always, were among the leaders on the water-for-growth issue). In addition, the black-and-white sound movie, *Thirst,* was running in theaters. Its narrator, MWD Chairman Whitsett, covered the dire consequences should the aqueduct not be built, described the route, surveys and studies, the site chosen for a reservoir on the river and, finally, announced impressive numbers: one billion gallons of water for Southern California, each and every day!

Was that the quantity of water needed if the theater audience was to avoid death by dehydration? Or was it, rather, an amount meant to accomplish far more than just personal "thirst-quenching"? In fact, Whitsett specifically admonished listeners that their focus should rest on *present* needs:

> We must not think that this is something for the future; it is of the most immediate and pressing necessity. . . . We must face the facts, for the value of our homes and our businesses, the security of our jobs, all depend upon an ample water supply. Out here in Southern California we are building a great empire on the edge of the desert. If we are to survive and to grow, we must have the water that will enable us to maintain our mastery over the desert. (MWD, 1931a)

MWD's groundwater overdraft estimate, around which they built their campaign, was 170 million gallons per day. The proposed aqueduct would deliver six times that amount. Those two figures were not juxtaposed for comparison in campaign literature or in the film.

The key to understanding the Colorado River water choice as a force for environmental change in California is quantity. Enough water was at stake to, by itself, serve a future population of more than 12 million people. Growth was not ignored in the campaign. "We must secure a large new supply of water, or we will be unable permanently to maintain our present population and property values—much less support future population increases and industrial expansion" (MWD, 1931a). Even in that statement acknowledging future growth, the emphasis remained, first, on present "needs," on bringing water that "means the very life of our Southern California."

Future population and industrial growth was part of the promise, but for farmers like Henry Warne and townspeople concerned with lowering groundwater levels, the compelling message was personal and immediate. It was hard to conceive that enough water was being considered to completely transform the region. How could they grasp what that quantity could do to farm property values and existing communities? And conceptualize a future population of 19 million people in the region, made possible by imported Eastern Sierra, Colorado River and Sacramento Valley water, and the consequences for quality of life and for the natural environment?

Los Angeles voters might understandably have wondered why they were even being asked to fund yet another aqueduct. Campaign literature explained: "By complete development of all remaining water in Owens Valley and the Mono Basin, Los Angeles is preparing to maintain an adequate supply UNTIL Colorado River water can be brought in" (MWD, 1931c). One year earlier, in May 1930, these same citizens had approved the Mono Basin extension of the Los Angeles Aqueduct—a $38.8 million bond election. With that action, the city assured itself enough water to grow for five decades. Nevertheless, the campaign message was of urgent need, even in

Los Angeles. Another theme appeared which would be repeated later in debates about northern California rivers emptying into the ocean through San Francisco Bay: "Water urgently needed by Southern California communities now is being *wasted* into the ocean by the Colorado River" (MWD, 1931c; my emphasis).

MWD's expenses to construct the aqueduct would be met from tax revenues based on proportional assessed values within each member-city. That structure fostered regional growth, because it ensured that outlying cities would purchase cheaper water. Los Angeles citizens, on the other hand, with higher assessments, would subsidize the growth of the entire region, covering 82 percent of aqueduct bond payments (and through the coming decades paying 62 percent of MWD's ongoing costs), though they received relatively little MWD water in return. MWD's assessment structure was designed to benefit individuals with land interests across the southland. Values would soar after new water was available, so the pressure from development-minded landowners was intense. The land barony pattern that began with Spanish and Mexican land grants was continuing to shape California's future.

One MWD campaign phrase was particularly revealing: "Water—The Destiny of a Mighty Empire Hangs in the Balance Now!" (MWD, 1931d). The writers of that phrase may have counted on the general public to be enthusiastic about the image invoked by "Mighty Empire." Or perhaps they knew what would best appeal to the "money people," the empire builders who funded and approved the campaign.

On September 29, 1931, $220 million in aqueduct bonds were approved by voters, by a 5-to-1 vote margin. The approval for a sum that large during the Great Depression was, in itself, amazing. In 1933, federal construction of Hoover Dam began—another amazing public works project of the Depression. The completed dam began impounding water to form Lake Mead in 1935.

In 1941, the 242-mile Colorado River Aqueduct began delivering "an everlasting supply of water" from Lake Havasu, behind MWD's Parker Dam, 155 miles downriver from Lake Mead. Within a few decades, average deliveries to MWD exceeded the agency's negotiated allotment by up to 800,000 AF each year (water for an additional 4 to 6 million people). The surplus would be available, and counted upon, by Southern California, until Arizona completed its own water project late in the century. Eighty percent of California's Colorado River entitlement (3.8 million AF) was dedicated to Imperial Valley agriculture. A half-century later, MWD would ask the U.S. Department of the Interior to consider the "higher use" served if MWD's urban population could receive a greater proportion of Colorado River water.

By 1970, with Colorado River water available, the counties of Los Angeles, Orange, San Diego and Ventura tripled their combined populations, growing from 3.3 million to 10 million people. In 2015, the MWD provided 60 percent of the water used by 19 million people living between Ventura and the Mexican border. It served twenty-six water agency clients, supplying 300 cities and unincorporated communities within six counties: Los Angeles, Orange, Riverside, San Bernardino, San Diego and Ventura.

When the Colorado River aqueduct choice was made, many Southern Californians, like Henry Warne, lived outside MWD's original thirteen cities. The district's charter was to provide municipal and industrial water *solely* to member cities. Because the aqueduct was completed in 1941, it has been said that its imported water arrived just in time to support the industrial and population buildup that came with World War II. Actually, most wartime expansion was handled with Los Angeles Aqueduct water and local sources. MWD water sales were too small during the 1940s to cover even ongoing pumping costs.

Japan formally surrendered on September 2, 1945, ending World War II. Ten days later, on September 12, the Orange County Water District announced a policy aimed at extending the use of Colorado River water throughout Orange County. They subsequently sent out 192 invitations—to cities, agricultural water users, the Orange County Board of Supervisors, irrigation companies, chambers of commerce and real estate associations—to join an effort to increase importation of water into the county. A new Central Basin Metropolitan Water District, serving twenty-seven communities, became a MWD client in 1951.

Such postwar annexations rapidly expanded the Metropolitan Water District's service area beyond cities, to include unincorporated, undeveloped and farm lands. The Navy town of San Diego made it through the war without Colorado River water, then joined MWD in 1946.

Early MWD policy had aimed at assuring adequate water to a specific service area, based on available Colorado River imports. Implicit in that policy was recognition that a limited water supply must dictate limits to growth. In 1952, meeting in Laguna Beach, the MWD board adopted a new policy committing the District "to provide its service area with adequate supplies of water to meet expanding and increasing needs in the years ahead. When and as additional water resources are required to meet increasing needs for domestic, industrial and municipal water, The Metropolitan Water District of Southern California will be prepared to deliver such supplies" (Gottlieb and FitzSimmons, 1991, 15). The concept of limits—which had been anathema to California's growth cartel—received a formal execution by the MWD Board of Directors on December 16, 1952, put to death by this "Laguna Declaration."

Problems addressed by the choice to bring Colorado River water were not as dire nor as dramatic as the opening scenes of *Thirst* suggested. Because of that choice, however, changes occurred on a dramatically massive scale.

At one end of the pipe, the mighty Colorado River was diminished, primarily by dams that trapped the warm, silty flow, releasing water that was cold and sterile. Sandy beaches began disappearing from the Grand Canyon. Water no longer reached the river's natural estuary and outlet in the Gulf of California except during a few flood years. The river's native fish joined the list of endangered species by late in the century. Humpback chub, bonytail chub, razorback sucker and Colorado squawfish depended on the colder water and unblocked spawning runs of an undammed river. Introduced game fish competed with the natives and exacerbated the declines. Fifteen million hatchery grown razorback suckers, planted as juveniles in Arizona streams from 1981 to 1990, mostly became food for nonnative predators.

Native Colorado River species had provided the first population of freshwater fish for the Salton Sea, arriving with the 1905 flood, but irrigated farms in the Imperial Valley utilized the Salton Sea as a sump for salts that would otherwise build up and contaminate their soils. About four million tons annually settled into the sea, increasing its saltiness 1.2 percent every year. By 1929, the Salton Sea became too salty for freshwater species, so the State Department of Fish and Game introduced salt-tolerant fish from the Gulf of California. During the 1950s, the state's highest catch per sport fisherman was from the Salton Sea; a healthy striped bass and corvina fishery persisted through the 1960s.

As salinity kept increasing, the Salton Sea fishery declined. Even the most salt-tolerant fish turn belly up when salinity reaches about 5 percent (Mono Lake, by comparison, has about 9 percent dissolved solids, the Great Salt Lake about 12 percent, and the Dead Sea in the Middle East 32 percent salinity). Nutrients from farm fertilizers entering the lake fed oxygen-consuming algae blooms, which led to massive fish kills. Tilapia, one of the smaller fish found in great numbers in the lake, began to die from botulism. About 7.6 million tilapia died in a single day, August 4, 1999. Sick fish, unfortunately, began producing sick birds.

Millions of birds had taken advantage of the new water source in the desert, and 380 species of migratory birds were spending parts of their year at the Salton Sea, including pelicans, herons, egrets, cranes, cormorants, ibises, various ducks, grebes, falcons, plovers, avocets, sandpipers and gulls. That is an astonishing number of species for one lake—about half of all bird species in the continental United States utilized the Salton Sea. Although not all of those are found in abundance, few places attract such a diversity. The "man-caused" lake and its fringing wetlands had become the key replacement for wetlands habitat that disappeared elsewhere in

Southern California. Migratory and nesting birds utilizing the sea's resources included several endangered species: brown pelicans, bald eagles, peregrine falcons and Aleutian Canada geese.

When 150,000 eared grebes died at the Salton Sea in 1992, it was an eerie echo of T.E. Jones's 1885 description of Owens Lake. Die-offs at the Salton Sea suggested that the fanciful idea of a "duck-killing" lake had become reality in the southern desert. Some of the grebes died from avian cholera; most of undetermined causes. In 1996, 1,400 brown pelicans (an endangered species), died after eating fish infected with botulism. Twenty-thousand birds died in 1994, including eared grebes, ruddy ducks and various ducks and shorebirds. In 1998, the year the Sonny Bono Salton Sea National Wildlife Refuge was established, another disease outbreak spread among fifty species.

Water that delivered salts and minerals to the Salton Sea was a problem, yet that same water kept evaporation from concentrating saltwater even further. Ideas for separating water from farm wastes before it reaches the lake range from dikes (to create settling and evaporation ponds) to high-tech desalting plants. Proposed solutions would cost hundreds of millions of dollars—a price tag necessitating political support. But the lake was often disparaged as a manmade, chemical sump. It lay far away from population centers and was not an integral part of the plumbing for urban-area drinking water.

The beleaguered lake became a threat to human health, too, as salt particles blown off the exposed lakebed carried harmful particulates across the Coachella and Imperial Valleys, violating air quality standards. When rotten-egg smelling hydrogen sulfide odors, related to fish die-offs at the sea, blew 150 miles westward and into coastal air basins of Southern California, the tension between urban water supply, environmental needs and agriculture became odiferously clear.

This dilemma in the desert was exacerbated by a 2003 Quantification Settlement Agreement negotiated by the state's Colorado River water users. The San Diego County Water Authority will receive 200,000 AF from the Imperial Irrigation District. That water transfer, set to begin in 2017, would accommodate more south coast urban development while leaving even less diluting water for the sea. To facilitate the agreement, the state promised to address impacts of a shrinking Salton Sea. Little action followed, however, until 2015, when the governor signed legislation requiring the Salton Sea Task Force to submit a list of "shovel-ready" projects by March 31, 2016, that could restore 12,000 acres of shoreline habitat by 2020 and up to 25,000 additional acres of exposed shoreline following that year. Funding sources, however, remained uncertain.

ELEVEN

BOOM! SPRAWLING GRIDLOCK

Walt [Disney] jumped in his car and headed south in the freshly-paved asphalt of the two-lane Santa Ana Freeway. As he drove . . . the brownish haze of the sky dissipated into a deep blue . . . and homes and businesses grew farther and farther apart. When he finally entered Orange County . . . open farmland scented with the fragrant perfume of orange blossoms stretched out before him. . . . Anaheim was a lot like Walt's boyhood home in Marceline, Missouri. Here, in the middle of orange groves, he had found the place for his magical park. (Colson and Black, 1993)

Traffic Supplants Crime Atop Bay Poll, Packed Freeways Are No. 1 Concern. (*San Francisco Chronicle,* January, 3, 1997)

Eight million soldiers, sailors, marines and airmen trained at California military bases or embarked for the Pacific theater from California. Thirty-five billion federal dollars were spent within the state during the war years (between 1940 and 1946). Those two sets of figures opened the curtain on a postwar boom that was utterly dependent on water via the Colorado Aqueduct. An immigration boom was closely followed by "the Baby Boom." They were booms funded by the Pentagon, whose war-year expenditures proved to be just preliminary excursions into lavish money-spending.

Some Californians hoped that peace would bring a respite from the frenzied buildup of the war years. Historian Carey McWilliams thought the state was ready to settle down, like a maturing adolescent, in 1948. "It is apparent that the period of runaway growth—the 'boom years'—have ceased . . . Southern California now faces for the first time since 1880, a period of relative stability during which it has at least a chance to consolidate its gains and to integrate its population" (1946, 373). It was a prediction that turned out to be wishful, wistful thinking.

In 1940, California held 6.9 million people. The census ten years later counted nearly 10.6 million residents. Two million of them, by then, lived in Los Angeles. The 1950s boom was still to follow. In the years after the war, California's economy feasted and fattened upon a high-calorie military menu. Aircraft and related electronics industries formed the core of the postwar military indus-trial boom. Lockheed, Douglas, North American, Northrup and Corvair were hiring. By 1965 a half million workers were employed by the aerospace industry. Bombers, fighters and missiles were needed, first for the Korean War, and then to maintain the nuclear deterrence capability of the Cold War. Then there were satellites and rockets to design and build for the space race. More than 40 percent of the billions of dollars devoted to beating Russia to the moon were spent in California.

New economic opportunities produced a surge in immigration rates. California's history of booms was repeatedly driven by such factors, rather than the state's persistent attractions of climate and environment. Jim Paravantes, who applied for a job at Lockheed in 1951, had passed through the state six years earlier as a sailor. He finished college in the East after the war, then joined the postwar immigration boom. His recorded voice became part of an exhibit on immigration in the Golden State Museum, in Sacramento: "The Navy is what got me to California, but it was the climate, econ-omy, and the California Dream that got me back" (Golden State Museum, 1997).

My father, Louis Carle, was one of the military millions who first saw Southern California under orders, riding a train car from Michigan:

We were forty air cadets, sent by train in 1943 from Michigan to the Santa Ana Army Air Base for further training. I was 18 years old and had never been west of the Mississippi River. A kid from the San Fernando valley spent 1,500 miles telling me how beautiful the orange groves would be with the beautiful San Gabriel Mountains in the beautiful background. They finally tied us to a freight train which, we were told, would take us through the beautiful Santa Ana canyon to beautiful Orange County where we would disembark at the beautiful freight yards in the beautiful city of Santa Ana. Mind you, because of the dense fog we disembarked there without ever seeing an orange tree. In time I learned that there *were* real beautiful mountains here and there *were* beautiful orange groves. (Louis Carle, 1999)

Finally, he could compare the citrus box images with which he had grown up to the reality of Southern California. He met a local girl from Anaheim, married her after the war, and started what would become the typical four-child family of the baby boom. Disneyland opened a few miles away from our home in 1955.

"Orange County was still a place of beauty and a source of pride to the 130,760 people who lived there in 1940. There were still thousands of acres of natural wilderness areas in the Santa Ana Mountains . . . miles of open fields, acres of orange groves, and forty miles of scenic coast. Orange County was as yet unspoiled and somewhat provincial" (Hallan-Gibson, 1986, 235). The 1950s boom pushed the county population to 703,925—more than five times the pre-war total. People, in such numbers, inevitably altered the "place of beauty."

Least terns returned to their nesting sites near Huntington Beach every April in numberless flocks. Each was " . . . a delicate, beautiful creature, like a spirit of the sand . . ." according to one early observer. Females scraped out simple nests while their male partners hunted over shallow water nearby. Successful courtship required formal presentation of a fish.

Not far from a female tern's new nest were thousands of other pairs, similarly courting or already incubating eggs—some feeding hatched young. The colony of least terns suddenly took to the air, then swept back down together to mob a cat. The besieged intruder raced back toward a house recently built nearby. It only dropped the chick from its mouth when it was startled by a growling bulldozer, suddenly cresting the dune in front of the cat.

California's least tern is the continent's smallest tern. The bird's forked tail, black cap and mask had been a common sight from April through September on the coast from San Francisco to Baja California. Accounts early in the century described hundreds of nesting pairs and "numberless" colonies on south coast beaches. Tern nests were little more than a scrape in the sand. The precocious chicks were termed "runners," because they wandered along the beach when just a few days old. Wildlife photographer B. "Moose" Peterson, whose cameras recorded nature's most dramatic wildlife scenes, described tern colonies as "one of the greatest wildlife spectacles" (Peterson, 1993, 145). It was an annual spectacle once, but one that nearly disappeared. Least tern beach habitat, near shallow lagoons for the best fishing, rapidly vanished during the postwar boom as wetlands were drained or filled, as coastal highways were widened and beachside homes were built. The population boom of the 1950s brought people—and their pets—to disturb those colonies that were not displaced outright by development.

Only six hundred pairs remained in the state by 1970. That year, under a new law prompted by two decades of postwar environmental loss, the least tern became one of California's first official endangered species.

Charles Holder's chapter on waterfowl in his 1906 book *Life in the Open: Sport with Rod, Gun, Horse, and Hound in Southern California* included a list of common ducks and shorebirds that is increasingly amazing today, when almost all of the listed species are unknown, uncommon or nearing extinction in that region. The list includes mallard, gadwall, baldpate, green-winged teal, blue-winged teal, cinnamon teal, spoonbill, sprig, wood duck, red-head, canvas-back, wing widgeon, bufflehead, American scoter, white-winged scoter, surf scoter, ruddy duck, lesser snow goose, greater snow goose, American white-fronted goose, Canada goose, Hutchin's goose, black brant and trumpeter swan.

> Here is the cinnamon teal with beautiful colouring . . . one of the commonest of Southern California ducks, found along shore all summer, spring, and fall. A few years ago I could count scores of herons in the country back of Playa del Rey, splashes of white against the green; and once I hunted a flock of the snowy herons [egrets] for hours in this lagoon. The sand-hill crane . . . makes the best displays spring and fall along the Sierra Madre. (1906, 57, 59)

Holder listed several kinds of gulls, the nesting least terns, avocets, black-necked stilts, marbled godwits, snipe and long-billed dowitchers, "great flocks" of western sandpipers, willets, tattler, spotted sandpiper, black turnstone and various plovers. "Where there are long stretches of beach and sand, behind which are pools and sea swamps . . . one may see the great blue heron, the least bittern, and at times, farther in, the wood ibis, that has a penchant for barley fields and rolling mesas near the sea" (Holder, 1906, 123).

Such descriptions, such experiences of waterfowl and shore-birds, became almost impossible to repeat. The declines were not a matter of hunting and not generally a matter of purposeful mortality. Habitat was overwhelmed by high-density humanity. Only a few remnant wetland marshes were preserved, totaling about 4,000 acres—places like the Seal Beach National Wildlife Refuge, Upper Newport Harbor and various creek mouths along the coast.

Walt Disney's cartoon studio was headquartered in Burbank, north of Los Angeles, but he came to Anaheim, 27 miles south, to build his famous amusement park. Orange County land was cheap, being still mostly citrus orchards. The new Santa Ana Freeway was not yet congested, making it feasible to think of downtown Los Angeles as only a short 27-minute drive from

Anaheim. Melbourne Gauer served on Anaheim's planning commission during those years of change:

> When Disneyland was coming in, it was quite a secretive movement. He bought one hundred and sixty acres or more. The Disneyland area was outside the city limits at that time. It was in the county, and they had to know whether the city would extend the water, sewer, and all the other city services. People said that we went over backwards to please Disneyland. The landowners around there said that they wouldn't be able to do anything with their land, and yet land was going up. . . . We weren't doing anything with their land except letting them get richer. (Gauer, 1974, 51–52)

Disney bought land from twenty owners. One family's condition-of-sale was that two large palm trees be preserved. They were incorporated into the Jungle Boat ride. An agreement with another family preserved their Spanish-mission style home as an administration building for the amusement park. The Disney Corporation later added more acres, but some local farmers resisted tremendous pressure to sell, in one case, for decades.

The Fujishige brothers turned down repeated multimillion-dollar offers for their 56-acre strawberry farm, a block away from Disneyland. They had purchased the land in 1954, a year before Disneyland opened. They had to fight off Disney, other developers and, during the 1980s, their own city: Anaheim went to court to force a road across their property to serve another hotel/condominium/office project. Publicity surrounding that court battle made them local folk heroes, yet the road was built. One of the brothers, Masao, died in 1986. In the 1990s, Hiroshi Fujishige reportedly turned down another offer for $32 million from Disney. Finally, in 1998, with Hiroshi in a coma, his descendants announced plans to sell, ending one California Dream.

As Disney realized *his* fantastic dream, Anaheim cashed in. When the park opened there were only seven hotels in Anaheim; by 1996 there were 150 hotels or motels. Throughout Orange County,

Disneyland under construction, January 3, 1955. The small community of Anaheim is beyond the new Santa Ana Freeway, with orchards and fields spreading toward the San Bernardino Mountains, visible through clean air. Courtesy Anaheim Public Library.

life was changing. The streets near Disneyland changed in ways that Walt Disney reportedly deplored. In those early years, the city did little to control the appearance of businesses near the park. Garish neon lights and a carnival atmosphere contrasted with Disney's classier tone. When Disney World was later built in Florida, the corporation bought enough land to control such problems.

Many people from Anaheim, focusing on the phenomenal growth that began in the mid-1950s, associated that era of change with the arrival of Disneyland. "This northern part of the county, [had been] one continuous citrus orchard. A lot of us that are going to be here with what few years we have left still miss those green orchards. About the time Disneyland opened, that's just about the time that we began to feel it" (Martenet, 1968, 21, 25). The amusement park brought in 60 million visitors in twelve years, but Orange County's permanent transformation from rural agriculture to, ultimately, one of the most densely populated counties in the nation was only coincidentally associated with the famous amusement park. Longtime mayor of Anaheim, Charles Pearson, who personally shepherded much of the transformation, more accurately perceived the real catalyst for growth: "If we had not had the Metropolitan Water District and the water which it produces from outside the area, Orange County . . . would now probably be where they were in every respect back in the early 1930s" (Pearson, 1968, 58).

Anaheim, during the 1950s, aimed to entice businesses. The city of four square miles annexed 1,500 acres in 1953, 2,700 acres in 1954, and in 1955, the year Disneyland opened, another 3,300 acres brought the city to four times its wartime size. Ultimately, a long, narrow industrial corridor was also added to the east along the Santa Ana River canyon. The interviewer for Pearson's oral history asked one particularly intriguing question about the expansion drive: "Why did the city of Anaheim want to annex so much territory?"

"Because those people want to come in to live there," Pearson answered, briefly.

"I see," his interviewer responded, with even more brevity.

Pearson expanded on his initial response: "There had to be places for people to build houses and live, and in order to do this they had to have services, sewer, and water. The only way they could get sewer and water, primarily, was through cities, through annexation. That's how the growth took place. We didn't try to develop these annexations, they instigated them themselves, and they're still doing it" (1968, 91).

The "they" who were doing it, never explicitly identified in that exchange, were developers controlling the large ranchlands of the county, moving to cash in now that Colorado River water was available. Planning commissioner Melbourne Gauer, who also helped shape that era of enormous change, said, "I said many times that we could have the type of city we wanted, if we just decided upon the type we wanted. We learned by our development and of course we had a great deal of pressure by the developer" (Gauer, 1974, 46).

Ellen Warne, speaking from the perspective of a longtime resident and farm family patriarch, eerily echoed the planner's phrase: "There was such pressure on the officials to build because people want it and developers want the work." Ellen, wife of Bolsa farmer Henry Warne, looked back on the 1950s, the earliest boom years, as the best time for raising a family. "The population was smaller. 'Dad' was still farming. We didn't worry about thieves or anything. We had to work hard, but there was still a sense of community." In 1960 the Warnes, feeling their own pressures, traded Orange County land that had been condemned for schools and freeways for farmland in the Imperial Valley. They continued to live in Bolsa; that was home. When asked what she thought about the changes that followed the Colorado River water choice, Ellen said, "It may have been fine, but we didn't realize growth would be so tremendous. It has far outgrown its usefulness" (Warne and Warne, 1997).

Eight new cities incorporated in Orange County during the 1950s, most to develop tools for controlling the new development pressures. Buena Park incorporated to fight off annexation threats from Anaheim. Costa Mesa did it to oppose oil drilling. Dairyland was a town with only 500 residents and 15,000 cows. Incorporation for Dairyland came in 1956, specifically to protect its agricultural character. Condemnation laws and the tax system, which had yet to develop tools for preserving agriculture, worked against Dairyland. Six neighboring school districts found it easiest to condemn property in Dairyland, avoiding condemnation battles within more heavily populated communities. So Dairyland changed its name to "La Palma" and became difficult to distinguish from any of the communities—residential with a mix of business and industry—that were merging into one vast sprawl across the county. "Longtime residents stood stunned as bulldozers swept away trees, hills, and history. They shook their heads in dismay, feeling frustrated and helpless, and unhappily chalked it up to progress" (Hallan-Gibson, 1986, 214).

San Juan Capistrano, the mission town, made a long, determined effort to resist the growth pressure. MWD water was the key to change, as in many places, but perhaps more blatantly than in the northern county where military-industrial expansion played a great role. Right after World War II, a majority of residents in the small agricultural town opposed an invitation to join MWD. Area farmers, reliant upon their own wells, were a particularly strong opposition bloc. "Behind the scenes plans quietly continued. . . . [In the early 1950s] boundary lines were proposed for the Southern Orange County Water District which would import Metropolitan Water. Ranchers protested; bitter words flew, and San Juan Capistrano quietly withdrew" (Hallan-Gibson, 1975, 132–33). The persistent pressure was again successfully opposed in 1958. But in 1960, the neighbor cities of San Clemente, Dana Point and Capistrano Beach joined MWD, responding to the "join now or pay higher future pipeline costs" threat.

> In August a committee was formed . . . to sell the idea to the public. The vote was held the following November with 356 people voting in favor and 56 against bringing Metropolitan Water to San Juan Capistrano. Some people claim that developers cast covetous eyes on the virgin hills and valleys of San Juan and immediately called in the bulldozers and public relations men. Others claim that the growth of San Juan was inevitable. (Hallan-Gibson, 1975, 133)

For a time, after tapping into the aqueduct, the little mission town grew faster than anywhere else in California.

Within Orange County, there were 6,109 farms in 1940. The boom years consumed 4,500 of them; only 1,642 farms remained in 1964. By 2012, the number was 312.

In 1950, rural Orange County had 275 residents per square mile. Its population density surged past Los Angeles County's in the 1960s. During the twentieth century, it grew from 20,000 people to become one of the most populous counties in the nation, with 3,871 people per square mile as of 2012. In California, only San Francisco

County, which is the city of San Francisco itself, has a higher density. With 3,090,132 people, 100 percent of the population was classified "urban" and 0 percent "rural" (City-Data.com, 2015).

California became the nation's most populous state late in 1962. To mark the achievement, Governor Edmund G. Brown proclaimed 'California First Days'—a three-day statewide celebration. Former Governor Earl Warren, then United States Chief Justice, spoke about the proclamation in a speech, in California, the next day:

> I told them I thought the governor was mistaken in his assessment of the importance of mere automatic growth; that there is no merit in simply being the largest . . . I told them that instead of dancing in the streets, we should . . . call the people of California to the schools, churches, city halls, and other places of public assemblage, there to pray for the vision and the guidance to make California the *finest* state in the Union as well as the largest.
> (Warren, 1977, 227)

Of all of the changes that Californians experienced, traffic congestion, with creeping, gridlocked freeways and surface roads, became perhaps the most widely shared manifestation of the deteriorating California Dream. The freedom that the automobile represented, including the opportunity to live in suburbs and commute to work, transformed into a daily ordeal of wasted time and pressure on raw nerves. "Road rage" joined the societal vocabulary. The media relished stories of brandished guns, shots fired, vehicles used as weapons, and of periodic tragedies whenever the various weapons became deadly. The phenomenon was so widespread that the Automobile Association of America published grin-and-bear-it advice for avoiding road rage incidents: allow more time for trips (accept the delays and slow pace), be patient, not aggressive (yield the road, nicely, when confronted by obscenities, gestures or threats).

Commuters creeping along the ever-expanding freeway system had plenty of time to read billboards designed for legibility at much higher speeds, advertising new subdivisions under construction nearby. Each time another hundred houses were completed and sold, a couple hundred more cars joined the daily stop-and-go masses, worsening the gridlock. But few objected to the construction itself. How could they object? The dogma pervading the region was that home construction equated with a healthy economy; growth was good.

The link between transport and urban sprawl had roots back in the early twentieth century, when citizens of Los Angeles were encouraged by the Pacific Electric trolley company to "Live in the Country and Work in the City." Pacific Electric "Big Red" trolley cars carried 110 million passengers in 1924 on 1,000 miles of track running as far south as Balboa and all the way north to San Fernando. Automobiles did not have to follow tracks or stick to timetables, though, and the convenience and freedom they represented doomed the region's mass transit trolley system.

The transformation was quickened by aggressive competition from the automobile industry and government-funded highway construction projects. On December 30, 1940, the first freeway opened in California: the six-mile Arroyo Seco Parkway, which connected Pasadena with downtown Los Angeles. In the 1960s alone, 450 miles of freeways were constructed in California. A phrase from Ian McEwan's novel *Amsterdam* (though concerning a different time and place) captured that decade's construction frenzy of "new roads probing endlessly, shamelessly, as though all that mattered was to be elsewhere" (McEwan, 1999, 68).

By 1996, the state was crisscrossed by 170,500 miles of streets, roads, highways. Yet California could not build roads fast enough to keep up. Not only was the "Red Queen" of highway construction running as fast as she could just to stay in one place, she constantly lost ground. The pattern repeated, over and over: gridlock conditions led to a highway-widening "solution"; construction slowdowns produced several years of increased frustration; after a few years of improved traffic flow on the wider highway, daily gridlock came back.

Ironically, the freedom from timetables and mobile convenience that cars represented was replaced by incarceration in traffic gridlock "prisons." Cars became cells, where major portions of life wasted away. Yet, commuters showed the amazing adaptability of human beings: frustration turned to resignation, acceptance and, finally, a loss of real understanding that there were alternatives to such a lifestyle. "If motorway driving anywhere calls for a high level of attentiveness, the extreme concentration required in Los Angeles seems to bring on a state of heightened awareness that some locals find mystical. . . . Yet what seems to be hardly noticed or commented on is that the price of rapid door-to-door transport on demand is the almost total surrender of personal freedom for most of the journey" (Banham, 1971, 214, 217). Banham's use of the word "rapid" is the part of his observation that became less accurate. More and more often, road rage burst forth while society's behavior modification experiment—the daily rush hour uncovered a fuming, frustrated subconscious in many drivers.

By 1990, supplemented by northern California water imports (see Part IV), the state would become the most urbanized state in the union, according to the U.S. Census. More than 80 percent of Californians lived in metropolitan areas with over 1 million people. The consequences of sprawl, including traffic congestion, air pollution, endangered species and permanent loss of open space and farmland, prompted publication of *Beyond Sprawl: New Patterns of Growth to Fit the New California,* in 1995. It was published by an unusual coalition of business, government and private interests: the California Resources Agency, Greenbelt Alliance, the Low Income Housing Fund and, most surprisingly (considering its stake in development financing) Bank of America. The report called for "smarter growth," for filling in open space within already developed areas, for redevelopment of older neighborhoods and business districts and for encouraging higher density living. It verified some facts that growth promoters hated the public to hear—that the costs of public services and infrastructure are seldom covered by development fees and taxes charged to new businesses and residents. Development that sprawled into the fringes of metro-politan areas, the report suggested, should finally start paying the full marginal costs inflicted on the region.

How much should they pay? Eben Fodor, author of *Better NOT Bigger* (1999) calculated infrastructure costs totaling $24,500 for each new single-family house in Oregon. That total considered schools, sewage systems, transportation facilities, water systems, parks and recreation facilities, stormwater drainage and fire and emergency services. *Not* included in those calculations were the capital costs of police facilities, open space, libraries, general government facilities, electric power generation and distribution, natural gas distribution systems and solid waste disposal facilities. Also not included were environmental and quality-of-life costs (decreased air and water quality, noise, traffic congestion, crime)—real costs to the community or region, but difficult to quantify.

Contrary to the myth that growth brought wide prosperity to communities and regions, most often the burden of new expenses fell on current residents, whose individually small tax and fee increases subsidized a relatively few profit-takers. Like a pyramid scheme, add-ing additional taxpayers to the "subsidy pool" was the only way the growth machine could stay ahead of the true costs of growth. While the list of costs applied particularly to local governments, in a similar manner the MWD subsidized sprawl by spreading costs of new pipe-line and infrastructure among all its customers, charging the same water rates to everyone in the region, new and old alike. The growth cartel dominating the political process, against only weak opposi-tion from the general population, was yet another example of "The Tragedy of the Commons" (Hardin, 1968). Costs spread among many individuals in a community (the "commons," in this case) meant less motivation to participate in government planning and decision-making processes. Direct benefits to developers, real estate agents and construction companies, on the other hand, ensured that they would be enthusiastic lobbyists for growth-inducing policies.

Predictably, the *Beyond Sprawl* (Bank of America et al, 1995) report was criticized as serving "no-growthers" and NIMBYs. The acronym NIMBY—"Not In My BackYard"—became a particular favorite of development interests. The critical label made the most sense when applied to "selfish" residents who would share benefits of essential developments (such as schools and fire stations), yet were adamant that such facilities be located in someone else's "backyard." The term was often applied, however, to opponents of strip malls and housing tracts. Whoever questioned growth, in general, was liable to be called a NIMBY. The label, like many derogatory terms, substituted emotion for fact. Carried to a logical extreme, its message was that it was wrong to cherish one's backyard—to be concerned with the environment and quality of life where one lived. Actually, NIMBYs included those who truly cared about communities and were willing to get involved in shaping their best future. Yet the label remains a powerful tool for developers confronting opposition.

In 1987, citizens (who would be labeled NIMBYs) placed a growth-control initiative on the Orange County ballot. "It had become painfully apparent to many that if regional limits on growth were not promoted and constructed from the bottom up, then such growth would most certainly be imposed by powerful interests from the top down" (Olin, Kling, and Power, 1991, 239). Organized opposition to the initiative came from the "ranches" controlling the only remaining undeveloped lands in the county—the 1980s corporate manifestations of the Stearns and Irvine families who had acquired the area's Mexican *ranchos* a hundred years earlier. They were joined by some of Orange County's multinational corporations. As noted in *Beyond Sprawl*: " . . . the complex of office centers around John Wayne Airport in Orange County—built on land that was, until a generation ago, cultivated for lima beans—recently surpassed downtown San Francisco as the second-largest employment center in the state" (Bank of America et al, 1995, 5). International corporations had little motivation to consider "backyard" quality-of-life concerns. "In *Your* BackYard"—IYBYism—might be the appropriate label for such developers. The well-financed opposition to the growth-control measure spent $2.5 million during an intense five-week saturation campaign. They defeated the initiative, 56 percent to 48 percent, in June 1988.

The measure had not actually been designed as a *"no*-growth" initiative. "Slow-growth" and "smart-growth" became the slogans for many organized efforts to redirect the state's future throughout California. "Slow" and "smart" sounded less negative than "no growth," and they seemed easier to sell to Californians whose history and culture had been built around a growth dogma. In an essay about the connections between water and "smart growth," the editor of *Western Water* pointed to a poll (in *Time* magazine, March 22, 1999), in which 57 percent of respondents favored greenbelts between their communities and new development. "Of course, Cliff Moriyama of the California Building Industry Association noted that poll and others do not include the opinions of the new Californians who are not here yet. Therefore, he said, the newcomers cannot participate in the debate" (Sudman, 1999, 2). That rather amazing concept in community planning suggested that the citizens the building industry association cared most about were theoretical, future customers. If these customers required land where greenbelt buffers might otherwise exist, they should be served. It was a logic that only made sense if one widely-held belief remained unquestioned—the idea that growth in California was inevitable and would be never-ending.

The same article added comments from a water agency spokesman offering both frustration and hope for Californians who might prefer that their government show concern for actual, living citizens. Randy Kanouse of the East Bay Municipal Utility District said districts like his "can't stop growth by constricting water supplies but first priority must be for utilities to protect existing water users" (Sudman, 1999, 2). If they actually followed that first priority, limits of the water supply *would*, ultimately, limit growth.

Tracing the story of the postwar boom and the environmental and quality-of-life changes it generated has led this narrative out ahead of its historic timeline. Key choices to construct additional massive water projects were still to come, choices that would shift northern California waters to cities and farms and further clarify the "water for growth" history that is still shaping California.

TWELVE

PEOPLE FUMES (I)

Smog first reached the front page of the *Los Angeles Times* on July 27, 1943, in a story headlined CITY HUNTING FOR SOURCE OF GAS ATTACK. (Rolle, 1995, 158)

In the context of the war years, it was understandable that Southern Californians looked for an outside enemy to explain air that burned throats and eyes. In time the source was clear: the enemy could be seen in our carports and in our mirrors. By the 1960s and 1970s, smog, as it eventually was named, became a challenge of daily life. The words "Los Angeles" and "dirty air" became closely associated, so that clear days with breathable air produced headlines.

"The purity of the air in Los Angeles is remarkable. The air . . . gives stimulus and vital force which only an atmosphere so pure can ever communicate" (Truman, 1874, 33–34). Benjamin C. Truman's 1874 description seems fantastic, almost unbelievable, today. Truman would become head of the "literary bureau" for the Southern Pacific Railroad's real estate marketing effort. He may have been tempted toward hyperbole, but not even the most manipulative real estate promoter would attempt such a description today.

Riverside became a particular example of the problem, where smog generated throughout the Los Angeles basin became trapped and concentrated against the mountain barrier. Yet, after a hike in the hills near Riverside, in March 1909, citrus scientist Harold

Powell wrote, "It is a joy to drink in this air and to feel it go down in your lungs" (1996). In Powell's letters to his wife, he exulted over the vistas and views everywhere in Southern California.

> My dearest Gertrude: I thought of you many times today and wished so much that you could have been with me and seen the magnificent hills and valleys with their seas of orange groves. Nothing I have seen in the East equals the magnificent panorama that spread out around me. . . . We went up the mountain foothills to a road . . . above all the groves. . . . From there the view is grand. You look down the valley to Riverside six or eight miles away, and . . . the groves extend as a single plantation across the valley to the foot hills up which the groves extend in spurs. The San Bernardino range is to the north east, the Cucamonga mountains to the north while the Sierra Madre range of which these are a part extend as far as you can see to the coast. If you were here today, we would take a trolley out on the hills and sit on a high knob and watch the changing moods of the valleys and mountains. (1996, 39–40, 45)

Just thirty years later, Riverside's vistas would be lost in the murk of pollution.

Earl Warren, governor during and after World War II, was concerned about the unknown hazards from the new phenomenon. He recommended legislation to authorize research

> to determine what the effect of smog is on the health of the people of the state. The reception given to that suggestion was really something. One would think I had robbed the treasury. Los Angeles was the only county in the state where smog was known to be a problem at that time, and the entire Los Angeles delegation rose in its wrath and declaimed, 'This is our own local problem and we will solve it ourselves.' They were cheered by the lobbyists for the oil refineries, the oil companies selling gasoline, the truckers who fouled the air with the exhaust of their diesel fumes,

Covina Valley, 1941; palm trees outline orchards, with the snowy San Gabriel Mountains in the background. Courtesy of University of Southern California, on behalf of the USC Library Department of Special Collections.

rubber manufacturers, garbage burners, and other elements of the smog culture. The legislators of the rest of the state were not particularly interested. . . . My bill went down the drain without a hearing. (Warren, 1977, 229)

A half-century after smog made the wartime headlines, air quality continued making front page news each time state or federal regulations were tightened, and, in a curious twist, after a solution to Eastern Sierra dust pollution became a threat to the Los Angeles water supply. When wind blows over the dry Owens Lake bed in the Eastern Sierra, a tremendous cloud of alkaline dust rises into the sky. It can grow oppressively dark; headlights come on in the middle of the day along Highway 395. Travelers may drive ninety miles before escaping the cloud. People living in the region shut their windows to seal out the fine particles and, at times, residents are warned to limit outdoor activity.

Water diversions were behind the Owens Lake dust problem. Yet connections between water and Southern California's smog generally have gone unnoticed. A December 17, 1996, story in the *Los Angeles Times* described an Air Pollution Control District plan to cover thirty-five square miles of the dry lake with sections of shallow water, gravel and vegetation. The city, because its water diversions were responsible for the pollution, would pay $70 million up front, and $25 million a year in maintenance and water replacement costs.

Ted Schade, heading the Great Basin Unified Air Pollution Control District's monitoring of the unhealthy particulates that afflicted the region and violated air quality standards, was publicly called a "zealot" during one court hearing. But by the time Schade ended a career dedicated to resolving the Owens dust problem, a viable plan was finally forged between DWP and the District. Schade said, at a gathering in his honor in April 2015, that being labeled a zealot "was one of the nicest things anyone ever said about me" (personal communication).

Back in 1996, Jim Wickser, assistant general manager of the DWP, had called the Owens dust effort "an exorbitant and unrealistic expense." He was further quoted in the *Los Angeles Times* story: "I don't see how we can in good conscience spend that amount of our customers' money for what I personally consider a very minor health problem and aesthetic problem."

The DWP manager's attitude was unfortunate, but understandable. That the DWP bureaucracy opposed the expense and use of water held no surprise, but the personal consideration mentioned was even more intriguing. Jim Wickser saw it as a minor problem. Was any other perspective likely from a resident of the South Coast Air Basin?

Consider the daily living conditions of Los Angeles residents, including most DWP employees, in 1996. "Millions of residents of the South Coast Basin . . . breathe dirty air some one-third the days of the year" according to the South Coast Air Quality Monitoring District (SCAQMD). Fourteen million Southern Californians were subjected to the worst air quality in the United States, one-third of the days of their lives.

Stage 1 smog alerts are called in reference to only one pollutant, ozone, but smog's other harmful ingredients include carbon monoxide, nitrogen dioxide and particulates, tiny dust and soot materials that can penetrate deep into lungs.

According to SCAQMD figures, the South Coast Air Basin has some of the worst particulate pollution in the nation, nearly twice the federal health standard. Meanwhile, Owens Lake dust storms had generated the nation's highest-ever particulate episodes, *"23 times greater* than a federal health standard allows. Keeler residents were exposed to unhealthful levels 25 days a year. . . . 40,000 people from Lone Pine to Ridgecrest . . . periodically choke on the eye-stinging, throat-burning grit that blows off the playa." (*Los Angeles Times*, December 17, 1996).

Keeler's dust comes off the salty bed of the lake, which was exposed by Owens River diversions to Los Angeles. What are the sources of smog? Ozone forms in a sunlight-driven reaction between nitrogen oxides and other emissions from cars, trucks, power plants and furnaces. Carbon monoxide comes almost entirely from motor vehicles. Smoke and diesel soot produce particulate pollution. Clearly, smog originates with the human population. It would be honest, and we might be more inclined toward realistic solutions, if we started referring to smog as "people fumes."

Southern California has had too many people "fuming" in too small a space. Their space was walled in by mountains on three sides, with onshore ocean breezes commonly forming the fourth "wall," and with a "roof" formed by a temperature inversion overhead.

The smog problem is diffuse, the shared fault of many "fumers." The costs of altering polluting behaviors, however, are personal and immediately felt. It is a classic condition described in Garrett Hardin's essay "The Tragedy of the Commons" (1968). Each user of a common resource (the atmosphere, in this case) makes choices based on individual benefits or costs, yet the consequences—the costs—of those choices are dispersed among the entire population. Benefits of car ownership were immediate and measurable, while the consequences to the common air of one car's fumes were just a minuscule fraction of the entire smog problem.

Each car, by itself, is a technological blessing, the solution to our individual transportation needs. It is only because millions of them are on the road that every car becomes a poisoner of the common air. The smog problem is too large for one person to feel much blame, and seems far too big for one person to solve.

Ozone damages lung tissues and reduces immunity. Bronchitis and asthma risks are higher in polluted areas. Children and athletes have a particularly high risk, partly because they spend more time outdoors doing mouth breathing, which bypasses the nose's filtering system. One study showed that children raised in the South Coast Air Basin suffered a 10 to 15 percent decrease in lung function. Loving, protective parents unwittingly let their children be harmed.

My high school cross-country coach told his runners to try to breathe in through our noses and out through our mouths. He was concerned with efficient running rather than air pollution. I never mastered the technique, and remained a mouth-breathing runner in Orange County in the late 1960s. I remember how many nights after a workout I could only take cautiously shallow breaths. All evening my irritated throat produced coughing spasms following any deeper breath. I put up with that, as "normal." What other kind of air could a boy raised in Southern California know?

Humans take a breath every five seconds or so every day of their lives—even in Southern California. Healthy air ought to be a basic right, a fundamental requirement to be insisted upon. That is the basis of clean air laws, of course, but Southern California struggled with this problem far too long without success.

There *has* been improvement. Despite Governor Warren's early setback, California eventually developed tougher state air pollution standards than the federal government required. Until the 1990s, ozone conditions regularly exceeded standards more than 200 days a year, but after 2005, the figure remained below 120 days. The severe Stage 1 episodes, occurring over 100 days a year in the 1970s, are *way* down. There were only twelve in 1998, and since then, only a single day in 2003. Credit has been given to cleaner burning gasoline introduced in 1996 and continued improvements in vehicle emissions control and mileage. Those are positive steps, but progress is not yet "success"—not when air quality still violates current standards in the South Coast Air Basin, as happened on 92 days in 2014. One-third of Californians, living in nineteen of the state's counties, breathe bad air. Southern California and the Central Valley still have the smoggiest cities in the nation.

On October 2, 2015, new, stricter national standards for ozone were set by the U.S. Environmental Protection Agency (EPA) that must be attained by 2037 in California (unfortunately, many people will wait twenty-two years to breathe that cleaner air). As has repeatedly happened when such regulations were announced, manufacturers and transportation interests vehemently protested, predicting dire economic consequences to their businesses if forced to comply with the tighter standards. They were ignoring forty-five years of improved air quality achieved through earlier regulatory changes that had also been accompanied by such dire warnings. In those decades, the gross national product (GNP) tripled and California, despite stricter fuel characteristics and emissions standards, remained one of the largest and most successful economies in the world. Such objections also showed no concern for evidence that thousands of asthma attacks and hundreds of early deaths will be prevented once the air is cleaned up. Cost savings from health benefits outweigh industry costs four to one, according to the EPA.

Fighting smog requires some of the same measures needed to fight global climate change, including increased reliance on renewable energy, stepping away from fossil fuels, increasing the number of electric vehicles on the highways and, with the help of the federal government, controlling emissions from ships, aircraft, and locomotives.

The Owens Lake dust problem is a water issue because Los Angeles' diversions dried up that large inland sea back in the 1920s. The smog problem that has plagued California's urban centers since the 1940s is also a water issue. Without imported water, the Los Angeles air basin and the greater San Francisco Bay Area might still be famed for healthful air, the images they sustained through the 1930s. Since the 1950s, emissions control technology improvements have had to work against the offsetting pressure of population growth. With per capita emissions dropping, if Los Angeles today had the population numbers found in 1970, or 1940, technological fixes *would* have worked.

PART IV

HISTORIC CHOICES—
NORTHERN
CALIFORNIA WATER

1913 Congress authorizes construction of a dam on the Tuolumne River at Hetch Hetchy Valley inside Yosemite National Park for the San Francisco Public Utility District (SFPUD); San Francisco's population (in the 1910 census) at 416,912

1930 East Bay Municipal Water District's Mokelumne River Project begins water deliveries to Oakland, Berkeley and other East Bay cities

1934 The Hetch Hetchy aqueduct system is finally completed, bringing water to SFPUD customers

1937 Rivers and Harbors Act authorizes the federal Central Valley Project (CVP)

1951 First deliveries from Shasta Dam to San Joaquin Valley, under CVP

1960 California Water bonds pass (barely); state population is at 15,717,204; Los Angeles is 2,702,500; San Francisco at 740,316

1962 Oroville Dam construction begins for the State Water Project

1969 California Legislature enacts Porter-Cologne Water Quality Control Act, establishing the State Water Resources Control Board and nine Regional Water Quality boards

State Water Project. Adapted from a map supplied by the Los Angeles Department of Water and Power.

1970 California is most urban state in nation, and most populous, at 19,953,134; Orange County doubled since last census, to 1,420,386; National Environmental Policy Act, California Environmental Quality Act and California Endangered Species Act pass

1971 California Aqueduct begins moving northern water into Southern California

1980 Federal Wild and Scenic Rivers Act protects Smith River and parts of other final free-flowing rivers in northern part of state

1982 Voters reject Peripheral Canal; first defeat of a major California water project

1983 Deformed and dead waterfowl at Kesterson Reservoir from toxic agriculture drainage

1990 State population 29,760,021; Los Angeles at 3,485,557

1992 Central Valley Project Improvement Act allocates water back to environment

1993 Court rules that CVP must obey state law and keep water for fish downstream from dams

1994 Los Angeles' water licenses amended to protect Mono Lake

2000 California enters the twenty-first century with over 33 million people

2010 On its fiftieth anniversary, the State Water Project is named one of America's greatest engineering achievements of the twentieth century by the American Society of Civil Engineers

2015 State population reaches 38.9 million; the greater Southern California statistical census area totals more than 19 million while the San Jose-San Francisco-Oakland population is over 8.6 million

THIRTEEN

A DAM WITHIN YOSEMITE NATIONAL PARK AND M.U.D. FOR THE EAST BAY

Considering that the Spring Valley Water Company provided
every gallon of water for San Francisco and the peninsula until
1934, it is obvious that when the Hetch Hetchy system came on
line, it practically flooded the city. (Righter, 2005, 135)

That summer [of 1919] the East Bay lost a huge Goodyear Rubber
factory because Los Angeles could promise the millions of gallons
of water the plant needed each day. (Noble, [1970] 1999, 20)

The damming and diversion of the Mokelumne and Tuolumne
Rivers was part of the San Francisco Bay area's effort to keep pace,
early in the century, with Los Angeles' water-driven growth. San
Francisco received Congressional approval to build a dam at Hetch
Hetchy in 1913, at the same time that Mulholland was completing
the Los Angeles Aqueduct, and finally began importing Tuolumne
River water in 1934 to serve the city and civic customers south
on the peninsula and the Santa Clara Valley. Mokelumne River
water reached the East Bay Municipal Utility District (East Bay
M.U.D.) in 1930.

With the promotion machine fostering growth in Southern
California, a perception began to spread across the nation and

around the world that "California living" meant the life of Hollywood and palm trees, Disneyland and surfers; that it never rained in eternally sunny California. People who settled along the south coast often seemed to have little awareness of their reliance on the rest of the state's rivers and the natural resources at the "other end of the pipe." A common Southern Californian perspective considers anything north of the transverse ranges—the San Gabriel and San Bernardino mountains—as "Northern California." Yet San Francisco Bay, over 350 miles north of Los Angeles, is more logically the upper boundary of the *central* state, which then extends yet another 350 miles north to the Oregon border. Three-quarters of the state's landmass is north of the transverse ranges.

California's border with Oregon lies 800 miles from its southern border with Mexico. If superimposed over the East Coast of the United States, the elongated state would touch Maine in the north while extending down to South Carolina. There is an enormous diversity of landscape and climate across that north–south expanse. Northern California has seasons, but Southern California does too, despite the persistent myth of eternal sunshine. Los Angeles averages fifteen inches of rain each year. Crescent City, on the north coast, has just as much claim to a California climate, with sixty-five inches of rain, annually.

Superlatives abound in California. The tallest mountain in the forty-eight states, Mt. Whitney, is just one of seven peaks rising over 14,000 feet in the southern Sierra Nevada. Not far east from Whitney is the lowest point in North America, Badwater, at 282 feet below sea level in Death Valley. The planet's oldest trees, bristlecone pines, grow on California's eastern border, in the White Mountains. The biggest trees on the planet are also found in the state, whether measured in height (the 360-foot-tall coast redwood, *Sequoia sempervirens*) or mass (the "Big Tree" or giant sequoia, *Sequoiadendron giganteum)*, found in scattered Sierra Nevada groves. The largest Big Trees are thirty feet thick and more than 270 feet tall.

As moisture-laden storms move inland from the coast, they pile up against the state's mountain backbone. The Sierra Nevada received its name on April 2, 1772, when mission *padre* Pedro Font stood at the western edge of the Central Valley and saw, one hundred miles to the east, *una gran sierra nevada*, a great snowy mountain range. The range runs northwest to southeast for 360 miles. With that orientation, Pacific Ocean storms coming out of the west crash against the range. The Sierra crest pokes into the jet stream at 8,000 feet in the northern range, but peaks rise higher and higher to the south, to over 14,000 feet. Air, colliding with the mountains, rises, cools and loses its hold on water vapor. Most of the condensation falls as winter snow. Seasonal snow totals are only two feet at the 3,000-foot elevation in the foothills, but increase to thirty-four feet on Donner Summit (the famous pass where the Donner party endured a tragic winter). Snowmelt runs into major rivers, down through the lower foothills (the scene of the Gold Rush).

Summers are hot and dry in those foothills. A great green wall of coniferous forest occupies the west slope of the mountains, including ponderosa, Jeffrey, lodgepole and sugar pines, Douglas firs and incense cedars. The pines and firs, along with coast redwoods, provided the lumber to build California's towns and cities.

HETCH HETCHY

Federal land ownership at the source was the primary difference between San Francisco's water imports and the Owens Valley land purchase for Los Angeles. Damming the Tuolumne River meant flooding Hetch Hetchy Valley inside Yosemite National Park. Secretary of the Interior James R. Garfield decided, in 1908, to approve the city's application for the project, despite the protections afforded the national park since 1890: "I appreciate keenly the interest of the public in preserving the natural wonders of the park. . . . Domestic use, however, especially for a municipal supply, is the highest use to which water and available storage basins therefor can be put" (Egleston, 1909, 7). Hetch Hetchy Valley was similar to the more famous Yosemite Valley, with granite cliffs and waterfalls. Garfield turned that similarity—an argument for preservation—on

Before: Hetch Hetchy Valley, 1913. The Yosemite Museum, Yosemite National Park.

its head, declaring that Hetch Hetchy, though "great and beautiful in its natural and scenic effects," was not unique! "Furthermore, the reservoir will not destroy Hetch Hetchy," he wrote. "It will scarcely affect the canyon walls. It will not reach the foot of the various falls which descend from the sides of the canyon. The prime change will be that, instead of a beautiful but somewhat unusable 'meadow' floor, the valley will be a lake of rare beauty" (Egleston, 1909, 7).

San Francisco voters passed a $45 million bond issue to build the city's dam, by a six-to-one majority, with 46,719 ballots cast. The character of the campaign was not unlike those in Los Angeles; preservationists were called, in the *San Francisco Chronicle*, "hoggish and mushy esthetes" (Egleston, 1909, 16). The opposition was led by John Muir, although the Sierra Club, which he had founded, split over the issue and took no official stance. Most of its members lived in the Bay Area; San Francisco's city engineer was a Sierra Club member.

After: Hetch Hetchy Reservoir, 1955. Robert McIntyre, NPS. The Yosemite Museum, Yosemite National Park.

Muir, 70 years old, had led the fight to create national parks in the Sierra; this became the eloquent writer's last great battle.

"Dam Hetch Hetchy?" he wrote, before 1913 Congressional hearings, "As well dam for water tanks the people's cathedrals and churches, for no holier temple has ever been consecrated by the heart of man" (Muir, 1912, 181). One of Muir's arguments was that there were other rivers available to San Francisco (the Mokelumne River, for one, which would be developed soon after for East Bay cities). But San Francisco coveted the Tuolumne because it was free of established water rights claims and would be the cheapest to acquire. "These temple destroyers, devotees of ravaging commercialism, seem to have a perfect contempt for Nature, and, instead of lifting their eyes to the God of the mountains, lift them to the Almighty Dollar," Muir raged (1912, 181).

The Raker Act, authorizing the Hetch Hetchy project, passed in the Senate by a 43-to-25 vote and was signed into law by President

Woodrow Wilson on December 19, 1913. San Francisco and the cities bordering the South Bay had the water and power they needed to grow. The principle that national parks should be forever protected had been undermined, yet, the decision also fostered a national awakening to that principle. "The damming of Hetch Hetchy was the event that turned the Sierra Club from an outings club to a political organization. Two years after Congress authorized the dam, they passed the National Parks Act, basically ensuring that we are going to preserve parks and not do anything like building the Hetch Hetchy dam ever again" (Spreck Rosekrans, in Carle and Carle, 2013, 206).

John Muir's death, in 1914, was due to pneumonia. Historians, however, have speculated that his passing, so soon after the Hetch Hetchy decision, was due to a broken heart over the loss.

As for the "lake of rare beauty" promised by Garfield, the reservoir in Hetch Hetchy valley, with a "bathtub ring" produced by each season's drawdown, is a seldom-visited part of the otherwise overcrowded Yosemite National Park. Restricting recreation use became San Francisco's policy for managing the reservoir, despite provisions in the Raker Act that required that the region remain open to recreation and that required the city to build roads and trails. "In 1928 the [San Francisco] supervisors and the city engineer seemed to have conveniently forgotten the very arguments that abetted the city in gaining the grant." The park service pushed back against city reluctance, enough to establish a nearby hikers' campground, but still, today, backpackers descending the Grand Canyon of the Tuolumne River must make long detours around the upper portions of the reservoir, where swimming and boating are also forbidden.

The San Francisco Public Utilities Commission had acquired far more Tuolumne River water than the city itself needed and, not confronted by the annexation requirement that restricted Los Angeles, began marketing surplus water and electricity generated by the system's power plants to cities south along the peninsula, across the Santa Clara Valley, and up the southeastern side of the Bay as far as Hayward. By 2015, the utility was delivering water to 2.6 million residents.

"Celebration of the First Delivery of Hetch Hetchy Water" program cover, 1934. Courtesy of the San Francisco History Center, San Francisco Public Library.

As bottled water became a popular phenomenon, San Francisco's Mayor Willie Brown suggested, in 1998, that the city bottle Hetch Hetchy water with a special label under that name. In 2003, the city did start marketing the bottled water, which prompted the *Los Angeles Times* to editorialize, on March 22, that year:

Shame. Hetch Hetchy may be as fresh and tasty as bottled water gets, but any good environmentalist with a sense of history would rather drink irrigation runoff. Someday, perhaps San Francisco will recognize that its pride in Hetch Hetchy is misplaced and that dismantling the dam is something that is really worth San Francisco's image of itself.

In the year 2000, the group Restore Hetch Hetchy had formed, aiming at that very dismantling project while promising no loss of water to San Francisco's customers, by relying on existing downstream storage on the Tuolumne River to replace the valley reservoir. Restoration had been given federal support during President Ronald Reagan's administration, when Don Hodel, Secretary of the Interior, suggested, in 1987, that restoring Hetch Hetchy could occur without harm to San Francisco. Feasibility studies supported that claim, including one by the National Park Service and U.S. Bureau of Reclamation in 1988 and another by the California Department of Water Resources in 2006.

In April 2015, Restore Hetch Hetchy filed a petition in the Superior Court in Tuolumne County asserting that the Hetch Hetchy Reservoir inside Yosemite National Park violated the reasonable use water diversion mandates in the California Constitution, because the value of restoration is greater than its cost. Their legal action does not ask for restoration to begin until necessary water system improvements can be made, so that "not one drop of supply will be lost."

THE VALLEY OF HEART'S DELIGHT

Beyond impacts at Hetch Hetchy, in the headwaters of the San Francisco Bay water systems, imported water facilitated major changes in the greater Bay Area. The alteration of the Santa Clara Valley, today commonly referred to as Silicon Valley, provided another graphic example of the close connection between imported water and growth.

The valley's formal name exists because the Mission Santa Clara was established there in 1777. During the Spanish era, up through the early years of California statehood, cattle ranching had been the primary activity. Wheat was widely grown for a short while, but by the 1870s, orchards found their niche. As of 1900, nearly 14,000 acres of orchards and vineyards were established in the Santa Clara Valley. With more rainfall than the citrus belt of Southern California, the fertile soil and local surface and groundwater nourished prunes, apricots, cherries, walnuts and other trees and vines. A new name for the fertile region became "the Valley of Heart's Delight." Drying and canning fruit became the dominant industries. Citrus labels and railroad shipping began marketing this produce, following the model of the Southern California citrus belt. Fruit drying and canning became dominant industries. Until the 1960s, the Santa Clara Valley remained the largest fruit-packing region in the world with thirty-nine canneries.

As in Orange County and parts of the Los Angeles basin, artesian wells that had gushed freely stopped producing as the water table diminished. Pumps chased after the descending water. By the 1920s, subsidence due to groundwater pumping was leading to saltwater intrusion into the aquifer from the bay. Regional reservoirs were constructed and attempts begun to recharge groundwater supplies. Across the Santa Clara Valley,

> . . . farmers frequently sold out to the realtors with sighs of relief. To be rescued handsomely just as their pumps started sucking air in wells drawn down by half a century of pumping or began salting up with ocean water seeping inland from the bay, was deliverance beyond dreaming. Pocketing rich sums as they turned their water worries over to their city cousins, the ranchers went seeking new fields to conquer or settled down in style in the latest luxury apartments. (Cooper, 1968, 209)

With water from the San Francisco Hetch Hetchy system, the population in Santa Clara County jumped from 30,000 in 1940 to 90,000 in one decade, then exploded to 291,000 by 1950. Palo Alto, Sunnyvale, San Jose, Santa Clara began sprawling. The northern

California version of the postwar population boom coincided with a major drought from 1940 to 1946. The local water supply was, in a familiar pattern, bumping against natural limits, although voters approved bonds to construct additional dams in the coast range hills. The lifestyle that had gone along with the "Valley of Heart's Delight" name was transformed.

The new appellation became "Silicon Valley" as a very thirsty computer industry grew up. Manufacturing computer chips required thousands of gallons of ultrapure water for each silicon wafer. Millions of gallons per day were required by the industry. By 2014, there were 1.89 million people in Santa Clara County. Such growth was only possible because of the imported water delivered by San Francisco, which was eventually supplemented with connections to federal and state aqueducts out in the Central Valley.

EAST BAY M.U.D.

Across the bay, the city of Oakland relied on surface streams and groundwater delivered by private water companies through the nineteenth century. Anthony Chabot's Contra Costa Water Company became the most important of the private suppliers. Chabot would also develop systems for the communities of San Jose and Vallejo. Oakland's population in 1870 was 15,000 and, with an active port on the bay to drive commerce, the numbers reached 34,000 by 1880. In the opening years of the twentieth century, Oakland's water system was serving 150,000 people.

Local reservoirs were constructed in the Oakland hills with plumbing to deliver water to homes and businesses, but water quality through the decades had been awful. In 1871, the *Daily Alta California* newspaper editorialized that the city's water "has such an offensive smell that, to say nothing of drinking it, it is not even '*goot vor vash*,' and . . . the muddy condition and terrible stench of the water now served Oaklanders renders it fearfully nauseating to the strongest of stomachs. Is there no remedy?" (Noble, [1970] 1999, 7). A majority of citizens placed blame for the lack of remedy on private ownership of the water system.

The East Bay Municipal Utility District, better known by its earthy nickname, East Bay M.U.D., was organized in 1923, as the Oakland and Berkeley region's population neared a half million people. A $39 million bond measure went before voters in 1924 to fund the new utility district, with aims to build an aqueduct from a source not yet identified. Future bonds, if the district was established, would require a two-thirds vote of the people. Private water purveyors fought energetically against the scheme they termed "socialism."

"The American people have not gone mad on socialism," retorted district proponents. "Neither will the people of this proposed district. Had we the foresight to see future needs we would never locate a city anywhere that did not have the natural advantages of good water, cheap transportation, and other fundamentals. We can't very well move the city to the water, so we must bring the water here" (Noble, [1970] 1999, 23).

The bond was approved by a 29,936 "yes" to 17,470 "no" vote. Two-thirds of those voters lived in Oakland. Only the cities of Piedmont and Richmond turned down the bond, by close margins (both cities joined the district later).

The former head of the U.S. Bureau of Reclamation, Arthur Powell Davis, became general manager and chief engineer for East Bay M.U.D. He was formally advised by two illustrious icons in the world of water development: Major General George W. Goethals, who had overseen construction of the Panama Canal, and Los Angeles' DWP Chief Engineer, William Mulholland. The president of the utility board was another luminary, Dr. George C. Pardee, who had served as Governor of California from 1903 to 1907, and as mayor of Oakland. He would be the utility president for seventeen years.

Water source options narrowed down quickly to the Mokelumne River, which had a Sierra Nevada watershed gathering runoff from 575 square miles in Alpine, Amador and Calaveras Counties. A suitable dam site was identified 38 miles upstream from Stockton. The utility purchased or condemned 30,000 acres in the watershed, acquired control over a 100-foot-wide corridor across the state, and added land for off-stream reservoirs in the East Bay hills. To acquire the reservoir site, they brought a condemnation suit against land-owner Stephen E. Kieffer, who had claimed a $22 million value; a court awarded him $337,450.

Construction of the East Bay Aqueduct finished in 1928 and the dam, named for Pardee, was dedicated in 1929. The first water made the 91-mile trip to the East Bay in June 1929. A second Mokelumne Aqueduct would be added in 1949, and a third in 1963.

East Bay M.U.D. today serves thirty-five communities in Alameda and Contra Costa Counties, including Berkeley, Oakland and parts of the San Ramon Valley. The population of Oakland, the city that drove so much of the initial demand, grew from 230,000 in 1930 to 413,000 in 2015. The utility's broader service area now includes about 1.4 million people.

FOURTEEN

BIG DAMS IRRIGATE BIG FARMS: THE CENTRAL VALLEY PROJECT

Historically, water development in California may have had more of an impact on biodiversity than any other single factor. (Andrew Cohen, in Thelander, 1994, 300)

During this season, which has been an unusually short one, the amount of fresh salmon which has been packed amounts to 451,957 Spring salmon, and 160,542 Fall salmon, aggregating 7,349,998 pounds. The amount of fresh Spring salmon sold in the markets was 115,004, and of Fall run 52,902, aggregating 2,235,684 pounds; total number of pounds sold and canned in the year 1883, 9,585,672 pounds. These statistics do not include 60,000 or more caught above Sacramento City. ("Report of the Commissioners of Fisheries for the State of California for the Years 1883–84" in Hinton, 1993, 10)

The northern half of California's Central Valley is drained by the Sacramento River, which gathers water from the Feather, Yuba, Bear and American Rivers, along with numerous smaller creeks. The San Joaquin River accepts runoff from the southern Sierra, with contributions from the Mokelumne, Calaveras, Stanislaus, Merced and Tuolumne Rivers. The Sacramento and San Joaquin

Rivers, draining the northern and southern halves of the Central Valley, merge into a complex of Delta channels that finally deliver water to San Francisco Bay and the Pacific Ocean. Over 30 million AF of annual runoff comes out of the Sacramento and San Joaquin Valleys.

A few rivers, in the southernmost portion of the valley, never reached the sea. The Kern River once terminated in Buena Vista Lake. The Tule, Kings and Kaweah Rivers (from the Sequoia National Park area) once formed Tulare Lake. James Carson described the southern San Joaquin conditions in 1852:

The oaks, in their majesty, thickly cover the plain for miles around, and stretch away to the shore of the Tulare Lake. Stretching beyond . . . to the west lie the placid blue waters of the Tulare Lake, whose ripples wash the foot of the low hills of the Coast range . . . [Tulare Lake] is about fifty miles in length by thirty in width. . . .

Buena Vista Lake is a beautiful sheet of water, twenty miles long, and from five to ten in width; it lays nestled in the head of the valley, and is fed by Kern River, and several small creeks. . . .

The slough connecting the Tulare and Buena Vista Lakes is about eighty miles in length. . . . Thousands of wild horses subsist on the grasses growing [west of] there now. . . . The Tulare Valley, perhaps, contains a larger portion of wild horses than any other part of the world to the same extent. On the western side of San Joaquin, they are to be seen in bands of from two hundred to two thousand.

Every beast and bird of the chase and hunt is to be found in abundance on the Tulares. Horses, cattle, elk, antelope, black tail and red deer, grizzly and brown bear, black and grey wolves, coyotes, ocelots, California lions, wildcats, beaver, otter mink weasels, ferrets, hare, rabbits, grey and red foxes, grey and ground squirrels, kangaroo rats, badgers, skunks, muskrats, hedgehogs, and many species of small animals; . . . swan, geese, brant, and over twenty different . . . ducks . . . in countless myriads from the first of October until the first of April, besides millions of . . . crane, plover, snipe, and quail. (Carson, [1852] 1931, 65–66, 68–69, 76, 80)

Both Tulare and Buena Vista Lakes are gone from today's California maps, their river sources diverted for irrigation and the dry lakebeds transformed into farm fields.

In one of John Muir's essays he described the flowery Central Valley as "a great bee garden" (Muir, 1961, 259). Other writers have called it "California's Kansas," "the Inland Sea," "California's Heartland" and "the Invented Garden." The valley became "the most productive unnatural landscape in the world," according to historian Kevin Starr, and "a triumph of irrigation technology" (Starr, [2004] 2006, 490). Its rivers once were thickly lined with trees: valley oaks, sycamore, cottonwood, willow and ash. Winter rains and spring runoff brought annual floods to soak a half-million acres of tule swamps. Those wet bottomlands were avoided by the first post–Gold Rush settlers. Farmers who settled, instead, on higher land were still called "rimlanders" in the 1990s, by their neighbors, long after bottomland reclamation made the rim of the "inland sea" little more than a memory.

The capital city of Sacramento was a seaport in the early years of statehood. In September 1857, twenty-three schooners, twenty-seven sloops and nine steamboats arrived or departed (Kelley, 1989). Steamboats needed fuel and growing towns needed wood for construction, so the nearby riparian forests were rapidly cut. Wetlands reclamation required drainage ditches—to drain off water—and levees—to hold back seasonal floodwaters from the developed lands.

Plant and wildlife populations that once thrived in the pristine valley were being displaced. "Weeds" and "varmints" were the new names for unwanted native plants and wildlife in direct competition with farms for habitat. That the transformation of the Central Valley into "an invented garden" was a war was made most blatantly clear during community rabbit drives. One such drive in Fresno County, on March 10, 1892, so impressed author Frank Norris that he built a chapter around it in his historical novel, *The Octopus*. Five thousand people participated, closing a great circle to drive rabbits from all sides toward a large corral:

Inside it was a living, moving, leaping, breathing, twisting mass. The rabbits were packed two, three, and four feet deep. They were in constant movement; those beneath struggling to the top, those on top sinking and disappearing below their fellows.

On signal, the killing began. Dogs that had been brought there for that purpose when let into the corral refused . . . to do the work. They snuffed curiously at the pile, then backed off, disturbed, perplexed. But the men and boys . . . were more eager.

Armed with a club in each hand, the young fellows . . . leaped over the rails of the corral. Blindly, furiously, they struck and struck. But only a few of the participants of the drive cared to look on. All the guests betook themselves some quarter of a mile farther on into the hills [to] the picnic and barbecue. (Norris, 1901, 363–64)

Twenty thousand rabbits were killed in that drive—probably the largest of many similar drives throughout the state as farmers fought to transform California.

The farmers won a costly victory. By the end of the twentieth century, choices made by Californians cost them 99 percent of their native grasslands, 89 percent of their riparian woodlands and 95 percent of their wetlands. The state became an "epicenter of extinction": at least 73 species are gone forever, including the California grizzly bear, the state's chosen symbol. Today, 291 California plant and animal species are officially listed as endangered or threatened, more than in any other state in the nation. Much of the loss was directly caused by water choices. Species that depended on water disappeared or declined wherever wet habitat was "reclaimed." A half million Tule elk once grazed the marshes of the Central Valley and central coast. By 1970, only 500 Tule elk remained alive, in three herds. The remnants were relocated to the Owens Valley, which, ironically, provided undisturbed grazing land, since Los Angeles had evicted Eastern Sierra farmers early in the century. The state later relocated animals from that herd and today, the remnant population totals about 3,800 Tule elk in twenty-one herds.

The southern half of the Central Valley was more susceptible to the region's periodic droughts and, so, more difficult to farm. It was also primarily owned by a few major landholders who could reap enormous benefits if water were delivered to their arid properties. The California State legislature approved a $170 million plan in 1933, to dam the Sacramento River above Redding and pump water from the Sacramento–San Joaquin Delta southward to the San Joaquin Valley. Those were Great Depression years, however, and the state could not market its construction bonds. They sought help from the federal government.

President Franklin D. Roosevelt signed an emergency relief measure in 1935, authorizing the Bureau of Reclamation to begin dam construction. Friant Dam, on the San Joaquin River, was completed in 1944; Shasta Dam, on the Sacramento River, in 1945; the canal system to deliver irrigation water from Shasta Dam to the San Joaquin valley opened in 1951.

The completed Central Valley Project (CVP) eventually added major dams on the Trinity, American and Stanislaus Rivers, ultimately totaling twenty reservoirs, eleven power plants and three fish hatcheries. Administered by the U.S. Bureau of Reclamation (though some of the facilities were built by the Army Corps of Engineers), the CVP would deliver seven million AF of water every year to three million acres of farmland. The Central Valley became one of the world's major agricultural regions. The Sacramento Valley today grows rice, wheat, orchard fruits, alfalfa and vegetable crops. The drier and hotter San Joaquin Valley counties of Fresno and Tulare became the top agricultural revenue–generating counties in the nation. With imported water to supplement groundwater wells, corn, grains, grapes, vegetables, fruit, nut and citrus orchards, cotton and alfalfa are produced to serve California and the nation, and to be imported overseas.

The 1902 Reclamation Act had established a 160-acre limit and a residency requirement for farms receiving Bureau of Reclamation water. That policy aimed to maximize small family farms. It was a goal that could not have been more at odds with the history and power structure within California, going back to Spanish and Mexican land grants, railroad land grants, and federal homestead grants that had been consolidated into immense holdings by a relatively few corporations and individuals. California's power-elite welcomed subsidized water, but 160-acre and residency limitations were anathema.

The controversy was particularly intense for a short while after World War II, when CVP water first became available. Small farmers, organized by local granges, gathered at a California Water Conference in 1945. The conference attendees extolled a populist vision of California's agricultural future built around federal acreage limitations and public power. Conference proceedings identified the "mouthpieces" of their primary opposition as "Pacific Gas and Electric Company, the Irrigation Districts Association, the California Farm Bureau Association, the State Water Project Authority" (Stene, 1998, 4). The concentrated power behind those organizations ensured that the conference's vision was never realized.

Yet the possibility that legal requirements actually might be enforced someday within California was a continual threat to the state's corporate farmers. That irritation was finally relieved by the Central Valley Reform Act of 1982, which raised the acreage limit to 960 acres and eliminated the residency requirement. This "reform" legitimized the actual pattern during thirty years of Reclamation water deliveries within the Central Valley, where 80 percent of the state's farmland was in holdings over 1,000 acres. Some of the state's agribusiness conglomerates included Standard Oil, Getty Oil, Southern Pacific Railroad and the Chandler family, publishers of the *Los Angeles Times*. Coincidental with the philosophy that the state's water distribution required "correction" was the general fact that the farther south one traveled through the valley, the higher was the percentage of corporate, absentee landholdings.

"Paper farms" came into a virtual existence, where "a large farming operation of several thousand acres . . . is operated as one enterprise, but on paper, it appears to be several smaller farms each

960 acres or less in size." Daniel P. Beard, a former Commissioner of the U.S. Bureau of Reclamation, drew that conclusion, in a book published years after his retirement from that agency, and added: "The Central Valley Project is the greatest water gift any group of farmers in America has ever received. . . . But our gift was not distributed evenly. There were winners, and then there were really big winners—the six hundred farming operations that make up the Westlands Water District" (Beard, 2015, 79–80).

Forty to eighty million migratory birds once used Central Valley wetlands for food, shelter or nesting habitat. Today, they number less than 3 million. Most of that decline was due to lost habitat, but some wetlands that accumulated toxic runoff water from Westlands Water District farms began killing birds outright. On the west side of the southern San Joaquin Valley water encountered a shallow hardpan layer in the soil, so the U.S. Bureau of Reclamation built a drain to carry off salt-laden irrigation water that would otherwise accumulate and make farming impossible. The San Luis Drain, concentrating runoff from 180,000 acres of southern San Joaquin Valley farms, dumped its water—carrying salts, pesticides and herbicides—into the Kesterson Wildlife Refuge. Problems appeared within a few years. In 1983, shocking photographs of grotesquely deformed hatchlings appeared in national magazines; 246 birds died at Kesterson that year. Selenium, leached from the valley soil, caused the deformities. The drain into Kesterson was shut down in 1986 and the deadly refuge was capped with dirt. Toxic pools form now only when it rains, yet the basic problem remains, shifted by new drains carrying the irrigation runoff into the lowlands of the former Tulare Lake.

After William Sweeney retired from the U.S. Fish and Wildlife Service, he spoke about his professional frustration over the conflict between water development and wildlife protection:

> Crops are being grown by taking huge quantities of water swiped from our migratory birds and anadromous fish and applying it to land, much of which is alkaline desert that should never have been

plowed. I tend to gag every time BuRec refers to the slopes on the west side of the valley as 'prime' agricultural land. . . . Construction and operation of the Central Valley Project . . . turned the San Joaquin River into the lower colon of California—a stinking sewer contaminated with salts, heavy metals, trace elements, and the residue from the annual application of hundreds of tons of insecticides, herbicides, and fertilizers. (In Lufkin, 1990, 210–11)

Changes in fish populations have been an even greater problem since so many rivers in the Sierra Nevada watershed were dammed. In an 1846 letter from California, William Garner wrote: "In the winter season, every rivulet that leads to the sea abounds in salmon" (1970, 100). Anadromous fish, like salmon and steelhead, are born in streams, migrate to the ocean, then return as adults a few years later, to spawn and die. They track the chemical signature of their birthplaces with noses that can detect dissolved substances diluted three quintillion (3,000,000,000,000,000,000) times! Steelhead used coastal streams throughout the length of the state. Coho (also known as silver salmon) were found in as many as 582 coastal streams from Monterey Bay north. In the Sacramento and San Joaquin river systems, over 25 Central Valley streams supported at least one chinook (king) salmon run each year. Four distinct chinook populations made fall, late-fall, winter and spring migration runs up the Sacramento River.

The first West Coast salmon cannery was established in 1864 in Sacramento. Eventually twenty-one canneries were operating, most capturing fish in the Delta area before they made it farther upstream. In the early 1880s, the canneries netted and processed 9 to 11 million pounds of fish, annually. Not surprisingly, given that harvest rate, by 1890 the take declined to one-eighth its 1882 peak. In 1919, the last operating cannery harvested only two percent of the peak harvest amount, then shut down.

Harvesting, clearly, cut deeply into the salmon runs, but other factors were at work. Hydraulic mining, railroad construction, dams and flumes—first for mining and then converted for

Spring-run chinook salmon caught on the San Joaquin river near Friant (ca. 1915). Courtesy of the California Department of Fish and Game archives, Fresno.

agriculture—destroyed or completely blocked river spawning habitat. Yet, as salmon numbers dropped, people blamed hungry sea lions or pointed fingers at ethnic fishermen as the problem. Finally, it was the era of major dam building that dealt the ultimate death blow.

In 1996, only about 1,014 miles of stream remained of 2,113 miles of Central Valley streams originally used by chinook salmon. Stream miles do not tell the complete story, however. Salmon must reach the upper branches of streams, where appropriate spawning conditions exist. Today, only 18 percent of the original spawning habitat remains accessible.

The spring run of chinook on the San Joaquin River once numbered up to a half million fish. Salmon runs ended, completely, on that drainage after Friant Dam was completed in 1942. The dam blocked fish from reaching spawning grounds, but even more decisive was the fact that the river channel was dried up for sixty miles *below* the dam, its water entirely diverted into irrigation canals.

From 1943 until the present, salmon heading north up the Sacramento River have encountered Shasta Dam. The depleted

Sacramento River winter run, by 1991, returned only 191 chinook. In 1982, spring-run chinook on the Sacramento still numbered 22,800, yet only 10 percent of that number, 2,300, returned to spawn in 1992. The Sacramento River winter-run has been declared endangered under federal and state listings. The threatened spring-run has been proposed for "endangered" status. The Sacramento Valley fall-run is considered threatened, as is the north coast run.

The historic coho population, numbering about 1 million in the mid-1800s, was down to 100,000 in the 1950s and 1960s. In 1996, less than six thousand returned to California's coastal streams to spawn. The coho population that ran south of San Francisco Bay has been listed by California as an endangered species. Genetically distinct coho populations in northern California and the central coast are officially "threatened."

Two steelhead populations utilizing streams along the southern coast were listed as endangered in 1997; four distinct central coast and northern populations are threatened or are being considered for listing.

The priorities of the federal CVP were dramatically realigned in 1992, when President George Bush signed a bill over the objections of California Governor Pete Wilson and Central Valley legislators. The Central Valley Project Improvement Act (CVPIA) elevated fish and wildlife protection and restoration to primary purposes of the project, in part because of the endangered species status for salmon. Water was reallocated back to fish, waterfowl and other wildlife in refuges and streams. The controversial 800,000 AF allocation was later modified to "amounts needed" in a given water-year to accomplish the same objectives. Water marketing was also authorized by the act, to allow conserved water to be sold to the highest bidder by Central Valley Project contractors.

After another water choice was made, in 1960, to construct the California Aqueduct, diversions from the Sacramento–San Joaquin Delta to serve agricultural and urban expansion accelerated. Many of the threats to ecosystems and wildlife that followed only became apparent in the final decades of the century.

FIFTEEN

TOO MUCH IS NOT ENOUGH: THE STATE WATER PROJECT

It's not a conspiracy—it's a religion. MWD has reached out to grab more and more of California's water so steadily over the last half century that growth has become the nature of the beast. (Mike Bradley, in Dennis, 1981, 14)

The far north simply doesn't understand the facts of life. It has no use for its surplus water. (*San Bernardino Daily Sun*, August 10, 1960)

The 1960 Federal Census showed the city of Los Angeles with 2.7 million residents, continuing to grow primarily with Owens River water delivered by the Los Angeles Aqueduct. The rest of the Southern California region was rapidly converting orchards to housing tracts with Colorado River water delivered by MWD. In the November 1960 election, the State Water Project bond issue came before voters, demonstrating that California's leaders still held firmly to the belief that "too much is not enough."

Many years after he led the political crusade to create the State Water Project, former governor Edmund G. "Pat" Brown explained why California's farm corporations were enthusiastic supporters of the effort, because it promised irrigation water without imposing acreage limitations.

You see, under the federal reclamation act they sell that water for $3.50 an acre-foot, and it cost about eighteen dollars to deliver.

So there's a fifteen dollars an acre-foot subsidy to these big
farmers—Southern Pacific, Standard Oil, Kern County Land—
and those people just reaped a terrific wealth. . . . Now, under the
state project . . . we charged them for—not the actual cost of the
water because the domestic user paid for most of it—but we did
charge them a much higher price for the water. . . .

This water project was a godsend to the big landowners of the
state of California. It really increased the value of their property
tremendously and people should realize that. But also the ordinary
citizen was helped by it too. I was willing to go for enrichment of
these rich people here because it was the lesser of evils.

If we put the acreage limitation into the California Water
Project as a lot of them wanted me to do—labor and other
people—I felt we'd incur the opposition of some of the large
landowners and they'd finance a campaign against my bond issue.
(Brown, 1981, 7–8, 61)

For the 1960 election, another well-financed water-cam-
paign machine sprang into action. In San Bernardino, a County
Supplemental Water Association was formed that distributed car
bumper stickers—the words "Water, Key to California's FUTURE"
topped the image of a dripping key. Editorial and news stories issued
dire warnings, once again, in Southern California newspapers:

WATER VITAL: STATE WARNS OF DISASTER. Harvey O.
Banks, state director of water resources, warned yesterday that
Southern California is headed for "economic disaster" unless
California's water development program proceeds on schedule.
Speaking at a Chamber of Commerce meeting, Banks said that
new water supplies must be found for the south by 1971 "to main-
tain the present economy as well as provide for future expansion."
(Daily Enterprise, March 24, 1960)

Project promoters knew that, unlike the negotiations between
states that culminated in Colorado River water imports, and unlike

the Los Angeles land grab that captured Owens Valley water for that city, a *statewide* vote must decide this bond election. Though Southern California held the majority of voters, Northern California voters, who were leery of losing control of local water, were motivated to participate in this election. One Southern California newspaper editorialized about its frustrations with northern voters' attitudes:

> What the north has not figured out is the vast benefit it would achieve from the doubling of population in Southern California. The San Joaquin and Sacramento valleys would provide the food for the additional population. The far north, which is dependent upon recreation, would have a greater potential upon which to draw. The far north simply doesn't understand the facts of life. It has no use for its surplus water. (*San Bernardino Daily Sun*, August 10, 1960)

Note the undisguised anticipation within that statement, of a "doubling of population" in the southern state if the bonds were approved.

Governor Pat Brown, who had been elected by a majority that gave him "the voters' mandate" and plenty of political momentum, took on the water project as a personal crusade. His message was that it was better to have water with problems, than problems without water. For an oral history, nineteen years later, he described the "missionary complex" that often develops in holders of high office; he felt he had been the one person to do the job and that, if *he* were not successful, there might never have been a State Water Project. "You've got to remember that I was absolutely *determined* that I was going to pass this California Water Project. I wanted this to be a monument to *me*" (Brown, 1981, 29; emphasis in original).

Uncertainty about the outcome of the bond election had more to do with statewide reactions to costs than with northern possessiveness regarding water. Proposition 1, on the November 1960 ballot, asked for approval of a $1.75 billion bond act, the largest ever considered by a state at that time. Brown proclaimed, with familiar hyperbole, that there was a critical water crisis that should override cost concerns: "The needs are desperate. We are in trouble now. Unless we act now to take care of that trouble, the growth and future of California is in mortal danger" (*San Francisco Chronicle,* May 14, 1959, 9).

There would be accusations, later, that Brown and his administration officials lied to voters about the project's real costs. An original plan, meant to solve the state's water problems through the end of the century, came with a $4 billion cost estimate. That amount was deemed politically impossible. A project to meet needs projected through 1990 came with an estimated price tag of $2.5 billion. Brown decided to ask for *only* $1.75 billion, intending to fund the balance by borrowing tideland oil revenues. In his oral history, Brown said he was copying a funding strategy of Governor Huey Long of Louisiana: if voters would not finance a road, then just go ahead and build from each end—a road with a big gap in the middle *would* eventually be finished.

On November 8, voters approved Proposition 1 by only 174,000 votes; 5.8 million votes were cast; the margin of victory was slim, at three percent. Out of fifty-eight California counties, forty-three voted "no." Predictably, the proposition was rejected in the north, but passed in the more heavily populated south.

SWP water began flowing down the California Aqueduct in 1971, sending 70 percent of its supply to urban users in the southern state, but also expanding farm irrigation even farther onto arid lands at the south end of the San Joaquin Valley. The State Water Project built twenty-two dams and a 444-mile aqueduct. Oroville Dam, on the Feather River, was the largest dam in the system, with the greatest hydroelectric generating capacity. It is an eerie experience to tour that power plant and to realize that 650 feet of reservoir water are directly overhead when you stand next to the turbines. The plant was built beneath the deepest portion of the reservoir, in a cavern blasted out of the bedrock, so that electrical turbines rotate with maximum efficiency from the weight of overhead water. That power plant can generate 2.2 billion kilowatt-hours (kwh) per year. Eight other generating plants at SWP reservoirs bring the system's total power generation to 5.8 billion kwh/year. Yet that is only three-fourths of the electricity *consumed* in pumping SWP water to Southern California. At the Tehachapi Mountains, north of Los Angeles, enormous pumps lift water 2,000 feet to crest the mountains. The annual electricity demand for SWP pumps is equal to all the electricity consumed by the City of San Francisco in one year, according to the California Department of Water Resources (1996, 10).

Why not tunnel through the mountains and avoid pumping costs, as was done for the Los Angeles Aqueduct? The route of the new California Aqueduct would encounter the San Andreas Fault not far from Tejon Pass and the Garlock fault in the Tehachapis, with a higher risk of damage from earthquakes if pipes were underground. Instead, engineers concluded that crossing the faults above ground, at right angles, was safer and earthquake damage would be far easier to repair. "The energy bill for pumping the water . . . is the earthquake insurance premium which the people of Southern California must pay . . . in every water bill for ever and ever" (Cooper, 1968, 214).

With California Aqueduct water added to the supply mix, Southern California's population grew by 45 percent between 1970 and 1990, as its developed land area increased 300 percent. Approaching the twenty-first century, the fastest growing California cities were on the fringes of the major metropolitan areas—in many cases, areas with true desert climates. Palmdale, on the Mojave Desert side of the mountains from the coastal basin, grew by 36 percent during the 1990s. Its neighboring community, Lancaster, increased 21 percent. Both cities had more than 100,000 residents by 1998, according to the California Department of Finance. Air-conditioning, the California Aqueduct and the region's freeway system helped explain the sprawling development pattern. During the same decades, the city of Los Angeles increased by a more modest 3.2 percent (to 3.6 million people).

Nineteen years after the water choice was made by a slim margin of voters, Pat Brown discussed population growth and environmental changes that followed in the wake of his State Water Project. "Today, of course, the environment—the quality of life—is very important. At that time, I was primarily dealing with the *quantity* of life" (1981, 34). Some of his advisors had suggested, back then, that it made more sense for people to come to the water, instead of shipping water great distances. "Well, I was a Northern Californian. I knew I wouldn't be governor forever. I didn't think I'd ever come down to Southern California and I said to myself, 'I don't want all those people to go to Northern California.' Now, it's arguable whether or not we shouldn't have limited growth by lack of water." He mentioned an effort in Santa Barbara, at that time, to manage population numbers by defeating water import measures. "It's a hell of a way to limit growth, but it's probably as good as any" (1981, 34–35).

William Mulholland and Pat Brown had much in common— though both were concerned about quality of life, nevertheless, both were driven to develop more water for ever more people. Despite the growth concerns Brown voiced, his oral history shows that he remained convinced that the state "must" eventually reach clear to Washington State and capture Columbia River water for California.

THE PERIPHERAL CANAL

To complete the State Water Project as originally envisioned, Governor Jerry Brown, Pat's son, signed a legislative bill in 1982, authorizing an $11.6 billion construction project whose centerpiece was a canal to move water around the San Francisco Bay Delta before shipping it south. Peripheral Canal opponents gathered 850,000 signatures to put a referendum vote into the 1982 election to cancel the project.

The Peripheral Canal was meant to keep fresh aqueduct water from mixing with the salty tidal waters of the Delta. Its backers hoped for support from the environmental community because the canal would end the need for pumping from the Delta itself—a major cause of fish mortality—and the legislation included permanent protection for undammed north coast rivers. While accomplishing those goals, however, up to 1 million AF of water would be diverted away each year from Delta and San Francisco Bay environments.

Before the Sacramento and San Joaquin Rivers converge to enter San Francisco Bay, they wind through a 1,130-square-mile maze of islands and channels forming the largest estuary on the West Coast. Estuaries, where freshwater mixes with saltwater, are some of the most productive biological habitats on the planet. The zone where freshwater mixes with saltwater is the key to productivity. The most fundamental environmental need is for water, in sufficient volume, to follow its original course through the Delta, through San Francisco Bay and out to sea, but the Delta is also the focal point for water distribution in California. Water passing through its channels runs out the faucets of two-thirds of the state's residents and irrigates over four million acres of farmland.

The campaign featured uncertainty and vacillating stances among all constituencies. The Sierra Club and the Planning and Conservation League each switched from initial support to opposition. The State Farm Bureau and some of the state's most influential farmers opposed the canal because, from their perspective, it gave too much protection—constitutional guarantees of protection—to north coast rivers and the Delta. Even the governor, Jerry Brown, although he had gone against his environmental constituency (one of his favorite slogans was "small is beautiful") to support the completion of his father's SWP legacy, stayed so far in the background during the divisive campaign that he was depicted in one political cartoon plucking petals from a "Peripheral Canal" flower, chanting "I love it . . . I love it not. . . ." The Metropolitan Water District was slow to join the pro-canal campaign at first, concerned that the new SWP bureaucracy would weaken its monopolistic control of water in the southern state. They also disliked the fact that the project would be paid for mostly by urban customers, despite most of the water going to agriculture. Late in the campaign, MWD began campaigning, however, with so much enthusiasm that they faced accusations of improperly using public funds to influence the election. MWD speakers blanketed the six southland counties.

To transform the Central Valley into a "garden" producing one-quarter of the nation's food and to keep Southern California's population growing required that an "accident of nature" be "corrected." Such terms were used repeatedly to justify shifting water from where it was abundant, in the north, to the drier parts of the state. "California is out of balance," the MWD film *Balance of Nature* told television viewers considering the Peripheral Canal referendum. "Nowhere is that imbalance more evident than in the state's distribution of water and people. Lacking the power or desire to move people to the water, it becomes a responsibility of government to bring water to the people." That logic contorted the fact that the canal was to be yet another water project meant to serve *potential* future users, rather than to meet the needs of existing urban residents.

The *Balance of Nature* narrative emphasized environmental benefits of the proposed canal, appealed for "fair play and sharing" (an appeal clearly aimed at Northern Californians), and threatened a dire future of water shortages (though less blatantly than in *Thirst*, their Colorado River aqueduct film a half century earlier):

> Taking advantage of every reasonable means of conservation and water reuse, Southern California will still be short of its needs by 1990. If that happens the state of economy will go out of balance and all Californians will feel the jolt.
>
> Opponents of the canal charge that it is unnecessary to move more water into Southern California. That charge is false, but we won't be able to prove that until 1990, and then it will be too late.
>
> The canal will be a monument to sharing, fair play, and mankind's awakening to the needs of our environment. The balance of nature does not always work in the best interests of people. Our dual responsibilities to people and to the environment require extending nature to bring about a balance nature did not provide. The peripheral canal is that extension. (MWD, 1981)

Both sides used television in their campaign efforts. Pros and cons of the issue, in fact, were more thoroughly presented to the public than in any of the earlier water project campaigns. The connection between more water and more people was an issue that MWD's general manager felt the need to address in an April 10, 1981, memo to his board of directors, with "Answers to Arguments against the Peripheral Canal." To the argument that more water would simply promote growth wanted by land developers, his answer was that experience in both parts of the state indicated population growth would continue whether or not additional water supplies were developed, ignoring the fact that only a small fraction—about one-sixth—of Los Angeles' 3 million and Los Angeles County's 7.5 million residents, in 1981, could possibly have been there if "additional water supplies" had never been developed.

The "Big Threat" tactic did appear, of course, during the campaign. In Long Beach, the Water Department put out a public education brochure with one of the most memorable images of the campaign. Beneath a photograph of a ball, a tricycle on its side and a seesaw abandoned on cracked, sunbaked ground, a caption read: "This must never be allowed to happen in Long Beach" (Dennis, 1981, 9). Echoing the *Los Angeles Times* on the Owens River issue seventy years earlier, the *Highland Park News* editorialized: "A Southern California voter who votes against the canal—Proposition 9—is clearly voting against himself." A *Sacramento Bee* story in April of 1982 was headlined: PERIPHERAL CANAL BACKERS WARN OF 'A DESERT.' That story quoted Anaheim mayor John Seymour telling several hundred Orange County business people: "The facts are, unless we develop new water sources, we will dry up. Failure to build the canal will force mandatory water rationing and severe conservation measures in Orange County." But there was a vocal opposition by then, much more organized than in earlier water campaigns, and in that same meeting Seymour was accused of using "big scare tactics."

Seymour responded, "*I'm* not saying the world will end. It won't. It will dramatically change unless Proposition 9, the Peripheral Canal, passes." Any admission that the world would *not* end marked a significant shift, bowing to the fact that the public was no longer going to swallow such pronouncements without skepticism.

Political cartoonists, especially in Northern California newspapers, picked up on the questions and doubts troubling many voters. The *San Jose Mercury News* ran a Wilkinson cartoon, on May 27, 1982, showing a bloated "Southern California" bully with near-empty bottles labeled "Mono Lake" and "Colorado River," turning its big "Peripheral canal" straw towards the Sacramento River bottle of a wimpy looking "Northern California," and saying, "I see you're not drinking all yours, sonny." *Sacramento Bee* cartoonist Renault drew a giant in a business suit (Agribusiness and Developers) wearing a Prop. 9 campaign button, who held a shovel ($20 Billion Peripheral Canal Scheme) poised to dig into Northern California, but the giant's foot pushed down, not on the shovel, but upon the back of a little figure labeled "South State Voters." That May 23, 1982, cartoon was captioned, "When Push Comes to Shove."

> Some [MWD] directors and staff members [began] to worry privately whether MWD was becoming overexposed by this high intensity rhetoric about the dire consequences that would follow defeat of the Peripheral Canal. The contrast between the widely disseminated public message of potential disaster and doom (one ally drew a portrait of future shortages where residents would be forced to drink toilet bowl water to meet mandatory cutbacks) and the less visible, more complex portrait of a district capable of relying on 'alternatives,' with a less dramatic projection of future shortages (offered for example to bond analysts) made the district more vulnerable when these conflicting assessments were made public. (Gottlieb and FitzSimmons, 1991, 20)

The Peripheral Canal was defeated on June 8, 1982, by a decisive 63 percent of the electorate. Despite immersion in the dogma of the eternal-growth religion, Californians said "no," by an overwhelming margin, to the Peripheral Canal. For the first time they defeated a major water project. Environmental and quality-of-life concerns, by then, had grown along with the population. By 1970 there were 20 million Californians to make their state the most populous in the

"When Push Comes to Shove." Cartoon by Dennis Renault; appeared in the *Sacramento Bee* on May 23, 1982. Courtesy of the *Sacramento Bee*.

nation. In that same year, the National Environmental Policy Act, California Environmental Quality Act and California Endangered Species Act all passed. Finally, there was recognition that the growth merchants—including public water agencies—were not primarily motivated by service to the existing population.

Between 1982 and 1990, Southern California, without the Peripheral Canal, did not become the predicted wasteland, but it did acquire more than 3 million additional residents—a population the size of Chicago—using imported water from the Colorado River, Eastern Sierra and State Water Project. During the last two decades of the twentieth century and first fifteen years of the twenty-first, about 15 million residents were added. With people throughout the state intimately connected by their water "pipes," each new water user meant less water reliability for everyone else in the system.

One approach to the limits of developed water supply could have been to approve only new construction with its own assured water supplies, placing no new demands on the statewide system. Yet, in December 1994, twenty-six of the twenty-nine contractors receiving SWP water signed an agreement favoring continued development and growth. Under the Monterey Agreement, allocations in dry years would be based on contractual proportions of the total supply, rather than actual amounts of water used. Though new customers would inevitably increase the demand for water, dry year shortages would be shared proportionally—treating everyone, including prior users, equally badly. In 1997, a new SWP aqueduct extension to the central coast of the state was completed. Santa Barbara and its neighboring cities hoped for increased water reliability during future droughts by tapping into the already overcommitted SWP. As it worked out, in the following fifteen years, full delivery of the region's water allotments occurred only 36 percent of the time. In an era of limits, the rest of the SWP's users might have wondered why adding new customers to compete for limited water was any cause for celebration.

By the 1990s, water supply reliability became a pressing issue for MWD and San Joaquin Valley corporate farms, because declining fish populations in the Sacramento–San Joaquin Delta had led to court-mandated shutdowns of the pumps serving the state and federal aqueducts. Those issues led, in 1994, to the CalFed Bay-Delta Accord—an effort at consensus-building between stakeholders. CalFed sought to accomplish environmental protection while improving water reliability for agricultural and urban users. The Accord established "solution principles" to reduce conflicts among beneficial uses of water, and avoid solutions that redirected impacts upon other parties.

Urban, agricultural and environmental advocates were the primary stakeholder categories. Those categorizations, in themselves, distorted some issues. The broad category of "agricultural interests" included farmers, farmer/developers and agribusiness corporations with a range of perspectives. "Environmental organizations" were overwhelmingly backed by membership from urban areas, yet their goals were not those of "urban interests." That last category might more accurately have been labeled "water-for-continued-urban-growth" interests.

In June 1999, CalFed published an environmental impact report (EIR), identifying their preference among alternatives for managing Northern California's water systems. Highlights included recharging underground aquifers, streamlining water transfers between farms and cities, studying the feasibility of new reservoirs and of raising dams to increase storage, promotion of water conservation on farms and in urban areas and cleaning contaminated agricultural runoff water. A new peripheral canal proposal was set aside (for the moment)—existing channels would instead be modified to carry more water south.

CalFed's proposal included a complex new idea for an "environmental water account." Water, taken from the environment, could be returned through purchasing power. There were plenty of doubters, concerned that an environmental account would never have enough money to compete successfully with other, richer interests. Environmentalists were not pleased with CalFed's focus on increased storage facilities, preferring that water conservation measures in farms and cities be emphasized. Farmers wondered if increased diversions would ever reach them. Coinciding with the release of the EIR, Delta smelt began massing near diversion pumps in the spring of 1999, and when too many of the endangered fish were killed, the pumps were shut down again. "All I know is, our farmers are on a 70 percent allocation this year, and that is following an extremely wet winter—there is plenty of water in the system, but we're not getting our share," said David Orth, general manager of the Westlands Water District, for a newspaper story on the EIR release (Martin, 1999, A1).

The CalFed effort had foundered by 2008. Jerry Brown was re-elected governor of California in 2010, and within two years, he announced his aim to finally resolve the problems of the Delta and achieve the original goals of the State Water Project by constructing twin tunnels to serve as an "isolated channel" *beneath* the estuary.

Cartoon by Ken Alexander predicting resurrection of the Peripheral Canal, which appeared in the *San Francisco Examiner* on June 11, 1982, just after its defeat. Courtesy of the *San Francisco Examiner*.

PART V

TOMORROWLAND: TODAY'S CHOICES IN A HOTTER, DRIER CALIFORNIA

SIXTEEN

WHO NEEDS FISH?
WHO NEEDS FARMS?

It's not rocket science: our salmon and our Delta estuary need fresh water to survive. The tunnels would hijack that water and deprive all but a fraction of Californians of its benefits. It's just a big straw with public trust resources on the Delta end, and industrial agribusiness sucking on the other. (Tim Sloane, Pacific Coast Federation of Fishermen's Associations, in Restore the Delta press release, October 30, 2015)

The choice, as we see it, is between two futures for the Central Valley: an agricultural future that maintains the ingredients for farming and attendant environmental benefits that farmland supports, or an endless sprawl of suburban development that provides no value for the environment and no future for farming. (American Farmland Trust, "California Farmland, An Irreplaceable Resource," in Reisner, 1997, 6)

Declines in smelt, shad and salmon species that rely on flows through the Sacramento–San Joaquin Delta may have been partially due to water pollution and competition by introduced species, but plummeting population numbers coincided tellingly with years of increased water diversions. Powerful pumps sucked water that would normally flow westward to the ocean, directing flows toward the aqueduct intakes instead. Migrating salmon trying to navigate upstream become confused and tiny Delta smelt, once the most abundant fish in the estuary, were pulled directly into the pumps and killed. Problems had been identified in plankton populations, the primary producers that support aquatic ecosystems at the base of the food web.

In 2008, a Delta Vision Blue Ribbon Task Force developed goals for managing the Delta, considering environment along with economic and social needs. The task force established coequal goals for 1) a sustainable ecosystem, and 2) a reliable water supply to users served by the aqueducts. Their findings called for statewide increases in conservation and water efficiency, new storage and conveyance facilities, and likely *reductions* in the water that had been taken away from the Delta in the early years of the twenty-first century.

An "elephant in the room" that some continued to ignore, but with influence over this debate, was the conclusion of a 2010 Flow Criteria Report for fish protection developed by the State Water Resources Control Board that current flows had not been sufficient to protect the Delta's resources (State Water Resources Control Board, 2010).

To address the coequal goals, Governor Brown's new alternative to a peripheral canal called for two tunnels, each forty feet wide, to capture water from the Sacramento River just before it entered the estuary, and move it *beneath* the Delta for thirty-five miles to the aqueducts. With tunnels periodically taking on about half of the diversions, the south Delta pumps would continue to be used, though at a lesser rate.

A first version of the project, known as the "Bay Delta Conservation Plan" (BDCP) included habitat restoration within the estuary, but in 2015, the tunnels and the habitat improvement efforts were separated. The tunnel concept moved forward with a new name: the "California Water Fix." Habitat elements were given the name "California Eco Restore."

Despite controversy that was sure to develop over this new manifestation of a canal to isolate water moving past the Delta, the administration decided *not* to put the project to a public vote or seek approval in the legislature. They declared that the original approval voters granted to the State Water Project in 1960, over a half century earlier, was sufficient authorization for a canal that had been intended from the beginning. That interpretation, in itself, was very controversial, and contrasted with the decision made by the Director of the Department of Water Resources during Brown's *first* administration, to seek authorizing legislation for the canal. "This was controversial," Ronald B. Robie recalled in 2010, as the agency marked the fiftieth anniversary of the SWP, "since I agreed the canal could be built without legislative approval, but I felt that nearly 20 years after the original authorization of the SWP this was an appropriate way to obtain consensus."

Though another thirty years had passed, the governor took a different approach the second time around and was in a more confrontational mood, as he explained to reporters at a press conference in Sacramento, on July 25, 2012:

> Analysis paralysis is not why I came back. We have farmers, we have fish, we have environmentalists, we have citizens, and we have to make this work. At this stage as I see many of my friends dying. . . . I want to get shit done. I want to get this thing done the best I can. You give me your analysis, I'll read it, but we're going to make stuff happen and that's why I'm here. We're going to take into account the opposition, but we're not going to sit here and twiddle our thumbs and stare at our navel. We're going to make decisions and get it done. If we have to fight initiatives or referendums, we'll fight those too. But somehow before I'm ready to turn in my payroll card I expect to get some very important things done and this is one of them.

In contentious debates about the tunnels idea, some characterized this as a "fish versus farmers" issue. Saving the Delta smelt had often been criticized by opponents, particularly San Joaquin Valley farm interests, who denigrated smelt as "tiny bait fish" and showed no concern for the declining species' role as a "canary in the coal mine," an indicator of the ecosystem's condition. Other farmers growing crops on 500,000 acres within the Delta were at odds with San Joaquin Valley farmers, seeing a threat to Delta farming should water flows drop within the estuary and their water supply be contaminated with saltwater.

Concerns similar to those expressed during the 1982 Peripheral Canal referendum persisted that, once massive tunnels were in place with so much capacity, the thirsts of powerful water users in the south might influence tunnel operations to actually take *more* water from the Delta, rather than less. The thirsts of farm irrigators in the San Joaquin Valley and development interests in Southern California historically have been accommodated by state and federal water projects. Leery opponents asked, why build on such a scale, otherwise? Why would those users, who must pay construction costs, be willing to pay billions of dollars unless they anticipate more, not less, water?

On May 6, 2015, at an Association of California Water Agencies conference in Sacramento, Governor Brown said to critics: "Until you've put a million hours into it [as the state's planners have], shut up. For fifty years we've been trying to deal with these problems." He added, to a room full of laughter, "If we don't solve the Delta problem this time, I'll just have to come back and run for Governor *again*." Jerry Brown appeared convinced that the tunnels, as planned, were the best way forward. He quoted E.O. Wilson, at that event:

> Surely one moral precept we can agree on is to stop destroying our birthplace, the only home humanity will ever have. The evidence for climate warming, with industrial pollution as the principal cause, is now overwhelming. Also evident upon even casual inspection is the rapid disappearance of tropical forests and grasslands and other habitats where most of the diversity of life exists. We are needlessly turning the gold we inherited from our forebears into straw, and for that we will be despised by our descendants.

Barbara Barrigan-Padilla, executive director of Restore the Delta, reacted to Brown's criticism of critics that day: "Brown has his fingers in his ears and will not listen. We will not go away and we will not shut up" (Siders and Kasler, 2015).

A coalition of environmental and business groups and some urban water agencies made an alternative proposal in 2013, for a western Delta conveyance system to allow flows to pass all the way through the Delta, restoring natural flow patterns and water conditions for endangered fish species. Water would then be diverted into a much shorter tunnel before the mixing zone of freshwater with salty ocean tides. A shorter tunnel would be less expensive to construct, so that money could be redirected to levee stabilization and water conservation, recycling and new surface or groundwater storage south of the Delta. Operable gates, normally kept open for navigation and fish migration, could be closed if catastrophic levee failures or super high tides caused saltwater intrusion. A western intake close to the saltwater–freshwater mixing zone would be, unfortunately, in the most critical habitat zone for the Delta smelt. Measures to reduce fish kills are important wherever water intakes are placed—that challenge had been a major problem for the existing pump intakes. The problem would not be eliminated after Delta tunnels were constructed, but the restoration of natural flows across the Delta made this western intake an appealing alternative, one that had not been fully analyzed in the BDCP environmental documents as of 2015.

An intriguing difference between the 1982 campaign for the Peripheral Canal and the 2015 "California Water Fix" was the leading advocacy role taken by San Joaquin Valley farm interests like the Westlands Water District, versus less enthusiastic support for tunnels from some Southern California cities. Though the MWD officially favored the tunnel project, several city clients within the MWD expressed concerns about the costs and need when compared to conservation and recycling alternatives.

WHO NEEDS FARMS?

As California dealt with the fourth year of severe drought extending into 2015, and urban water users faced cuts mandated by the governor, fingers began to point at agricultural water use, where 80 percent of the state's developed water (held behind dams and running through pumps, aqueducts and pipes) is used. This was not a new concern; urban growth interests had long coveted that water, but the drought heightened the focus on how much water is required for crop production. Economist David Friedman, in an opinion piece in the *Los Angeles Times*, had made that point back in 1998:

> Contrary to popular belief, California does not have a water shortage. Urban communities, moreover, the backbone of the state's mammoth economy, use just a fraction of what's available. Agriculture uses 32 million AF [per year]. California's municipalities make do with about 7 million AF a year. What the state does have . . . is a critical water-allocation crisis. (Friedman, 1998)

Where fruits, nuts or vegetables are served in this country, the odds favor them being from California—55 percent of the nation's produce is grown in the state. About a third of the state's 100 million acres were in agriculture in 2015. California has been the leading agricultural state in the nation for sixty years. It is also the exclusive origin (greater than 99 percent) of a long list of specialty crops, including almonds, artichokes, dates, figs, olives, pistachios, prunes, raisins and walnuts.

If urban communities are the "backbone" of the state's economy, in Friedman's (1998) anatomical analogy, farms might be its vital organs, considering the biological imperatives they address. Agriculture has a significant financial role in the economy, too. The state's production was valued at $54 billion in 2014. According to the State Department of Food and Agriculture, after the third year of severe drought, California's top-ten valued commodities were: milk, almonds, grapes, cattle, strawberries, lettuce, walnuts, tomatoes, pistachios and hay. One in ten of California's jobs had ties to agriculture.

Within that list, the acreage planted to permanent orchards of almonds and pistachio trees increased enormously after 2010, even during years of severe drought, despite the hardening of water demand that perennial trees absolutely require, unlike the flexibility that had existed when that acreage was used for annual crops. Nuts had become an extremely profitable crop, despite being relatively thirsty, so farmers pumped groundwater and record levels during the drought to sustain the trees and threw their political support toward surface water solutions like the Delta tunnels.

Much wiser use of agricultural water is possible. According to the Pacific Institute, from 4.5 million AF to 6 million AF could be saved by using local climate and soil information to help farmers be more precise about scheduling irrigation that meets crop water needs, by shifting away from flood irrigation to drip and sprinkler systems for some crops, and by practicing "regulated deficit irrigation." Deficit irrigation applies water during drought-sensitive growing stages, but limits or stops watering during the vegetative stages or late ripening period. These startlingly large savings were similar to findings in two studies done by CalFed in 2000 and 2006 (Cooley et al, 2009).

If 17 percent of the water going to agriculture could be conserved, farmers should stop overdrafting groundwater basins, even during droughts. They might also return some, at least, of that water to beleaguered rivers and wetland environments and back off on the pressure to build new dams and Delta tunnels. Alternatively, Californians might choose a future that continues their state's historical pattern of population increase, shifting agricultural water to serve even more domestic growth. If so, 5 million AF *could* translate into another doubling of the state's human population. What should the choice be? Who needs farms?

My day began with a drive on stop-and-go freeways; forty-five-miles to downtown Los Angeles that took two hours. I was heading to a water policy conference, in October 1997, to hear presentations on "The Search for Certainty."

Later that day, I came out of a conference session on the "Urbanization of Agricultural and Natural Lands," mulling over an experience akin to Hans Christian Andersen's story "The Emperor's New Clothes." The panel had represented a water agency, farm interests, a planning institute and a Realtors' association. The moderator, an academic, began by stating that population growth projections suggested there would be another doubling of California's population by the year 2025, to over 68 million people. That daunting growth projection (an overestimate, as the years between 1997 and 2015 have shown), set the stage for the conversation that followed. The moderator first addressed the real estate lobbyist:

> *Moderator:* "What is your organization's stance on refitting houses with low-flush, water efficient toilets as a requirement of sale or transfer?"
>
> *Lobbyist:* "We're opposed. It raises costs and will hurt sales. Realtors aren't toilet experts, after all."
>
> *Moderator:* "Water conservation measures, even the most aggressive ones, won't keep up with the demands of the increased population."
>
> *Voice from the audience:* "I'm from Oregon and maybe I see things a little differently [general laughter], but I can't imagine any way to protect agriculture in the face of such population growth. If you figure one acre-foot is needed for every five people, then another 34 million people need almost 7 million acre-feet more water. A low estimate of that relationship is one acre-foot per eight people; you'll still need over 4 million acre-feet."
>
> *Water agency:* "Well, certainly some farmlands will have to give up *some* water."
>
> *Farm Bureau* (when asked by the moderator if agriculture could survive with less water): "Yes, of course, but not *much* less. There's less room to cut than people think. Anyway, people love the open space and esthetic value of agricultural land."
>
> *Planner:* "If we want to protect agriculture, we should do it directly, through zoning ordinances, for example, not just by protecting farm water rights."

Real estate lobbyist: "The sale of farmland to developers is a private property right; we don't want those rights taken away, and we don't think farmers do either."

Moderator: "Let's keep in mind that Fresno, today, is the number one farm county in the United States, and forty years ago, Los Angeles was the number one farm county."

Real estate lobbyist: "People shouldn't be so concerned; the Central Valley is not that attractive a place for development. It's hot and muggy. Development is going to focus around developed areas, especially near the coast."

Remember "The Emperor's New Clothes"? Tailors "sewed" a new set of (expensive) royal clothing that no one could see, but no one was willing to speak up and say so. The tailors had manipulated public opinion so that seeing the "beautiful new clothes" became a measure of each person's cultural and esthetic discernment. It took a child, too innocent to be blinded by society's posturing, to force everyone to acknowledge that the emperor was naked (and that the tailors had been fleecing the royal treasury while making fools of the populace).

The "tailors" in the water conference session also weaved familiar patterns of "cloth." They were not deliberate villains, like those in the fairy tale, but their messages seemed analogous: population growth is inevitable; water conservation is good—but let's not be restrictive; saving *some* farmland would be nice, but if more money can be made through development, well, that's the way the economy works.

The session title sounded appealing. There might be discussion of realistic, effective measures to not just slow, but actually halt the urbanization of farm and natural lands. Some specifics *were* mentioned, including transfers of development rights, agricultural zoning, and state regulations (recently passed) forcing planners to consider water supplies before approving large development projects. But the atmosphere in that room (and throughout the water conference) made it difficult for participants—primarily water agency professionals, immersed in the dogma of their profession—to reveal fundamental doubts about the tailoring process. A few voices (the Oregonian, for one, with the objectivity of an outsider) tentatively probed the assumptions driving the whole consideration. Yet, no hint of desperate urgency came from the farm organization representative; he never addressed the Oregonian's observation that too much population growth *must* overwhelm farmland and take his constituents' water. Was that because so many "farmers" in his organization were corporate entities, as interested in protecting development rights as in long-term farming? No one asked. Overall, the panel presented a mannered analysis that never dented the real estate lobbyist's polite intransigence. I left the session feeling that farmlands, despite all the talk, would continue to drown beneath urban sprawl.

Despite the real estate lobbyist's lack of concern, from 1984 to 2010, farm and grazing lands in California decreased by more than 1.4 million acres, averaging almost 54,000 acres per year lost, or about one square mile every four days, according to the California Department of Conservation. About half of the loss has been "prime" farmland, which has the best soils for agricultural production. That is a particular concern because only one-third of the state's irrigated acreage (about 9,000 acres) is considered "prime." Urbanization accounts for the majority that has been lost. Most of the farms closed or sold were small, at less than fifty acres.

And despite the real estate lobbyist's assertion that the Central Valley was too hot to attract development, the San Joaquin Valley (the southern half of the Central Valley) has led in farmland conversion in recent decades. Keep in mind that today's fully urbanized Southern California coastal basins and the Santa Clara Valley (better known today as Silicon Valley) in the southern San Francisco Bay Area were the nation's leading agricultural counties during the first half of the twentieth century. Those transformations should be remembered as a cautionary historic lesson about complacency toward farmland conversion ongoing in the Central Valley.

Sixty years ago, the Los Angeles County Board of Supervisors published "1925–1955 Crop Acreage Trends for Los Angeles County and Southern California" (California Farm Bureau Federation [CFBF], 1999). Change was happening fast after World War II. Possible choices for addressing the problem were fundamentally the same then as today:

> The southern portion of the State is . . . outstanding in the magnitude, diversity, and value of its farm enterprises. Conversion of agricultural land to urban uses will not stop in Southern California unless the increase in population stops or is appreciably reduced. Renewed interest in the use of zoning for protection of agricultural lands may result in some protections against premature subdivision.

Compare that historic assessment to the American Farmland Trust's (AFT) 2007 "Paving Paradise" report, which stated:

> As long as the state's population continues to increase, the tide of development will not abate and the Golden State will continue to lose farmland to urban development. Given this state of affairs, the challenge for California is to assure that the best farmland remains available for agriculture and that urban development doesn't convert any more land than is truly necessary to accommodate its expanding population and economy. This challenge is made more difficult by the fact that most of the state's cities, where more than 90 percent of the population lives, are located in the midst of California's most productive farmland, generally in valleys and on coastal plains where the soil is deep, water is relatively abundant, and the climate is mild. (American Farmland Trust, 2007, 1)

AFT predicts that another 2.1 million acres of California farmland will be lost by the year 2050, if the current trend continues. A rapid and disturbing transformation is underway.

There are ways to slow and ways to stop the loss of farmland. The California Land Conservation Act was enacted in

1965. Commonly called the "Williamson Act" after its legislative author, it established voluntary land enrollment contracts where landowners agree to keep their land in agriculture or open space for ten years. Contracts automatically renew each year. In return, taxes on the land are based upon agricultural income, rather than open market values. Ten year contracts slow, but do not stop, agricultural conversion.

Recognizing that problem, the alternative "Super Williamson Act" became law in 1996. Formally titled the Agricultural Lands Stewardship Program (ALSP), it is a voluntary program for permanent protection of agricultural land. Landowners receive a onetime payment in exchange for voluntarily giving up the right to develop their land for non-agricultural uses. The conservation easement transfers to a new owner, should the land be sold. "Permanent" protection in this case allows a review of the agreement after twenty-five years.

Such voluntary programs have not stopped cement from being poured over the state's most productive soils. For the September/October 1998 edition of *Western Water*, which focused on "The Future of Central Valley Agriculture," farmer Cliff Coster was interviewed: "He believes in placing one's land in the Williamson Act as a matter of principle vs. expediency, something that '*separates farmers from farmer/developers*'" (McClurg, 1998, 6, my emphasis).

One of the obstacles to preserving farmland in California is rooted in the state's historical trend toward large, absentee land-holdings and corporate "farmers." Consider, for example, the Newhall Ranch subdivision proposal for over 20,000 houses and a commercial center in the hills of northern Los Angeles County. In the 1870s, Henry Mayo Newhall had acquired five Mexican land-grant *ranchos* totaling 143,000 acres, including the Santa Clara River watershed. Grazing livestock and vineyards were, for many decades, the primary activities of the company. By the late twentieth century, the Newhall Land and Farming Company's primary interests were in real estate development. In 1998, the proposed Newhall Ranch subdivision gained the initial approval of Los Angeles County, but legal objections to the project's environmental impact report (EIR) and uncertain water supply, along with economic downturns during the "great recession" (2007–2009) kept the project on hold. The developers again received permission from Los Angeles County in 2012, but the project remained stalled by lawsuits. The California Supreme Court ruled, in November 2015, that the EIR was inadequate because it provided no evidence to support a claim that the development would not significantly affect greenhouse gas emissions. A plan to capture and relocate the endangered unarmored three-spine stickleback was also deemed to be illegal.

Zoning may be the most effective tool for farmland protection. Because zoning is not voluntary, it is controversial. Yet California's agricultural lands are *valuable* to nearby communities, to the state, the nation and, since the state is a major exporter of food, to the world. When nothing else stops the bulldozers, landholders may feel compelled to care about the special values of their lands and businesses.

In 1998, "the citizens of Ventura declared that half a century of rape and pillage by land developers had come to an end, at least in their county. They stripped the Board of Supervisors of the power to approve new subdivisions on land zoned for open space or agriculture. They reserved that power to themselves. In the future, any such proposals will go on the ballot" (Jones, 1998, B1). The Save Open Space and Agricultural Resources (SOAR) initiative was approved by 63 percent of the voters in Ventura County. In the same election, four cities in that county also voted to confine their future growth within specified boundaries; majorities in some of the city initiatives were 70 percent. Because of the SOAR initiative, almost all of the lands already zoned as farmland or open space within Ventura County can now only be rezoned for development *after voter approval*. "Owners of land zoned agriculture do not have any more right to develop a housing tract on their land than you or I have to put a McDonald's in our front yard" (SOAR, 1998).

The votes for SOAR showed that citizens, overall, were no longer willing to swallow the historic dogma that damaged so much that was good about California living. Because their government representatives were not ready to step away from that historic pattern, their constituents took direct control through the initiative process.

Zoning controls apply at local or regional levels. At the state and federal levels, where primary control over irrigation water resides, water reliability may be a feasible tool for saving open space. Marc Reisner, author of *Cadillac Desert*, wrote an analysis for AFT (1997) suggesting that increased water reliability be exchanged for permanent farmland protection. Providing subsidized water for agriculture has long been controversial. Increasing benefits even further, though, recognizes the societal value of standing up to multimillion-dollar development offers that consume farmland. Californians, looking to alter their historic growth patterns, may wish to accept some costs of farmland protection for the return benefits of food production within the state's borders, the quality of life that comes with a mix of rural and urban living, and avoidance of those tax increases that generally subsidize urban development (farm animals don't go to school). There are environmental benefits, too. Though California farmers' heavy reliance on fertilizers and pesticides have sadly exacerbated the state's environmental losses, "nearly any bird, mammal, amphibian, or insect is apt to prefer a farmed field to a treeless new development or shopping mall" (Reisner, 1997, 2).

Will tools for farmland preservation be broadly implemented with enough zeal to actually save the state's agricultural productivity? Some of the most forthright "tailors" have revealed their vision for the future, the logical outcome of their work:

> We must learn to let go of farming and ranching. In the short run, this means eliminating the subsidies that delay the inevitable *development of our nation out of agriculture and into more profitable industries.* In the long run, this means becoming citizens of the world, dependent on others for our food commodities while we produce the marvels and know-how for the future. *We have to do these things to become King of the Hill.* The first step is to accept that farming, although it enabled us to move into our

dynamic future, is part of our proud past. (Blank, 1998, 195–96, my emphasis)

Some farmers, pointing fingers from their perspectives, had been fond of blaming shortages on water "wasted" to protect fish and maintain aquatic ecosystems. The environment, as always, remained the ultimate source of water that Californians might tap, if that was their choice for the future.

SEVENTEEN

THE FATE OF MONO LAKE

The public trust . . . is an affirmation of the duty of the state to protect the people's common heritage of streams, lakes, marshlands and tidelands. (Supreme Court of California, 1983)

"We have legal rights to that Mono Basin water and we won't reduce our exports one bit unless someone sues us and we lose. The odds of that happening are mighty small." That quote is tacked to the office wall in the Mono Lake Committee Information Center, an ironic record of a conversation with a Los Angeles Department of Water and Power engineer in 1976. Against all odds, DWP was sued and lost the case. From another perspective, Mono Lake won—along with a million migratory birds, several trillion brine shrimp and a quarter of a million tourists who visit the lake each year.

In 1941, Mono Lake began shrinking due to stream diversions to Los Angeles. Since it is a saltwater lake, as it declined the water became concentrated: with half as much water, the lake salinity doubled. The naturally harsh environment of uniquely beautiful Mono Lake, which was incredibly alive with brine shrimp, alkali flies and water birds, grew ever harsher. The inland sea, east of Yosemite National Park, was in danger of becoming California's Dead Sea.

The shrinking lake also exposed a land bridge to Negit Island, where almost all of the state's California gulls (*Larus californicus*) nested. The gull colony was forced to relocate to small islets in the lake to be safe from coyotes and other land predators. Even the

Birds among tufa towers at Mono Lake. Photograph by David Carle.

Mono Basin's normally pristine air began violating federal air quality standards whenever wind picked up caustic, unhealthy dust from the exposed lakebed.

In 1978, the Mono Lake Committee and National Audubon Society began a seemingly hopeless quest; they sued a giant—the city of Los Angeles. Against all odds, a superior court judge ruled, in 1983, that the public trust doctrine applied to Mono Lake. The ruling stood up to every legal appeal.

The public trust decision declared that society could reconsider and revise water licenses that had been granted a half century earlier, when new information made it clear that the lake's environmental, recreational or aesthetic values were being destroyed. Such values, held in trust for the public, deserved and required government protection. The judgment shocked water agency executives who, until then, firmly believed that their water rights had been granted in perpetuity.

While years of legal appeals dragged on and on, a separate court ruling came in 1988, declaring that the city's water diversions also violated fish and game law by totally drying the streams. Minimum flows were reestablished by court order, and active steps mandated to restore fish habitat along those streams.

On September 24, 1994, the sixteen-year battle to protect Mono Lake concluded with an order by the State Water Resources Control Board to amend Los Angeles' water licenses and protect the lake. Mono Lake would rise seventeen feet (still twenty-five feet lower than it was in 1941) and be managed around an elevation that would reduce salinity and provide a buffer against droughts. Enough salt flat should be covered to end dust storms that caused air quality violations. The nesting islands will be surrounded by a protective moat of water.

Sixteen years in court culminated in a victory for citizen groups: the Mono Lake Committee, with legal aid from the National Audubon Society, and CalTrout, which entered the fray on behalf of the streams that had been desiccated by diversions. Government actions to implement the legal victories came as a result of court orders. A handful of caring citizens built the Mono Lake Committee, an organization with 16,000 members. Their commitment forced a fundamental change in Californians' relationships with natural water systems. The public trust doctrine, following this decision, became a powerful legal tool for protecting other bodies of water.

A powerful tool, but not a certain one. The courts did not declare that Mono Lake must *absolutely* be protected, but rather that *balancing* must occur between "beneficial domestic uses" of diverted water and the lake's public trust values. Public trust values are, in great part, a subjective product of changeable attitudes and beliefs. Society's concern for ecosystems, such as Mono Lake's, changed dramatically in the half-century between the 1930s (when the choice was made to extend the Los Angeles Aqueduct to the Mono Basin) and the 1980s (when the public trust decision was made). As California changed and so much was lost, the surviving natural environment took on new value. Yet, the same doctrine that allowed prior water rights to be re-evaluated also permits future revisions to that protective decision, should that become society's choice.

Because California's population growth continues to be seen as "inevitable," water entering salty lakes and the salty ocean continues to be seen by some people as "wasted" (particularly during droughts). The perception of "greatest good" *can* change. The Mono Lake decision was a sign of hope that society can mature enough to exercise restraint and preserve something of the California Dream. Yet that victory may ultimately fail unless Californians continue to affirm the importance of environmental protections and a sustainable relationship with water.

Although the plan has been in place since 1994 to raise Mono Lake and manage it at an elevation that will protect the ecosystem, by 2015 the lake stood only a few feet higher than it had been twenty-one years earlier. It *had* risen almost nine feet, due to wet years following the 1994 Water Board action, but then, as the state experienced long and severe drought conditions, most of those gains evaporated away. The return of average-or-better snow seasons will be needed to reverse that trend and achieve full recovery.

The million-year-old inland sea survived prehistoric dry cycles and century-long medieval droughts, yet a sufficient buffer to protect the lake against lethal salt concentrations may have been removed by the half-century of stream diversions to Los Angeles. It would be heartbreaking if global climate warming undermines society's best intentions to restore and protect the Mono Lake ecosystem.

We know about two mega-droughts because of research done at Mono Lake, analyzing growth rings in tree stumps exposed when the lake declined due to modern stream diversions. Mono Lake (and other lakes in the region) declined far enough for trees to grow, and long enough for them to live more than a century.

> Since statehood, Californians have been living in the best of climatic times. And we've taken advantage of these best of times by building the most colossal urban and agricultural infrastructure in the entire world, all dependent on huge amounts of water, and all based on the assumption that runoff from the Sierra Nevada will continue as it has during the past 150 years. (Stine, 1994, 548)

EIGHTEEN

PEOPLE FUMES (II): CLIMATE WARMING AND THE CHANGING WATER CYCLE

Anthropogenic greenhouse gas emissions have increased since the pre-industrial era, driven largely by economic and population growth, and are now higher than ever. This has led to atmospheric concentrations . . . that are unprecedented in at least the last 800,000 years. Their effects . . . are *extremely likely* to have been the dominant cause of the observed warming since the mid-twentieth century. (Intergovernmental Panel on Climate Change, 2014, 8)

The ideological warriors . . . have concluded that there is really only one way to beat a threat this big: by claiming that thousands upon thousands of scientists are lying and that climate change is an elaborate hoax. (Klein, 2014, 43)

The forest seemed grim, even threatening, with at least half the pine trees brown, apparently dead. If anyone was foolish enough to ignite a fire, I thought, this whole area around the Bass Lake reservoir was going to explode in flames, just like the 152,000-acre Rough Fire that had burned out of control most of that summer of 2015, not many miles south in parts of this Sierra National Forest and Sequoia National Forest. That September, with the weather oppressively hot and dry—perfect fire hazard conditions—I was heading toward Bass Lake to speak to a Conference of County Directors of

Environmental Health about two hundred years of water choices that shaped California's history (in fifty minutes!), hoping to provide some context to the challenges they faced in their counties after four years of extreme drought.

Forest trees fight off bark beetles by flooding them with sap as they bore into the tree to lay eggs. But during droughts, when the trees are water-stressed, beetles more often win those battles and as their larvae chew and grow, the assault can kill trees. After four years of drought, the U.S. Forest Service estimated that there were 22 million dead trees on California's wildlands, an exceptional level of tree mortality. Tens of millions more were likely to die by the end of that year. What was happening in the Ponderosa pine forest along the road to Bass Lake was part of an unprecedented epidemic of tree mortality. Later that fall, the governor would declare a state of emergency and seek federal help in expediting removal of dead trees to reduce the hazards of falling trees and wildfire.

Governor Brown had earlier declared a *drought* state of emergency in January 2014 as the state entered its third dry year. The year 2014 would be the hottest on record (until it was surpassed in 2015), as scientists analyzing tree-ring records called it the most severe drought in the last 1,200 years. There was no relief in the winter that followed, and when the 2015 annual spring snow survey found only 5 percent of normal snowpack conditions in the Sierra Nevada, Brown announced the first-ever mandatory 25 percent statewide water reductions.

With few exceptions, Californians responded with unprecedented conservation efforts—cumulatively 28 percent—exceeding the governor's water reduction target in each of the summer months. In October, however, Beverly Hills, Indio, Redlands and the Coachella Valley Water District were fined $500 per day for not reaching the mandatory goals; the fines were retroactive to June, so each would pay $61,000.

Hopes for breaking the drought during the winter of 2015–2016, as a strong El Niño pattern developed in the Pacific, were balanced by worries about flooding from violent storms and long-term worries about the "new normal" weather and climate extremes that are predicted to accompany global climate warming.

In 2015, the population of California approached 39 million people, while around the world human numbers had surged past 7 billion. Certain "people fumes," particularly emissions of carbon dioxide, methane and nitrous oxide released from burning fossil fuel, were trapping heat in the atmosphere at levels that generated a host of changes to the global water cycle.

Atmospheric carbon dioxide levels have risen since the nineteenth century, from about 270 parts per million (ppm) to over 400 ppm. The rise accelerated after the 1970s, during four decades when the Earth's human population doubled. The atmospheric greenhouse effect makes life on Earth possible, by trapping heat that would otherwise escape into space. But by *enhancing* that effect, energy has been added into the atmosphere and the ocean, with disquieting consequences.

Modeling all the variables that drive natural global climate changes, such as variations in solar radiation and in the Earth's rotation and volcanic eruptions, cannot match the observed greenhouse gas and temperature trends until emissions by human burning of fossil fuels are incorporated into the calculations.

Around the world, the year 2014 was the warmest year since temperatures began to be recorded in 1880. California's average temperature was more than four degrees above the twentieth-century average. A rising temperature trend in California accelerated over the last thirty years and shot up in the last ten years.

Climate warming affects us, and every other life form on the planet, by altering the planet's water cycle. Higher atmospheric and ocean temperatures translate into winter precipitation in California that is more likely to fall as rain instead of snow. My family has lived for thirty-four years at the 7,000-foot elevation in the Eastern Sierra, and that trend has become clear to us as less snow is deposited at our elevation and rain (an unfamiliar sight in past decades) now dominates the local pattern. Water planners in California figure on a 40 percent smaller Sierra Nevada snowpack by the year 2050.

The ocean has been absorbing much of the heat and CO_2 humans send into the sky. Though that reduces impacts in the atmosphere and on land, there are consequences for ocean ecosystems. Dissolved carbon dioxide made seawater 26 percent more acidic between 1901 and 2010, which interferes with shell formation of oysters, clams, plankton and corals. Warmer oceans are behind coral reef "whitening," as symbiotic algae is expelled by coral when the water is too warm; without the photosynthesis contribution, the coral ultimately starves and dies.

The ocean also expands as its water warms. Along the California coast, the sea rose by seven inches in the twentieth century, on average. That rate was larger than during the previous two thousand years. Climate models suggest another sixteen-inch sea-level rise is possible by 2050, and a rise of fifty-five inches by 2100, bringing major challenges to coastal cities and Delta levees.

While the levels of greenhouse gases in the atmosphere result from emissions around the world, California has recently been generating 450 million tons of CO_2 a year, or two percent of the world's fossil fuel burning. Clearly, cutbacks within California can only address so much of the problem, but doing nothing until *all* nations adopt appropriate measures is a recipe for a disastrous status quo. Instead, California has taken measures within the state and assumed a leadership role in negotiations with other states and other nations.

In 2002, Governor Gray Davis signed the most aggressive renewable energy requirement in the country, at that time, to curtail vehicle emissions of greenhouse gases with a target of 20 percent renewables in the state's energy portfolio. That became a 33 percent target with Governor Schwarzenegger's "California Global Warming Solutions Act of 2006." Schwarzenegger said that he wanted California to be "Number 1 in the fight against global warming, as something owed to our children and our grandchildren." Under Governor Jerry Brown, the objective became 50 percent renewables, with a target date of 2030. Cars and trucks are responsible for over a third of the state's greenhouse gas emissions, while electrical power generation and industry account for most of the rest.

"Look! It's that crazy Jerry Brown!" cartoon by David Horsey, which appeared July 9, 2015, in the *Los Angeles Times*. © Tribune Content Agency, LLC. All Rights Reserved. Reprinted with permission.

Conserving water is a key to reducing energy consumption. Nineteen percent of the state's electricity and 33 percent of the natural gas that is used in California (beyond what is burned in power plants) goes toward pumping water from the ground; moving water over mountains and through pipes, cleaning it to potable standards or heating and chilling water. So, beyond the water supply and environmental benefits of conservation, recycling and reuse, water efficiency reduces the state's energy use and carbon footprint of greenhouse gas emissions.

In a speech at a climate conference in Canada in July 2015, Brown said, "Oil, gas, coal has created the wealth we enjoy. What was the source of our wealth, now becomes the challenge of our future. We're demonstrating that you can de-carbonize and improve the well-being of your state. California is the best example. They're all looking to California" (quoted in Megerian, 2015). While in Canada, Brown also addressed the problem that vexes those who recognize the threats posed by climate change: "We have a lot of troglodytes south of the border," the governor said.

The "troglodytes"—determinedly unenlightened "cave-men"—have been effective at confusing public opinion in the United States. While they have worked to spread doubt about science regarding this topic, there is little doubt about the motives behind most of the big money fueling the denial agenda. "The real reason we are failing to rise to the climate moment is because the actions required . . . spell extinction for the richest and most powerful industry the world has ever known—the oil and gas industry, which cannot survive in anything like its current form if we humans are to avoid our own extinction" (Klein, 2014, 63).

And so, the State of California's online climate change information includes a web page (www.opr.ca.gov/s_denier.php) that addresses the contentions of "deniers."

> Deniers continue to repeat several arguments long after they have been debunked by experts. In the past, deniers have contended (and some continue to argue) that the world is not warming. Overwhelming amounts of data from throughout the world have made that argument so fallacious that the deniers have now shifted their contention; claiming that humans are not responsible for the warming. Because the basic physics of greenhouse gases has been well-established, along with the fact that human activity has generated billions of tons of greenhouse gases, make this argument untenable, the denier argument has shifted further. Some deniers now concede that warming will occur, but that impacts will be minimal, and some argue that even if climate change will have impacts, it will cost too much for us to do anything about it. Of course, the cost of failing to act will be much higher.

One of the challenges, beyond that posed by powerful, selfish, fossil fuel interests, may be simple terminology. Neither "global warming" nor "climate change" seem to successfully communicate that the issue is too much energy being released into the atmosphere and absorbed into the ocean. It is that energy that drives super winter storms, as atmospheric energy redirects storm tracks and dynamically powers both hurricanes and heat impacts. If impacts already being manifested within the water cycle are changing conditions for life on Earth, is that not enough motivation? There is a sense of urgency because greenhouse gases already "up there" will remain in the atmosphere for a century; they break down very slowly. Continuing to "dig," when you realize you are already "in a hole," shows an appalling disregard for the future—that of ours and our descendants.

Pope Francis spoke before the United Nations General Assembly in September 2015, when he identified climate change as a moral issue that must not be left to future generations. Later, during a gathering on the White House lawn, the pope praised President Obama's initiative to reduce air pollution. Three months later, the president presented that plan to reduce overall U.S. carbon emissions by one-fourth within the next ten years, during the international meeting on climate change in Paris. At that 2015 gathering, 196 nations agreed to a plan to reduce greenhouse gas emissions, with a goal to hold global warming to less than 2 degrees centigrade (3.6 degrees Fahrenheit). President Obama declared the Paris climate agreement "a turning point for the world." Yet, in the face of that action by almost every nation on Earth, the Republican Party leader in the U.S. Senate, Mitch McConnell, remained adamantly defiant. In a statement McConnell released after the conference, he declared that the agreement may be "shredded in 13 months," should his party prevail in the next presidential election (Zaroya, 2015).

Global climate change is exacerbating every water challenge facing California in the twenty-first century. With effects manifested via the changing planetary water cycle, one choice now is whether to stubbornly seek ever more water to serve unending growth—the historic paradigm—or, instead, to develop a new relationship with water in an era of limits.

NINETEEN

USE LOCAL WATER AGAIN AND AGAIN, BECAUSE DAMS ARE LITTLE HELP

It may be that people have difficulty visualizing how a water conservation initiative can solve a problem. A dam is a highly visible solution to a problem, a toilet rebate program isn't. (Beard, 2015, 117)

What L.A. has done, all of the state of California can do. It's not the exception. It's the future. (Davis, 2014, at the "Mono Lake @ 20" symposium)

Faced with cuts from its Eastern Sierra supplies serving the Los Angeles Aqueduct, the Los Angeles Department of Water and Power instituted aggressive water conservation measures (aided by over $100 million in grants that the Mono Lake Committee helped secure) including a free low-flush toilet replacement program for all of the households they served. The results were amazing: though the city population has grown by 1 million people between 1970 and 2015, per capita daily water use has dropped so much that the city's total water consumption each year is the same, today, as it was forty-five years ago. Conservation and recycling of wastewater explain that very positive pattern, and yet there is much more that still could be saved, enough perhaps to end the reliance on imported water by Los Angeles. And as Martha Davis, the former director of the Mono Lake Committee, pointed out at a symposium to mark the twentieth anniversary of the decision to protect Mono Lake: "What L.A. has done, all of the state of California can do."

In 2014, the mayor of Los Angeles issued an executive directive to reduce the city's water use by 20 percent by the year 2017, and cut imported water by 50 percent by 2024. Going even further, the City of Long Beach and the West Basin Municipal Water District are aiming for 100 percent reuse of local water to *wean themselves completely from imported water.* If those cities can do that, so can other water importers, and the historic paradigm that has driven so much environmental change in California will be transformed.

There is a long way to go. Consider how much urban water is in place at this moment, available and being used today in communities at the delivery end of water aqueducts. Most of that water, cleaned to drinking water standards before being piped to households, has been used to flush toilets or water lawns, the two biggest water uses in California homes. Through recycling, water can be reused again and again. Recycled water is a drought-proof supply, because it is already "at hand," immune to cyclical droughts.

Of course, *all* water is recycled, returning to us after being cleaned by natural processes and distilled when it evaporates back to the atmosphere. People in any city that is downstream from other municipalities (Sacramento is a good example) drink water that has already been used, cleaned to societal standards, then passed along. In the past, most of the water carefully gathered behind dams and moved hundreds of miles, at great expense, has been used just once and then sent away (into rivers, the ground, or the ocean) after being cleaned up enough to avoid polluting the environment.

Instead of passing treated wastewater back into the planetary water cycle, technological innovations can now take a shortcut and keep it recirculating locally. Societal attitudes had to change, along the way, to overcome what is often called the "yuck factor" by news reporters. In 1994, an editorial cartoon appeared in the *San Diego Union-Tribune*, depicting a dog drinking from a toilet with a man telling the dog, "Move over. . . ." The newspaper later coined the phrase "Toilet to Tap" to describe wastewater recycling, and those words have been far too catchy for reporters to avoid ever since. Opposition stopped a $55 million recycling project back in the '90s that would have provided enough water for 120,000 Los Angeles homes, part of a suite of conservation efforts prompted by the 1994 Mono Lake decision.

With twenty-first-century recycling techniques, the water produced is far cleaner than ever before, akin to distilled water. Orange County served as a leader in this field by reusing water to replenish groundwater basins and supplement domestic supply drawn from wells. Today's treatment systems use reverse osmosis filtering membranes, microfiltration and ultraviolet radiation. In 2015, the Orange County Sanitation District's new state-of-the-art plant began sending 139 million gallons of such highly treated wastewater to the Orange County Water District, which puts 100 million gallons per day in the coastal groundwater basin.

The West Basin Municipal Water District partners with the Water Replenishment District of Southern California to put recycled water below ground to hold back seawater intrusion and for future extraction in domestic water wells. The Replenishment District has reduced its reliance on imported water from 60 percent of its supplies to just 20 percent today, and intends to stop importing any water in the near future. Los Angeles announced recycling efforts in 2008 for treating 4.9 billion gallons of wastewater to drinking standards by 2019. San Diego's "Pure Water Project" plans to provide one-third of its water supply with recycled water by the year 2035.

"Today, Los Angeles is managed as a drain," Andy Lipkis told us, on September 1, 2015, speaking to a "Walking Water" group during a three-week pilgrimage between Mono Lake and Owens Lake in the Eastern Sierra. As president of the organization TreePeople, Andy has been working with the City and the County of Los Angeles to change that systemic "drain" into a "catchment" that could capture almost half of the fifteen inches of annual rainfall that comes to that semiarid region. Fifteen inches a year does not sound like much, yet one inch of rain deposits 7.6 billion gallons of water across Los Angeles. Instead of funneling into gutters and drains that direct runoff straight out to the ocean, stormwater *could* soak into swales and be stored in cisterns for later use. TreePeople has shown the water supply and sanitation agencies of the Los Angeles Basin that, through collaboration, more than 40 percent of the local water demand could be met with local rainfall, improving flood protection and reducing treatment costs and reliance on imported water.

> Each rainy season, even in the driest years, greater Los Angeles throws away billions of gallons of water—and hundreds of millions of dollars to deal with flooding and the polluted water that overwhelms our storm drains, threatens our neighborhoods, and fouls our ocean. At the same time, the region spends billions of dollars, and a significant amount of California's total energy use, to import water from hundreds of miles away, with all the costs—economic, health, and environmental—that entails. (Bloome and Lipkis, 2015, 12)

As California endured four years of severe drought, conserving water used to irrigate urban landscapes became a major effort. By the summer of 2015, the state was supporting local and regional lawn-removal rebate programs with a "Model Water Efficient Landscape Ordinance" to limit grass to about 25 percent of a home's combined front, back and side yards in all new construction and eliminate turf grass or other thirsty landscaping plants around commercial landscapes. "You have to find a more elegant way of relating to material things. You have to use them with greater sensitivity and sophistication," Governor Brown explained that June.

He might have illustrated that more elegant and sensitive approach, with a reminder that, since *all* Californians use water, we are *all* part of the problem and each should participate in the solution. Yet, there always seem to be people who declare, when faced with new restrictions, "I won't reduce *my* water-use until *they* go first"—with "finger-pointing" aimed at whatever large-scale water-waster they perceive as the real problem. "There is plenty of water; it just hasn't been distributed properly" commonly accompanies such pronouncements. Of course, "proper distribution" means, in their opinion, that the water come *their* way in unrestricted quantities.

"Make Conservation a Way of Life" was the excellent advice heading a list of ten key actions for the next five years, published in the *California Water Action Plan* in January 2014 by the California Natural Resources Agency. Two other important actions on the list were "Manage and Prepare for Dry Periods" and "Expand Water Storage Capacity and Improve Groundwater Management."

STORAGE BEHIND DAMS
OR IN THE GROUND?

As California voters considered a water bond proposition on the November 2014 ballot that included billions of dollars for new water storage infrastructure, a Stanford think-tank published a research brief titled *Storing Water in California: What Can $2.7 Billion Buy Us?* The bond, ultimately passed by the voters, authorized that much matching-fund dollars toward either surface storage (dams) or storage in the ground. During years of drought, farmers have always turned to groundwater pumping from wells to keep producing crops, and the overdrafting problem in the San Joaquin Valley had become extreme by 2014. Replenishing that aquifer not only became imperative, but also provided capacity and an opportunity for storage in basins close to the use-areas and without the evaporation losses and environmental impacts that occur with reservoirs. The California Water Commission will consider proposed projects during 2016 to authorize matching funds with dollars provided by project proponents. Eligible projects must provide measurable benefits to the Delta ecosystem or its tributaries.

Findings by the Stanford researchers were intriguing. They calculated that the available bond money, based on median costs of dam construction, could provide about 1.4 million AF of new surface storage. Alternatively, about 8.4 million AF of groundwater storage capacity was possible: *six times more than surface storage behind dams.*

New reservoirs being proposed might be constructed at Temperance Flat, on the San Joaquin River upstream from Friant Dam, and an off-stream reservoir near the town of Sites, in the Sacramento Valley. The Sites reservoir would be filled by pumping in Sacramento River water during years of surplus. Another proposal would raise Shasta, the largest of the federal Central Valley Project dams, which spans the Sacramento River. Construction costs (many billions of dollars) and capacity versus actual water yield estimates are numbers that add to the controversies surrounding these surface storage projects.

Dams do not create water, and reservoir capacity does not translate into an equivalent yield of water supply. This has become very clear on the Colorado River, where two large reservoirs, Mead and Powell, compete for a diminished amount of water. So much is diverted from the Colorado River, while extended drought and climate warming have reduced watershed runoff in the last few decades, so that neither reservoir can be kept anywhere near full. Some people suggest it would be wisest to drain Powell and handle all of the Colorado River storage within Mead, allowing that reservoir to continue to generate electricity and not drop below the intake that serves Las Vegas.

California's human thirst has reached and exceeded the limits of its water supply. UC Davis researchers analyzed the state's water rights allocations in a 2014 study, providing numbers that explained the increased tension in the state's water situation during the twentieth century: California has granted water rights to five times more surface water than actually runs off our watersheds each year! The situation is even more out of balance on specific watersheds. Rights to withdrawals from the San Joaquin River are nearly nine times more than the river annually delivers. Kern River allocations are six times what actually flows. Water rights exceed average natural runoff on sixteen major rivers (Grantham and Viers, 2014).

Far too many demands placed on our rivers, along with multiple dams that already exist in almost every watershed, help explain why the yield versus capacity figures for the proposed Temperance Flat and Sites reservoirs are disturbing. Temperance Flat, with a $2.5 billion price tag, would have a 1.26 million AF capacity, but yield a much more modest 180,000 AF per year. Of course, Millerton reservoir already exists behind Friant Dam on the same river, with its 520,000 AF capacity.

The off-stream Sites reservoir could cost $4 billion; and yield 164,000 AF in average years, despite a capacity of 1.8 million AF. It would only be filled when enough floodwater comes down the Sacramento River to deliver a "big gulp."

Three alternative heights have been considered for elevating the crest of Shasta Dam: by 6.5, 12.5 or 18.5 feet. Those height increases would increase reservoir capacity by 256,000 AF, 443,000 AF or 634,000 AF, respectively, yielding about 10 percent of those amounts, and with construction costs ranging from $827 up to $1.07 billion. An 18.5-foot raise, however, would inundate another half-mile of the lower McCloud River, which lost fifteen of its thirty-five miles when the original reservoir filled. Sacred sites and burial grounds of the Winnemem Wintu Indians were covered when the reservoir was first filled, and elevating the dam would inundate additional sacred sites upstream.

California's 2014 water bond prohibited funding projects that could have an adverse effect on wild and scenic rivers, however, and as the McCloud River fits that category, it appears that state money cannot be spent there. The U.S. Bureau of Reclamation concluded, in the final feasibility report that evaluated the potential for enlarging Shasta, that without a cost-share partner, no recommendation for moving ahead could be made.

The overblown promise of new dams brings attention back to groundwater storage and possible solutions to the extreme overdrafting that occurred during the extreme drought of 2012 to 2015. Until the Sustainable Groundwater Management Act of 2014, California was the only state government in the nation without authority over groundwater. "Sustainable yield" is now the goal, but the pace of planning for management of each groundwater basin is excruciatingly slow, with compliance not mandated until 2040.

There is another focus for the future of the state that has never received enough attention: a vision of stability that would help reduce California's carbon emissions, while taking pressure off almost every other stress we face. Motivation to shape a different future in the twenty-first century can emerge from the tattered condition of the California Dream.

TWENTY

VISUALIZE TOMORROW—
A CALIFORNIA DREAM

> I was born and raised in Los Angeles around the San Gabriel River,
> the Los Angeles River and the Rio Hondo, which were concrete
> channels, a little old trickle down the center through most of the
> year. I've left Los Angeles. The rest of California is something I
> want to protect. I want it to stay a special place and I don't find
> strip malls and concrete water courses with carp in them aesthetic.
> (Bruce Herbold, in WEF, 1999, 13)

> There's the shock of raising kids with public schools ranked among
> the worst in the nation, and public universities that have more
> than doubled in cost since 2007. Most of my outdoor pleasures
> are still available, but it's getting scary with the desertification of
> subalpine ecosystems, Sierra snowpack at a historic low, as much
> as 20 percent of California's once-majestic forests at risk of dying,
> and freeway traffic so ubiquitous that it can be soul-destroying just
> getting out of town to see all this stuff. (Duane, 2015)

The key to today's choices, those that will shape California in the
twenty-first century, continues to be water, but human population
numbers matter, too.

As of May 2015, there were 38.9 million Californians,
according to the California Department of Finance. The state's
population is projected to reach 50 million in the year 2051. Those

numbers are lower than had been predicted before California and the nation experienced several years of economic contraction between December 2007 and June 2009. Back in 2007, the forecast had been that the state would reach the 50 million benchmark as early as 2032. The slower pace of population growth is encouraging for those who recognize that "too much is more than enough," but the next generations still face that looming 50 million mark and what lies beyond. State estimates only extend out to 2060, and they forecast a society of 51.7 million. With such a large population, an average growth rate below 1 percent still adds a lot of people. A point where the population peaks has not yet made it into the forecasts.

The United Nations does attempt to predict peak world population numbers, but does not foresee that happening before the end of the century. In 2015, the U.N. adjusted its world population projections upward, predicting that the world's 7.3 billion inhabitants could increase to between 9.5 billion and 13.3 billion by 2100. They foresee only a 23 percent chance of human numbers peaking before then. Median projections (with a 50/50 chance of occurring) are for 9.7 billion in 2050 and 11.2 billion by 2100. These numbers were higher than given in a report just two years earlier, due to increases in fertility and reduced mortality, particularly in African and Asian nations. Developed nations, as a group, will barely increase; Europe will see a decrease (www.unpopulation.org, 2015).

In the twentieth century, as the world population tripled, water use increased by six times. That corresponded with movement out of rural areas; half of people on the planet now reside in cities, where resources have to be delivered to the populace.

> You just can't live the way you always have. For over 10,000 years, [native] people lived in California, but the number of those people were never more than 300,000 or 400,000. Now we are embarked upon an experiment that no one has ever tried: 38 million people with 32 million vehicles, living at the level of comfort that we all aspire to attain. This will require

adjustment. This will require learning. (Governor Jerry Brown, quoted in Nagourney et al, 2015)

Contemplate the future someday soon, as you perhaps are stalled in commuter traffic, or battling crowds in a store, or standing in line, almost anywhere. Considering quality of life, and the resource challenges we face today, try to envision a future with another 10 million people in California. Though the rate of growth *has* been slowing down, if stabilization will not happen before 2050, when might that happen? Never?

A viable future must begin with a vision, an alternative to the status quo. Considering the lessons to be learned from the state's environmental history, Californians might adopt a radically different path for the coming century. They might choose to stabilize their state's population, as soon as possible.

California's population has not been stable since the Gold Rush, over 150 years ago, so this visualization may be very difficult for citizens of the state. "Stability" and "sustainability" are related concepts, but the latter term has been increasingly coupled with "growth," in recent years, by well-intentioned people who should know better. "The finite size of resources, ecosystems, the environment, and the Earth, lead one to the most fundamental truth of sustainability: When applied to material things, the term 'sustainable growth' is an oxymoron" (Bartlett, 1997). Long-term thinking is essential to avoid that mistake.

It is interesting that, in a state with officially-declared water shortages, with mandatory water restrictions and concerns that drought may become the "new normal" condition due to climate warming, few calls were heard for moratoriums on new water connections. Of course, the working assumption of water providers had long been that they would acquire whatever water was needed to meet demands of growth.

It bears repeating: if no water had ever been imported to Los Angeles, the population, using local sources, could not have grown beyond 500,000 to 800,000 residents.

Politicians shy away from population issues. The term "control," when coupled with "population," conjures draconian images of interference with reproductive freedom. Though people also fear the consequences of unlimited population growth, few are ready to face the problem directly. Yet water limits can be the stimulus prodding us toward a stable population without any need for unpalatable reproductive restrictions. Limits to water availability *and* the growing threats from climate change can be embraced as the opportunity to stabilize population numbers.

Many Californians find it nearly impossible to believe that their society can do anything but grow, given their personal experiences. They seem oblivious to the fact that there are states in this country that do have stable populations. The list includes Connecticut, Pennsylvania, Rhode Island and the State of New York. Each of these dealt with challenging transitions from industrial economies toward service economies.

Every nation in Europe, except Iceland, had a stable or declining population in 2015, with birthrates below 2.1 children per couple. While there are challenges to address during the decades after birthrates fall, until a balance is restored between children and the elderly, there are many countries on this list that are successfully addressing those problems while maintaining vibrant economies.

Economists have traditionally been trained in a dogma that economies *must* grow. But some are watching Japan, the nation with the lowest birthrate in the world today, and realizing that such economic concerns, while challenging, may have been overstated.

"Japan's economy has been growing slowly for two decades now. But that . . . is deceptive," says William Cline of the Peterson Institute for International Economics in Washington DC. Thanks to the falling population, individual income has been rising strongly—outperforming most US citizens'. With 127 million people, Japan is hardly empty. But fewer people in the future will mean it has more living space, more arable land per head, and a higher quality of life. Its demands on the planet for food and other resources will also lessen. (Pearce, 2014)

A benevolent phenomenon is happening around the world—where infant mortality rates drop, where women are educated and empowered, and where birth control measures are widely available, people choose smaller families to raise cherished, better-advantaged children. "The study of population has always been a subject that makes people uncomfortable. One fundamental reason for this is that it treats people as numbers, or as a 'stock,' and not as individuals. The great merit of the new population policies, centered on rights and security, is that they see people as individuals and not as numbers" (Rothschild, 1994, 406).

To achieve a stable population, the government does not have to specify family sizes—the pattern in developed nations shows that a replacement level birth rate will be the preference of enough individual families. We do not need new border fences or beefed-up Border Patrol forces to control immigration. Immigration need not stop, but the fluctuations that follow economic ups and downs show that rates drop on their own whenever the state stops sending eternal-growth economic signals to the world.

Immigration has driven California's population growth ever since the 1849 Gold Rush. The efforts of the state's boosters were devoted, from the early days of statehood, to attracting newcomers. Yet the entry rate has never been constant—"booms" manifested themselves because immigration rates varied, generally responding to economic cycles.

In 2015, thousands of refugees fled war in Syria. Though violence was the primary force driving that exodus, the crisis emerged following an extreme drought from 2006 to 2011, when water shortages prompted two million people to relocate to Syria's cities. *Time* magazine quoted Richard Seager, a climate scientist at Columbia University's Lamont-Doherty Earth Observatory, in a 2015 article about perceived connections between water shortages and the crisis: "We're not saying the drought caused the war. We're saying that added to all the other stressors, it helped kick things over the threshold into open conflict. Global warming is desiccating the region in two ways: higher temperatures that increase evaporation in already parched soils, and weaker winds that bring less rain from the Mediterranean Sea during the wet season" (Baker, 2015).

People will always move toward relative opportunity. Yet, California's history of immigration driving population growth has been, primarily, the overheated product of a state that was actively attracting new arrivals. Immigration need not stop, and compassion toward refugees must be the humane response during a crisis, but a well-structured level of immigration *can be* consistent with a stable population.

California's economy will, of course, be different when the state achieves this goal. Those whose businesses have been based on everlasting growth will have to adjust, as all states and nations with stable populations are adjusting. There are vested interests who will fight to protect the growth industries, just as powerful people, serving personal interests, "bulldozed" over the jobs of the state's salmon fleet fishermen, and literally bulldozed over the farm and agribusiness jobs in regions that became buried beneath suburbia. To continue in the old pattern requires acceptance of plant and wildlife extinctions, continued introductions of toxins into waterways and air, and acceptance of increased traffic gridlock, crime, crowded schools and higher taxes for public services. Some industries and some jobs, by their very nature, cannot continue forever on a finite planet.

Is seeking population stabilization "selfish"? That powerful question connects to the guilt U.S. citizens *should* feel about our extravagant resource consumption rates that, if practiced by every person on the planet, would require the global population to be less than one-fifth its present size. The question suggests that Californians have a moral obligation to keep their state growing. When would that process end? When life everywhere on Earth was equally unattractive, so that no one had any incentive to move anywhere else?

California *can* plan for stability, instead of planning for growth. Is there enough motivation? Consider that, in 2014, California ranked only fortieth among the states in the annual *Kids Count* comparison of conditions for children in the fifty states, looking at economic well-being, education, health, and family and community status.

Recognizing that Los Angeles successfully reduced overall water consumption during recent decades as the city grew by a million people, some voices proclaimed that population and water supply had been "decoupled." Yet, when evaluating how well cities and water districts are conserving to meet water restrictions, the key units of measurement remain: gallons used . . . *per person* . . . per day. Conserving water is important, of course. So is the number of people in that calculation. Improvements in water use must inevitably be overwhelmed by never-ending population growth.

If we wish to protect what remains of the California Dream, to continue feeding the nation and much of the world with California's agricultural output (arguably a moral imperative), and to halt the flood of species extinctions in California's environment (another moral imperative for many people who find it wrong for humans to terminate other species' very existence from this planet), then a choice for population stability should be made soon.

Californians should seek every opportunity to help improve conditions in underdeveloped nations. Again, proof is widespread today that stable birth rates follow when child mortality rates drop, when women are educated and birth control means are easy to find. We should push to see that the United States commits to support such benevolent international population stabilization measures.

The good news is that we know how to do this without coercion and abuse. A half-century of experience has shown that the best way to slow population growth is not by limiting family size but by ensuring that all people are able to make real choices about child-bearing. That means access to voluntary family planning and other reproductive health information and services. It means education

and job opportunities, especially for women. And it means tackling
the deep inequities—gender and economic—that prevent people
from determining the course of their lives. (Mazur, 2015, A13)

How can one oppose a doctrine that pursues "the greatest good
for the greatest number"? That has been the mantra in California
for 165 years, but it became twisted along the way, becoming heresy
to oppose the similar sounding, yet critically different formula—"the
greatest number equals the greatest good." Author James Houston
quoted a "young fellow," soon to graduate from a California university, who stepped away from the cultural dogma in which he had
been reared: "I see how my first reaction represents one of the mis-
conceptions we all are raised on—that progress is good, and bigger
is better. It makes me think of people I used to know who would rip
off their younger brothers and sisters by trading them pennies for
dimes. The pennies were bigger, so the young kids automatically
figured they were worth more" (1982, 268).

Raymond Dasmann, in closing his environmental classic, *The
Destruction of California*, called for "a vision, an ideal, of what the state
can be—a land that would permit the greatest diversity of human
activities and fullest expression of human freedom in a setting of natural splendor and man-made beauty." Dasmann eloquently called
for action "now" to stop the destruction, or "the state that once was
green and golden may become an object lesson that shows only what
other areas must avoid" (1965, 225). Fifty years later, there has been
some action, yet the negative object lesson continues.

In another '60s classic, *Desert Solitaire*, Edward Abbey wrote,
"It's only the old numbers game again, the monomania of small
and very simple minds in the grip of an obsession. They cannot see
that growth for the sake of growth is a cancerous madness. . . . They
would never understand that an economic system which can only
expand or expire must be false to all that is human" (1968, 145).

This book has relied upon the voices of many people, famous
and obscure, who participated in or commented upon California's
history. Here is a final quotation: "Ordinary citizens have . . .

substantial psychological as well as social and economic investments in a stable and quiet life, and activism on principle is avoided" (Kelley, 1989, 76).

Author Robert Kelley was describing the slow response among Central Valley farmers and townsfolk to the floods and farm losses caused by hydraulic mining, but the concept is universal. It took *ordinary citizens*, transformed into activists, to turn Californians from spectators, passively watching a slow death, into the saviors of Mono Lake. Like Californians of the late 1800s who philosophically supported the mining industry that built their young state, and like Mono Basin residents through the middle decades of this century, most of us practice denial, first, and continue avoiding problems for as long as possible. That is the most comfortable way to go through life. However, it is long past time to stir ourselves and address the population stabilization issue.

The issue is not a simple one, but it is simply true that water limits *can* be accepted. Stability need not bring the disasters predicted by fearmongering campaigners each time one of the state's water choices was made (but the state's history does suggest that similar campaign rhetoric will keep emerging).

The shape of the future remains a matter of choice, as it was throughout the state's history. The people of the Golden State can step away from their historic path and, for the new millennium, choose to stop drowning the California Dream.

REFERENCES

Abbey, Edward. 1968. *Desert Solitaire.* New York: Ballantine Books.

Abel, Heather. 1999, January 20. "Water Wars, California's proposed water plan is a disaster for fish, family farmers, and farmworkers—but not for suburbs and sprawl." *San Francisco Bay Guardian.*

Alcorn, J.R. 1991. *Tinnemaha.* Fallon, NV: Fairview West Publishing.

American Farmland Trust. 2007. *Paving Paradise: A New Perspective on California Farmland Conversion.* American Farmland Trust. www.thegreenhorns.net/wp-content/files_mf/1345131218pavingparadise.pdf.

An Act to Aid in the Construction of a Railroad . . . from the Missouri River to the Pacific Ocean [Pacific Railway Act]. 1862, July 1. *U.S. Statutes at Large,* Vol. 12, p. 489ff. www.pbs.org/weta/thewest/resources/archives/five/railact.htm.

Annie E. Casey Foundation. 2014. *Kids Count: State Trends in Child Well-being 2014 Data Book.* www.aecf.org/2014db.

Armor, Samuel. 1921. *History of Orange County, California, with Biographical Sketches of The Leading Men and Women of the County Who have been Identified with its Growth and Development from the Early Days to the Present Time.* Los Angeles: Historic Record Company.

Austin, Mar. 1905, September 5. "The Owens River Water Project." *San Francisco Chronicle.*

Baker, Aryn. 2015, September 7. "How Climate Change is Behind the Surge of Migrants to Europe." *Time.* http://time.com/4024210/climate-change-migrants/.

Bakker, Elna. 1984. *An Island Called California.* Berkeley: University of California Press.

Bancroft, Hubert Howe. [1890] 1967. *History of California, Vol. VII, 1860–1890.* San Francisco: The History Company. Reprint. New York: Arno Press/McGraw-Hill.

Banham, Reyner. 1971. *Los Angeles: The Architecture of Four Ecologies.* New York: Harper and Row.

Bank of America, California Resources Agency, Greenbelt Alliance and Low Income Housing Fund. 1995. *Beyond Sprawl: New Patterns of Growth to Fit the New California.* San Francisco: Bank of America Corp.

Bartlett, Albert A. 1997. "Reflections of Sustainability, Population Growth, and the Environment—Revisited." *Renewable Resources Journal.* 15:4 (Winter): pp. 6–23.

Bean, Walton and James J. Rawls. 1983. *California: An Interpretive History.* 4th ed. New York: McGraw-Hill.

Beard, Daniel P. 2015. *Deadbeat Dams: Why We Should Abolish the U.S. Bureau of Reclamation and Tear Down Glen Canyon Dam.* Boulder, CO: Johnson Books.

Bishop Chamber of Commerce. 1920. *Owens River Valley, Inyo County, California, the Field of Opportunity, The Land of Promise.* Bishop, CA: Inyo Register Printing.

Bixby-Smith, Sarah Hathaway. 1925. *Adobe days; being the truthful narrative of the events in the life of a California girl on a sheep ranch and in El Pueblo de Nuestra Señora de Los Angeles while it was yet a small and humble town. . . .* Cedar Rapids, IA: Torch Press.

Blank, Steven C. 1998. *The End of Agriculture in the American Portfolio.* Westport, CT: Quorum Books.

Bloome, Deborah Weinstein and Phoebe Lipkis. 2015 (February). *Moving Towards Collaboration: A New Vision for Water Management in the Los Angeles Region.* Beverly Hills, CA: TreePeople. www.treepeople.org/sites/default/files/pdf/publications/Moving%20Towards%20Collaboration_e-version.pdf.

Bohn-Spector, Claudia and Jennifer A. Watts. 1997, June 3. "Envisioning Eden: Water and the Selling of Los Angeles, 1880–1930." Wall text, Huntington Library. San Marino, CA.

Bolton, Herbert Eugene. 1927. *Fray Juan Crespi, Missionary Explorer on the Pacific Coast.* Berkeley: University of California Press.

Bouvier, Leon F. 1991. *Fifty Million Californians?* Washington, DC: Center for Immigration Studies.

Boyle, Robert H., John Graves and T.H. Watkins. 1971. *The Water Hustlers.* San Francisco: Sierra Club Books.

Brewer, William H. 1966. *Up and Down California in 1860–1864.* Berkeley: University of California Press.

Brower, Kenneth. 2013. *Hetch Hetchy: Undoing a Great American Mistake.* Berkeley: Heyday.

Brown, Edmund G., Sr. 1981. "The California Water Project: Personal Interest and Involvement in the Legislation, Public Support, and Construction, 1950–1966." Oral history conducted in 1980 by Malca Chall: in *California Water Issues, 1950–1966.* Berkeley: University of California, Bancroft Library, Regional Oral History Office.

Brown, Lester R. 2009. *Plan B 4.0: Mobilizing to Save Civilization.* Earth Policy Institute. New York: W.W. Norton & Company.

Bryan, George W. 1911. *The Lure of the Past, the Present and Future.* Los Angeles: E.G. Newton Co.

Bulpitt, Harriett B. 1954, February 5. Oral history interview. Eastern California Museum, Independence, CA.

Burcham, Lee T. 1957. *California Rangeland: An Historico-Ecological Study of the Range Resource of California*. California Department of Natural Resources, Division of Forestry.

California Department of Conservation. 2014. *Farmland Conversion Report: 2008–2010*. Sacramento. www.conservation.ca.gov/dlrp/fmmp/Pages/FMMP_2008-2010_FCR.aspx.

California Department of Finance. 2015, May. *E-1 Population Estimates for Cities, Counties and the State with Annual Percent Change—January 1, 2014 and 2015*. Sacramento. www.dof.ca.gov/research/demographic/reports/estimates/e-1/view.php.

California Department of Fish and Wildlife. 2015. *Threatened and Endangered Fish*. www.dfg.ca.gov/wildlife/nongame/t_e_spp/fish.html.

California Department of Water Resources. 1996. "California State Water Project." Pamphlet. Sacramento.

———. 2006. "Hetch Hetchy Restoration Study." www.water.ca.gov/pubs/environment/hetch_hetchy_restoration_study/ hetch_hetchy_restoration_study_report.pdf.

———. 2013. "California Water Plan: Bulletin 160-13, Update 2013." Sacramento. www.waterplan.water.ca.gov.

———. 2016. "Drought Information: California Water Year 2016." www.water.ca.gov/waterconditions/.

California Farm Bureau Federation. 1999. "1925–1955 Crop Acreage Trends for Los Angeles County and Southern California." California Farm Bureau Federation. www.cfbf.com/CFBF/Issues/Issue_and_Regulations/CFBF/Issues/Central_Valley_Land_Use_Report_-_Sidebar__Can_the_Central_Valley_Learn_from_the_Experience_of_Los_A_.aspx.

California Farm Water Coalition. 2016. www.farmwater.org/about-california-farm-water-coalition.

California Natural Resources Agency. 2008. *Our Vision for the California Delta. Governor's Delta Vision Blue Ribbon Task Force: Final report*. Sacramento. http://deltavision.ca.gov/index.shtml.

———. 2014. *California Water Action Plan*. Sacramento. http://resources.ca.gov/california_water_action_plan/.

California State Water Resources Control Board (SWRCB). 2010. *Final Report on Development of Flow Criteria for the Sacramento-San Joaquin Delta Ecosystem*. www.waterboards.ca.gov/waterrights/water_issues/programs/bayDelta/delta-flow/index.shtml.

Cameron, Michael. 1991, April 1. "Unclogging the Highways and Clearing the Air." *Environmental Defense Fund Newsletter*, 22:2.

Canfield, Chauncey L., ed. [1920] 1993. *The Diary of a Forty-Niner*. Boston: Houghton Mifflin. Reprint. New York: Turtle Point Press.

Cannon, Frederick. 1993 (June/July). "Economic Growth and the Environment." *Economic & Business Outlook*. Bank of America.

Carle, David. [2004] 2015. *Introduction to Water in California*. Berkeley: University of California Press.

Carle, David and Janet Carle. 2013. *Traveling the 38th Parallel: A Water Line Around the World*. Berkeley: University of California Press.

Carle, Louis. 1999. Personal correspondence.

Carrillo, Leo. 1961. *The California I Love*. Englewood Cliffs, NJ: Prentice-Hall.

Carson, James H. [1852] 1931. *Early recollections of the mines, and a description of the great Tulare valley. . . . steamer edition of the San Joaquin Republican*. Tarrytown, NY. Reprint. New York: W. Abbatt.

Caughey, John Walton. 1948. *Gold is the Cornerstone*. Berkeley: University of California Press.

Caughey, John and Laree Caughey, eds. 1977. *Los Angeles: Biography of a City*. Berkeley: University of California Press.

Chalfant, W.A. 1922. *The Story of Inyo*. Bishop, CA: Chalfant Press.

Chandler, Raymond. [1949] 1976. *The Little Sister*. New York: Random House.

Chatterjee, Pratap. 1998. *Gold, Greed & Genocide in the Americas: California to the Amazon*. Berkeley: Project Underground.

Children's Rights Council. 1999, July 27. "Top Ten States to Raise a Child." www.crckids.org.

Citizens Colorado River Water Committee. 1931, July. "We Need It! Let's Go and Get It!" Campaign brochure. Los Angeles.

Clappe, Louise A.K.S. (Dame Shirley). 1970. *The Shirley Letters: From the California Mines, 1851–1852*. San Francisco: T.C. Russell. Reprint. Santa Barbara: Peregrine-Smith.

Cleland, Robert Glass. 1941. *The Cattle on a Thousand Hills: Southern California, 1850–1880*. San Marino, CA: Huntington Library.

———. 1947. *California in Our Time (1900–1940)*. New York: Knopf.

Cleland, Robert Glass and Glenn S. Dumke. 1966. *From Wilderness to Empire: A History of California*. New York: Knopf.

Clifford, Frank. 1999, February 28. "Headwaters a Case Study in Forest Policy Failure." *Los Angeles Times*.

Cohen, Andrew. 1994. "The Hidden Costs of California's Water." In *Life on the*

Edge: A Guide to California's Endangered Natural Resources. Vol. 1, Wildlife, edited by Carl G. Thelander. Berkeley, CA: BioSystem Books.

Cohen, Michael P. 1988. *The History of the Sierra Club.* San Francisco: Sierra Club Books.

Colson, Brett and Geoff Black. 1993. *Dreams to Reality: A Profile of Modern Day Anaheim.* Anaheim, CA: Pioneer Publications.

Cooley, Heather, Juliet Christian-Smith and Peter H. Gleick. 2009. *Sustaining California Agriculture in an Uncertain Future.* Oakland: Pacific Institute. www. pacinst.org/wp-content/uploads/sites/21/2014/04/sustaining-california-agriculture-pacinst-exec-sum.pdf.

Cooper, Erwin. 1968. *Aqueduct Empire: A Guide to Water in California, Its Turbulent History and Its Management Today.* Glendale, CA: Arthur H. Clark.

Council on Environmental Quality. 1970. *Environmental Quality: The First Annual Report of the Council on Environmental Quality.* Washington, DC: U.S. Government Printing Office.

Dana, Richard Henry, Jr. 1949. *Two Years Before the Mast: A Personal Narrative of Life at Sea.* New York: Doubleday.

Daniels, Tom and Deborah Bowers. 1997. *Holding Our Ground: Protecting America's Farms and Farmland.* Washington, DC: Island Press.

Dasmann, Raymond F. 1965. *The Destruction of California.* New York: Macmillan.

Davis, Margaret Leslie. 1993. *Rivers in the Desert: William Mulholland and the Inventing of Los Angeles.* New York: HarperCollins.

Davis, Martha. 1998. "Stepping Outside the Box: Water in Southern California." From a speech at the University of California at Los Angeles Environment Symposium. Reprinted at Mono Lake Committee site: www.monolake.org/mlc/outsidebox.

_____. 2014, November 17. "Mono Lake @ 20: Past, Present, Future." In Part 6. Video. Sacramento: State Water Resources Control Board. www.waterboards.ca.gov/board_info/video.shtml.

Dawson, Robert and Gray Brechin. 1999. *Farewell, Promised Land: Waking from the California Dream.* Berkeley: University of California Press.

DeDecker, Mary. 1992, May 22. Oral history interview by Richard Potashin, for Eastern California Museum, Independence, CA.

Dennis, Harry. 1981. *Water and Power: The Peripheral Canal and Its Alternatives.* San Francisco: Friends of the Earth.

Dillon, Richard. 1981. *Fool's Gold: The Decline and Fall of Captain John Sutter of California.* Santa Cruz, CA: Western Tanager Press.

Dinno, Rachel, ed. 1999, February. *Restoring the California Dream: Ten Steps to Improve Our Quality of Life.* Sacramento, CA: Planning and Conservation League Foundation.

Duane, Daniel. 2015, October 25. "My Dark California Dream." *The New York Times*. www.nytimes.com/2015/10/25/opinion/sunday/my-dark-california-dream.html?_r=0.

Dumke, Glenn S. 1944. *The Boom of the Eighties in Southern California*. San Marino, CA: Huntington Library.

Egan, Ferol. 1985. *Frémont, Explorer for a Restless Nation*. Reno: University of Nevada Press.

Egleston, N.H. 1909, February 8. *Granting Use of Hetch Hetchy to City of San Francisco*. Report to 60th Congress. Washington, DC.

Erie, Steven P. 2006. *Beyond Chinatown: The Metropolitan Water District, Growth, and the Environment in Southern California*. Stanford, CA: Stanford University Press.

Evans, Taliesin. [1883] 1981. "Hydraulic Gold-Mining in California in 1883." *Century Magazine*. Reprint. Golden, CO: Outbooks.

Farmer, Jared. 2013. *Trees in Paradise: A California History*. New York: W.W. Norton & Company.

Fodor, Eben. 1999. *Better NOT Bigger: How to Take Control of Urban Growth and Improve Your Community*. Gabriola Island, B.C., Canada: New Society Publishers.

Fogelson, Robert M. 1967. *The Fragmented Metropolis: Los Angeles, 1850–1930*. Cambridge, MA: Harvard University Press.

Frémont, John C. 1848. "Geographical Memoir upon Upper California, in Illustration of His Map of Oregon and California." In *The Expeditions of John Charles Frémont*, vol. 3, edited by Mary Lee Spence. 1984. Urbana: University of Illinois Press.

Friedman, David. 1998, April 19. "The Divining Rod of Water Politics." *Opinion, Los Angeles Times*.

Fulton, William. [1997] 2001. *The Reluctant Metropolis: The Politics of Urban Growth in Los Angeles*. Baltimore: John Hopkins University Press.

Garner, William Robert. 1970. *Letters from California, 1846–1847*. Berkeley: University of California Press.

Garrett, Wilbur E., ed. 1988. *Historical Atlas of the United States*. Washington, DC: National Geographic Society.

Gauer, Melbourne A. 1974, March 16. "Anaheim Area Since 1925." Oral history interview by Kathy Landis. California State University, Fullerton, Community History Project.

Gilbert, G.K. 1917. *Hydraulic-Mining Debris in the Sierra Nevada*. Professional paper 105. Washington, DC: U.S. Geological Survey.

Golden State Museum. 1997. Jim Paravantes interview. "The Journey." immigration exhibit. Sacramento: California State Archives.

Gottlieb, Robert and Margaret FitzSimmons. 1991. *Thirst for Growth: Water Agencies as Hidden Government in California*. Tucson: University of Arizona Press.

Gottlieb, Robert and Irene Wolt. 1977. *Thinking Big: The Story of the Los Angeles Times, Its Publishers, and Their Influence on Southern California*. New York: Putnam.

Grantham, Theodore E. and Joshua H. Viers. 2014. *One Hundred Years of California's Water Rights System: Patterns, Trends and Uncertainty*. Environmental Research Letters 9. https://watershed.ucdavis.edu/files/content/news/WaterRights_UCDavis_study.pdf.

Graves, Jackson Alpheus. 1927. *My Seventy Years in California, 1857–1927*. Los Angeles: Times-Mirror Press.

Greenwald, John. 1995, September 25. "Arsenic and Old Mines." *Time*. 146:13, p. 36.

Hall, Clarence A., Jr., Victoria Doyle-Jones and Barbara Widawski, eds. 1992. *The History of Water: Eastern Sierra Nevada, Owens Valley, White-Inyo Mountains*. White Mountain Research Station Symposium, vol. 4. San Francisco: Regents of the University of California.

Hallan-Gibson, Pamela. 1975. *Dos Cientos Años en San Juan Capistrano*. Irvine, CA: Lehmann Publishers.

_____. 1986. *The Golden Promise: An Illustrated History of Orange County*. Northridge, CA: Windsor Publishers.

Hammer, Joshua. 2013, June. "Is a Lack of Water to Blame for the Conflict in Syria?" Washington, DC: *Smithsonian*. www.smithsonianmag.com/innovation/is-a-lack-of-water-to-blame-for-the-conflict-in-syria-72513729.

Hardin, Garrett. 1968. "The Tragedy of the Commons," in *Science*, 162, pp. 1243–48.

Harrison, Paul. 1992. *The Third Revolution: Environment, Population and a Sustainable World*. New York: I.B. Taurus & Co.

Hayes, Benjamin. 1929. *Pioneer Notes from the Diaries of Judge Benjamin Hayes, 1849–1875*. Edited by Marjorie Tisdale Wolcott. Los Angeles: Margorie Tisdale Wolcott, private publisher.

Heizer, Robert F., ed. 1978. *Handbook of North American Indians, Vol. 8, California*. Washington, DC: Smithsonian Institution.

Hendry, George. 1931. "The Adobe Brick as a Historical Source." *Agricultural History*. Berkeley: University of California Press, 4: pp. 110–127.

Henstell, Bruce. 1984. *Sunshine & Wealth: Los Angeles in the Twenties and Thirties*. San Francisco: Chronicle Books.

Hinton, Ralph N. 1993. "History of the Winter-Run and other Sacramento River Salmon." Unpublished manuscript.

Hoffman, Abraham. 1981. *Vision or Villainy: Origins of the Owens Valley–Los Angeles Water Controversy*. College Station: Texas A&M University Press.

Holder, Charles Frederick. 1906. *Life in the Open; Sport with Rod, Gun, Horse, and Hound in Southern California*. New York: Putnam.

Holliday, J.S. 1981. *The World Rushed In: The California Gold Rush Experience*. New York: Knopf.

Houston, James D. 1982. *Californians: Searching for the Golden State*. New York: Knopf.

Hundley, Norris, Jr. [1992] 2001. *The Great Thirst: Californians and Water—A History*. Berkeley: University of California Press.

Intergovernmental Panel on Climate Change (IPCC); R.K. Pachauri and L.A. Meyer, eds. 2014. *Climate Change 2014: Synthesis Report. Contribution of Working Groups I, II and III to the Fifth Assessment*. Geneva, Switzerland: IPCC. www.ipcc.ch/report/ar5/syr/.

Inyo Register. [1912] 1983. *Inyo County California: Anno Domini 1912: Beautiful Owens Valley*. Bishop, CA: Inyo Register. Reprinted by Bishop Chamber of Commerce and Chalfant Press.

Isbell, F.S. [ca. 1871] 1994. "Market Hunting in the San Jose Valley." In *Life on the Edge: A Guide to California's Endangered Natural Resources. Vol. 1, Wildlife*, edited by Carl G. Thelander. Berkeley, CA: Biosystem Books.

Isenberg, Andrew C. 2005. *Mining California: An Ecological History*. New York: Hill and Wang.

Jackson, Donald Dale. 1980. *Gold Dust*. New York: Knopf.

Jacobs, Josephine Kingsbury. 1966. "Sunkist Advertising—The Iowa Campaign." In *Los Angeles: Biography of a City*, edited by John Caughey and Laree Caughey. Berkeley: University of California Press.

Johnson, Paul C. 1970. *Pictorial History of California*. New York: Bonanza Books.

Jones, Robert A. 1998, November 8. "Ecotopia Comes South." *Los Angeles Times*, p. B1.

Kahrl, William L. 1982. *Water and Power: The Conflict over Los Angeles Water Supply in the Owens Valley*. Berkeley: University of California Press.

Kattelmann, Richard. 1995. "Impacts of Gold Mining on Water Resources of the Sierra Nevada." Paper presented at American Institute of Hydrology conference, Mammoth Lakes, CA.

Kelley, Robert. 1989. *Battling the Inland Sea: Floods, Public Policy, and the Sacramento Valley*. Berkeley: University of California Press.

Kirsch, Robert and William S. Murphy. 1967. *West of the West: Witnesses to the California Experience, 1542–1906*. New York: E.P. Dutton & Co.

Klein, Naomi. 2014. *This Changes Everything: Capitalism vs. The Climate*. New York: Simon & Schuster.

Kohlenberger, George F. 1974, March 19. "Life in Anaheim, California 1904–1920." Oral history interview by Vivian Allen. California State University, Fullerton.

Kroeber, Theodora. 1976. *Ishi in Two Worlds*. Berkeley: University of California Press.

KTEH-TV Foundation. 1997. *Cadillac Desert—An American Nile, Pt. I*.

Langsdorff, Georg von. 1927. *Langsdorff's Narrative of the Rezanov voyage to Nueva California in 1806.* San Francisco: Thomas C. Russell. www.archive.org/stream/langsdorffsnarra00lang#page/n13/mode/2up.

La Rue, Steve. 1998, July 3. "Bass Brothers' Quest for Water Contract with Agency Told." *Los Angeles Times.*

Lassiter, Allison, ed. 2015. *Sustainable Water: Challenges and Solutions from California.* Berkeley: University of California Press.

Leopold, A. Starker. 1985. *Wild California: Vanishing Lands, Vanishing Wildlife.* Berkeley: University of California Press.

Los Angeles Department of Water and Power. 2016a. "A New Supply." www.ladwp.com/ladwp/faces/wcnav_externalId/a-w-fact-hist.

———. 2016b. "Whoever Brings the Water, Brings the People." www.ladwp.com/ladwp/faces/wcnav_externalId/a-w-fact-hist.

Lucas, Greg. 1997, March 18. "Southern California Water Crisis Looms, Colorado River is Key to Disagreement." *San Francisco Chronicle.*

Lufkin, Alan. 1990. *California's Salmon and Steelhead: The Struggle to Restore an Imperiled Resource.* Berkeley: University of California Press.

Madina, Frank M. 1990. "Where Have All the Ranches Gone. . . ." *The Album, Times & Tales of Inyo-Mono,* 3:3, pp. 22–29.

Marcum, Diana. 1999, August 12. "7.6 Million Fish Die in a Day at Salton Sea." *Los Angeles Times.*

Margolin, Malcolm. 1978. *The Ohlone Way.* Berkeley, CA: Heyday.

Martenet, Morris W., Jr. 1968, April 19. "Discussions of Anaheim Urban Renewal." Oral history interview by Richard D. Curtiss. California State University, Fullerton oral history program.

Martin, Glen. 1999, June 25. "Divvying Up Our Water." *San Francisco Chronicle.*

Mason, Richard Barnes (Colonel). 1848. "Official Report on the Gold Mines, August 17, 1848." Virtual Museum of the City of San Francisco. www.sfmuseum.org/hist6/masonrpt.html.

Mayo, Morrow. 1933. *Los Angeles.* New York: Knopf.

Mazur, Laurie Ann, ed. 2009. *A Pivotal Moment: Population, Justice, and the Environmental Challenge.* Washington, DC: Island Press.

———. 2015, November 3. "Ban the 'Population Bomb.'" *Los Angeles Times.*

McCarthy, John Russell. 1937, November 13. "Water: The Story of Bill Mulholland." *Los Angeles Saturday Night.*

McClurg, Sue. 1998. "Saving the Salmon." *Western Water: Journal of the Water Education Foundation* (January/February): pp. 4–13.

———. 1999. "The Future of Central Valley Agriculture." *Western Water: Journal of the Water Education Foundation* (September/October): pp. 4–13.

McEwan, Ian. 1999. *Amsterdam*. New York: Nan A. Talese imprint, Doubleday, Anchor Books edition.

McWilliams, Carey. [1946] 1973. *Southern California: An Island on the Land*. Santa Barbara, CA: Peregrine Smith, Inc.

————. 1949. *California: The Great Exception*. New York: Current Books.

Megerian, Chris. 2015, July 8. "World is on a collision course with fossil fuels, Governor Jerry Brown says." *Los Angeles Times*. www.latimes.com/local/political/la-me-pc-jerry-brown-speech-toronto-climate-change-20150708-story.html.

Mells, William V. [1860] 1978. "How We Get Gold in California. [By] . . . a Miner of the Year '49." *Harper's*. Reprint. Golden, CO: Outbooks.

Metropolitan Water District of Southern California (MWD). 1931a. *Thirst*. Film produced by Gilliam and Reed, Hollywood, for MWD.

————. 1931b (June). "It's Your Move." Colorado River election campaign brochure. Los Angeles: MWD.

————. 1931c (March). "The Metropolitan Aqueduct." Colorado River election campaign brochure, Number 4. Los Angeles: MWD.

————. 1931d. "Water—The Destiny of a Mighty Empire Hangs in the Balance Now!" Colorado River election campaign poster. Los Angeles: MWD.

————. 1981. *Balance of Nature*. Film produced by Metropolitan Water District of Southern California.

Muir, John. 1912. *The Yosemite*. New York: The Century Co.

————. 1961. *The Mountains of California*. Garden City, NY: American Museum of Natural History and Doubleday.

Mulholland, Catherine. 1987. *The Owensmouth Baby: The Making of a San Fernando Valley Town*. Northridge, CA: Santa Susana Press.

Mumma, Phil. 1998. "The Dark Legacy of the Gold Rush." *Museum of California*, 22:2, pp. 20–26.

Nadeau, Remi. 1974. *The Water Seekers*. Bishop, CA: Chalfant Press.

Nagourney, Adam, Jack Healy and Nelson D. Schwartz. 2015, April 4. "California Drought Tests History of Endless Growth." *The New York Times*. www.nytimes.com/2015/04/05/us/california-drought-tests-history-of-endless-growth.html.

Newmark, Harris. 1916. *Sixty Years in Southern California, 1853–1913, containing the reminiscences of Harris Newmark*. . . . New York: Knickerbocker Press.

Noble, John Wesley. [1970] 1999. *Its Name Was M.U.D.* Oakland, CA: East Bay Municipal Utility District.

Nordhoff, Charles. 1873. *California: For Health, Pleasure, and Residence*. New York: Harper and Brothers.

Norris, Frank. 1901. *The Octopus: A Story of California*. New York: Doubleday.

Older, Fremont. 1919. *My Own Story*. San Francisco: The Call Publishing Co.

Olin, Spencer, Rob Kling and Mark Poster. 1991. "Intraclass Conflict and the Politics of a Fragmented Region." In *Postsuburban California: The Transformation of Orange County Since World War II.* Berkeley: University of California Press.

Oliver, Dennis. 1997, December 28. "Gold's Tarnished Legacy," *Alameda Times-Star.*

Orange County Water District (OCWD). 1947. "Progress Report on the Policy for Balancing the Present Supply and Draft on the Orange County Underground Water Basin." Directors of the Orange County Water District.

Orsi, Richard J. 1991. "Railroads and Water in the Arid Far West: The Southern Pacific Company as a Pioneer Water Developer." *California History,* 70:1 (Spring), pp. 46–61.

Ostrom, Vincent. 1953. *Water and Politics: A Study of Water Policies and Administration in the Development of Los Angeles.* Los Angeles: Haynes Foundation.

Paddison Joshua, ed. 1998. *A World Transformed: Firsthand Accounts of California Before the Gold Rush.* Berkeley, CA: Heyday Books.

Parcher, Marie Louise and Will G. Parcher. [1934] 1970. *Dry Ditches.* Reprint. Bishop, CA: Inyo Register Press.

Pavlik, Bruce M., Pamela C. Muick, Sharon G. Johnson and Marjorie Popper. 1993. *Oaks of California.* Los Olivos: Cachuma Press and the California Oak Foundation.

Pearce, Fred. 2014, January 11. "Japan's ageing population could actually be good news." *New Scientist:* 2951. www.newscientist.com/article/dn24822-japans-ageing-population-could-actually-be-good-news.

Pearson, Charles A. 1968, April 10, 18, 26; May 7. "Politics, Growth, and Development of Anaheim, California." Oral history interview by Richard D. Curtiss. California State University, Fullerton oral history program.

Perrone, Debra and Melissa Rohde. 2014. *Storing Water in California: What Can $2.7 Billion Buy Us?* Stanford, CA: Stanford Woods Institute for the Environment. http://waterinthewest.stanford.edu/resources/publications-directory.

Peterson, B. "Moose." 1993. *Nikon Guide to Wildlife Photography.* Rochester, NY: Silver Pixel Press.

Pimentel, David and Marcia Pimentel. 1997. "U.S. Food Production Threatened by Rapid Population Growth." Washington, DC: Carrying Capacity Network.

Pimentel, David and Mario Giampietro. 1994. *Food, Land, Population and the U.S. Economy.* Washington, DC: Carrying Capacity Network.

Pitt, Leonard. 1971. *The Decline of the Californios: A Social History of the Spanish-Speaking Californians, 1846–1890.* Berkeley: University of California Press.

Population Reference Bureau (PRB). 2016. www.prb.org.

Powell, G. Harold. 1996. *Letters from the Orange Empire.* Los Angeles: Historical Society of Southern California.

Preston, William. 1998. "Serpent in the Garden." In *Contested Eden: California Before the Gold Rush,* edited by Ramón A. Gutierrez and Richard J. Orsi. Berkeley: University of California Press.

Putnam, Jeff and Genny Smith, eds. 1995. *Deepest Valley: Guide to Owens Valley, Its Roadsides and Mountain Trails.* Mammoth Lakes, CA: Genny Smith Books.

Rarick, Ethan. 2005. *California Rising: The Life and Times of Pat Brown.* Berkeley: University of California Press.

Reisner, Marc. 1986. *Cadillac Desert: The American West and Its Disappearing Water.* New York: Viking Penguin.

_____. 1992. "High-rise Urban Shrimp Fishing." The History of Water: Eastern Sierra Nevada, Owens Valley, White-Inyo Mountains. White Mountain Research Station Symposium, Vol. 4. Berkeley: University of California.

_____. 1997. "Water Policy and Farmland Protection: A New Approach to Saving California's Best Agricultural Lands." American Farmland Trust. www.farmlandinfo.org/sites/default/files/WATER_POLICY_AND_FARMLAND_PROTECTION_SEPTEMBER_1997_1.pdf.

Restore the Delta. 2015, October 30. "30,000 Californians Speak Out Against the Delta Tunnels." Press Release. http://us3.campaign-archive2.com/?u=0 6887fa70084fef8e939fef63&id=fddd175d58&e=3ad9c4895b.

Righter, Robert W. 2005. *The Battle Over Hetch Hetchy: America's Most Controversial Dam and the Birth of Modern Environmentalism.* New York: Oxford University Press.

Ring, Bob, Steven Charles Ring and Al Ring. 2008. *Detour to the California Gold Rush: Eugene Ring's Travels in South America, California, and Mexico, 1848–1850.* Tucson, AZ: U.S. Press & Graphics. http://web.archive.org/web/20000302052210/ http://uts.cc.utexas.edu/scring/index.html.

Risebrough, Robert. 1994. "Environmental Contaminants. . . ." In *Life on the Edge: A Guide to California's Endangered Natural Resources. Vol. 1, Wildlife,* edited by Carl G. Thelander. Berkeley, CA: BioSystem Books.

Robie, Ronald B. 2010. "Highlights of the State Water Project" in *SWP, 50 Years & Counting,* DWR News: "People." www.water.ca.gov/pubs/dwrnews/dwr_ news_people_fall_2010/news-people-fall2010.pdf.

Robinson, W.W. 1948. *Land in California.* Berkeley: University of California Press.

_____. 1953. *Panorama: A Picture History of Southern California.* Los Angeles: Title Insurance and Trust Co.

Rolle, Andrew F. 1963. *California: A History.* New York: Thomas Y. Crowell.

_____. 1995. *Los Angeles, From Pueblo to City of the Future.* Reprint. San Francisco: MTL, Inc.

Rose, Gene. [1992] 2000. *The San Joaquin: A River Betrayed.* Clovis, CA: Word Dancer Press.

Roosevelt, Theodore. 1907, December 3. "The Conservation of Natural

Resources." *Seventh Annual Message to Congress.* www.pbs.org/weta/thewest/resources/archives/eight/trconserv.htm.

Rothschild, Emma. 1994. "Population and Common Security." In *Beyond the Numbers: A Reader on Population, Consumption and the Environment,* edited by Laurie Ann Mazur. Washington, DC: Island Press.

Saga of Inyo County. 1977. Oral history collection of Southern Inyo American Association of Retired Persons, Chapter 183. Covina, CA: Taylor Publishing Co.

San Francisco Chronicle. 1959, May 14. "State Water Needs Critical, Brown Warns Legislature," p. 9.

Schoenherr, Allan. 1992. *A Natural History of California.* Berkeley: University of California Press.

Schrank, David L. and Timothy J. Lomax. 1996. *Urban Roadway Congestion—1982–1994, Vol. 1. Annual Report.* Texas Transportation Institute. Texas A&M University, College Station, Texas.

Sedlak, David. 2014. *Water 4.0: The Past, Present, and Future of the World's Most Vital Resource.* New Haven, CT: Yale University Press.

Seidenbaum, Art. 1988. *Los Angeles 200: A Bicentennial Celebration.* New York: Harry N. Abrams.

Sherman, William T. (General). 1945. *Recollections of California, 1846–1861.* Oakland, CA: Biobooks.

Shinn, Charles Howard. [1885] 1948. *Mining Camps: A Study in American Frontier Government.* Reprint. New York: Knopf.

Shippey, Lee. 1948. *It's An Old California Custom.* New York: Vanguard Press.

Siders, David and Dale Kasler. 2015, May 6. "Jerry Brown to water tunnels critics: Shut up." *Capitol Alert,* in the *Sacramento Bee.* www.sacbee.com/news/politics-government/capitol-alert/article20375127.html.

SOAR. 1998. Save Open Space and Agricultural Resources. www.soarvc.org.

South Coast Air Quality Monitoring District (SCAQMD). 1996. "Smog and Health." www.aqmd.gov/home/library/public-information/publications/smog-and-health-historical-info.

Spence, Mary Lee, ed. 1984. *The Expeditions of John Charles Frémont.* Vols. 1–3. Berkeley: University of California Press.

Spriggs, Elisabeth Mathieu. 1931. "The History of the Domestic Water Supply of Los Angeles." Master's thesis. Los Angeles: University of Southern California.

Standiford, Les. 2015. *Water to the Angels: William Mulholland, His Monumental Aqueduct, and the Rise of Los Angeles.* New York: Ecco.

Starr, Kevin. 1973. *Americans and the California Dream, 1850–1915.* New York: Oxford University Press.

————. 1985. *Inventing the Dream: California Through the Progressive Era*. New York: Oxford University Press.

————. [2004] 2006. *Coast of Dreams: California on the Edge, 1990–2003*. New York: Vintage Books.

Stene, Eric A. 1998. "The Central Valley Project." U.S. Bureau of Reclamation. www.usbr.gov/history/cvpintro.htm.

Stine, Scott. 1994. "Extreme and persistent drought in California and Patagonia during mediaeval time." *Nature* 369: pp. 546–49.

Storer, Tracy I. and Lloyd P. Tevis, Jr. 1955. *California Grizzly*. Berkeley: University of California Press.

Storper, Michael and Richard A. Walker. 1984. *The Price of Water: Surplus and Subsidy in the California State Water Project*. University of California at Berkeley, Institute of Governmental Studies.

Sudman, Rita Schmidt, ed. 1993, September. "Memories of the Early Days of California Water Development." Sacramento: Water Education Foundation.

————. 1999. "Editor's Desk" column. *Western Water: Journal of the Water Education Foundation*. Sacramento: Water Education Foundation (March/April): p. 2.

Swatt, Steve, with Susie Swatt, Jeff Raimundo and Rebecca LaVally. 2015. *Game Changers: Twelve Elections That Transformed California*. Berkeley: Heyday.

Taylor, Bayard. [1850] 1983. *Eldorado: Adventures in the Path of Empire*. New York: Putnam. Reprint. New York: Time-Life.

————. 1862. *At Home and Abroad, Second Series*. New York: Putnam.

Thelander, Carl G., ed. 1994. *Life on the Edge: A Guide to California's Endangered Natural Resources. Vol 1, Wildlife*. Berkeley, CA: BioSystem Books.

Thomas, Bob. 1976. *Walt Disney: An American Original*. New York: Simon and Schuster.

Truman, Ben. C. (Major). 1874. *Semi-Tropical California: Its Climate, Healthfulness, Productiveness, and Scenery*. San Francisco: A.L. Bancroft.

U.S. National Park Service. 1988. "Alternatives for Restoration of Hetch Hetchy Valley Following Removal of the Dam and the Reservoir." http://vault.sierra-club.org/ca/hetchhetchy/nps_hh_restoration.pdf.

Vail, Mary C. 1888. *Both Sides Told, or Southern California As It Is . . .* Pasadena, CA: West Coast Publishing.

Vallejo, Guadalupe. 1890. "Ranch and Mission Days in Alta California." *The Century Magazine* 41 (December): pp. 183–92.

Walton, John. 1992. *Western Times and Water Wars: State, Culture, and Rebellion in California*. Berkeley: University of California Press.

Warne, Henry and Ellen Warne. 1997, July 7. Personal correspondence. Westminster, CA.

Warner, Charles Dudley. 1891. *Our Italy*. New York: Harper & Brothers.

Warren, Earl (Chief Justice). 1977. *The Memoirs of Chief Justice Earl Warren*. Garden City, NY: Doubleday.

Water Education Foundation (WEF). 1999. "Where Science and Public Policy Meet: A Roundtable Discussion." *Western Water: Journal of the Water Education Foundation*. Sacramento: Water Education Foundation. (May/June): pp. 3–13.

Watkins, T.H. 1969. *The Grand Colorado: The Story of a River and its Canyons*. Palo Alto, CA: American West Publishing.

_____. 1983. *California: An Illustrated History*. New York: American Legacy Press.

West, G. James. "Pollen Analysis of Three Adobe Brick Samples from Johnson-Taylor Adobe, San Diego County, California." Unpublished manuscript.

West, G. James and Catherine V. Fossberg. 1980. "A Pollen Record of Historic Changes in a California Grassland Community." Department of Anthropology, University of California Davis. Paper presented at Workshop in Historical Archaeology, Reno, NV.

Western Water Policy Review Advisory Commission. 1998, June. "Water in the West: The Challenge for the Next Century." Report to the U.S. Congress.

Wheeler, Keith and editors of Time-Life Books. 1973. *The Railroaders: Old West series*. New York: Time-Life Books.

Wheelwright, Jane Hollister. 1988. *The Ranch Papers: A California Memoir*. Santa Monica, CA: Lapis Press.

Wilson, E.O. 2012. *The Social Conquest of Earth*. New York: Liveright Publishing (W.W. Norton).

Woehlke, Walter W. 1912, April. "The Land Before-and-After." Palo Alto, CA: *Sunset Magazine*.

Wood, Richard Coke. 1973. *The Owens Valley and the Los Angeles Water Controversy: Owens Valley As I Knew It*. Stockton, CA: University of the Pacific.

Work, John. 1945. "Fur Brigade to the Bonaventura, John Work's California expedition, 1832–1833, for the Hudson's Bay Company." Edited by Alice Bay Maloney. San Francisco: California Historical Society.

Worster, Donald. 1992. *Rivers of Empire: Water, Aridity, and the Growth of the American West*. New York: Oxford University Press.

Yoshiyama, Ronald M., Eric R. Gerstung, Frank W. Fisher and Peter B. Moyle. 1996. "Historical and Present Distribution of Chinook Salmon in the Central Valley Drainage of California." In *Status of the Sierra Nevada, Final Report to Congress, Sierra Nevada Ecosystem Project, Vol. 3*. University of California, Davis, Centers for Water and Wildland Resources.

Zaroya, Gregg. 2015, December 13. "Kerry: Climate deal will transform economy." *USA Today*. www.usatoday.com/story/news/nation/2015/12/13/senate-leader-says-climate-deal-mean-job-losses-and-rate-hikes/77245216.

INDEX

ACKNOWLEDGMENTS

From the first edition:

I must thank: Genevieve Troka and the curators of the California State Archives; Ellen Harding and the California Room librarians (State Library); Dace Taub (University of Southern California Regional History Center); Cathy Cherbosque and the curatorial staff of the Huntington Library; Linda Eade, librarian at Yosemite National Park; Noella Benvenuti (San Bernardino County Museum); Joy Neugebauer (Westminster Historical Society); the librarians and curators of the Water Resources Center Archives and Bancroft Library at University of California, Berkeley, Laws Railroad Museum, Eastern California Museum, Mono County Library, Anaheim Public Library, Scripps Institution of Oceanography and the California State University Fresno library; Mike Lynch (park ranger, Auburn State Recreation Area) and Sandy Taugher (State Museum Resource Center, both with California State Parks); and Sue McClurg and Rita Sudman (Water Education Foundation).

A quest for historic salmon photographs led me to an astonishing number of helpful people, including (in part): Ralph Hinton (U.S. Fish and Wildlife); Jeff Seigel (Natural History Museum of Los Angeles County); Ron Yoshiyama and Peter Moyle (UC Davis); Buford Holt (Department of Water Resources); Marilyn Coulter and Dean Gormby (Tehama Museum); author Alan Lufkin; Bill Kier, Dick Hallock and Phil Pister (retired Department of Fish and Game [DFG] biologists) and Bill Loudermilk (DFG, Fresno office).

The Library of Congress maintains an incredible internet resource: *California as I Saw It, First-Person Narratives of California's Early Years, 1849–1900,* (http://lcweb2.loc.gov/ammem/cbhtml/cbhome. html) with digitized images of complete texts (including illustrations).

My heartfelt thanks go to literary agent Julie Popkin, who pushed me beyond fiction and persisted until this book found a publishing home; to Becky Ward, who found the Warne family; and to Sally Gaines (cofounder of the Mono Lake Committee); Rick Kattleman (hydrologist); and Janet (park ranger, job-sharing partner, my wife) who read installments, caught typographical errors, made great suggestions and kept me on track.

The first edition was published in hardcover by Praeger, with the title *Drowning the Dream: California's Water Choices at the Millennium.* I am grateful to Sierra Club Books editors Danny Moses and Helen Sweetland for bringing the book out in paperback with the new title.

For this second edition, I must thank Alex DeGeorgey with Alta Archaeological Consulting for pointing me toward a letter by Mariano G. Vallejo and to Carol Dodge, with California State Parks, Bay Area District for providing a copy of that letter. Also Tami J. Suzuki, archivist with the San Francisco History Center (San Francisco Public Library), for help with a Hetch Hetchy dedication program cover used as an illustration.